The Versatile Profession

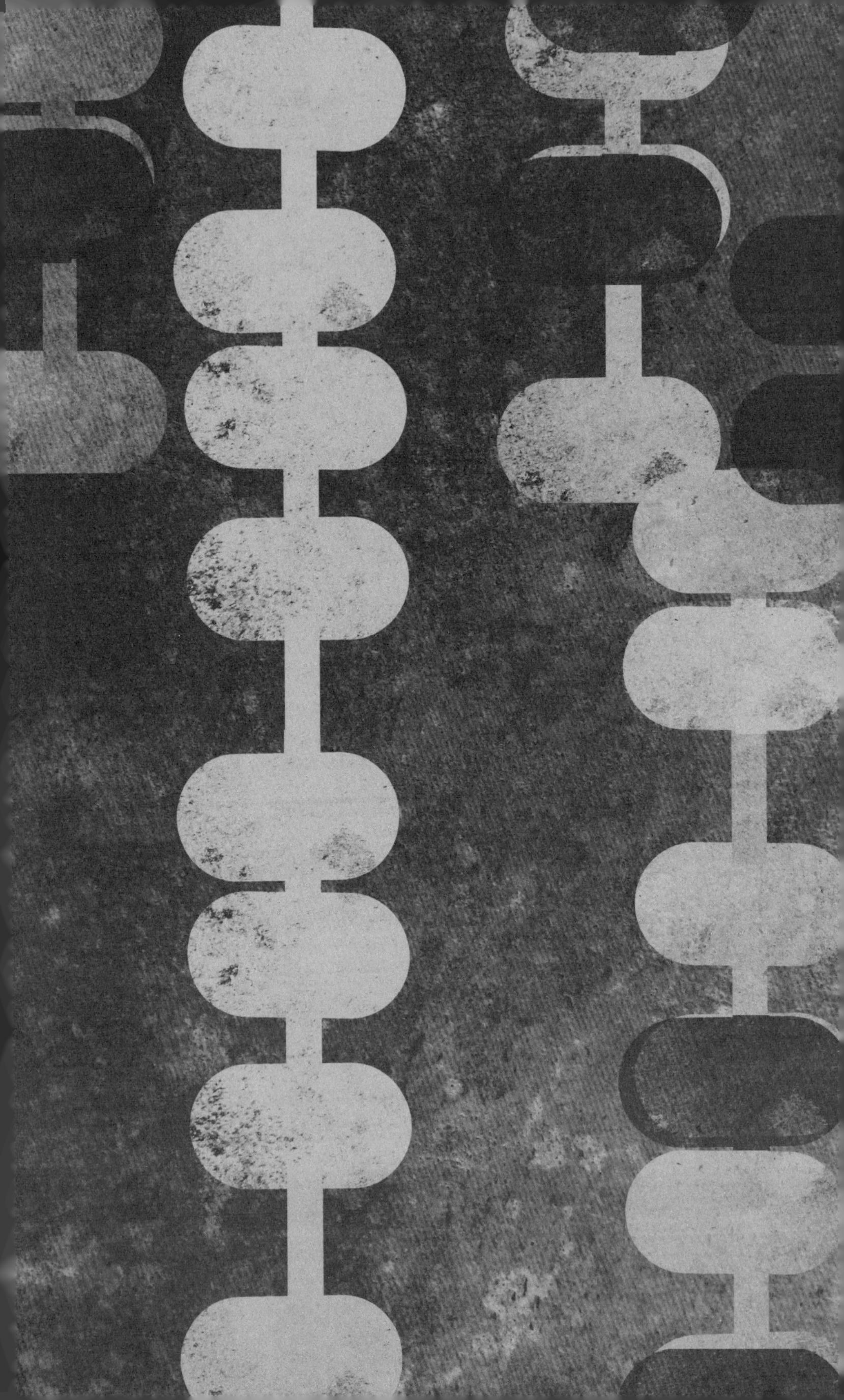

The Versatile Profession

A History of Accountancy in Ireland since 1850

Tony Farmar

Chartered Accountants Ireland

Published by
Chartered Accountants Ireland
Chartered Accountants House
47–49 Pearse Street, Dublin 2
www.charteredaccountants.ie

ISBN Hardback: 978-1-908199-82-9
ISBN Paperback: 978-1-908199-29-4

Text Design and layout by A & A Farmar Ltd
Index by Helen Litton
Cover design by Graham Thew
Printed by Turner's Printing Co. Ltd, Longford
Bound by Robinson & Mornin Bookbinders Ltd, Belfast

The publishers wish to acknowledge the support of the Chartered Accountants Ireland Educational Trust for the research and authoring of this history.

Contents

Preface

I am delighted to have the opportunity to preface this special book, which is being published in the year that we celebrate our 125th anniversary as a professional body.

It has always been curious to me in explaining the significance of this anniversary that I start by saying that we are definitely not celebrating the birth of accountancy in Ireland. As you will see within these pages, by the 1870s there were already numerous public accounting firms in Dublin, Belfast and Cork.

So what are we celebrating? In 1888, Queen Victoria granted us a Royal Charter thereby allowing us to form a special type of company to organise as a professional body – special in the sense that does not exist for the benefit of its members or its shareholders. The main purpose of forming this special company was to deliver a number of services for the community, for the public benefit. The Institute of Chartered Accountants in Ireland (now styled as 'Chartered Accountants Ireland' but retaining its original, legal name) at its heart is about delivering for the public a class of persons to do important and difficult work. These days I do not think there is a doubt that chartered accountants do such work. We deal with people and businesses at all the important junctures and difficult periods in their lives. Capital markets, creditors and lenders rely heavily on us. Governments in a very practical sense rely on us, for example, for efficient operation of the taxation system.

Historically, matters were not as clear and we are celebrating the first formal and public recognition, in 1888, that what we do for a living as chartered accountants is important and difficult work; that it requires a high level of skill and training and that therefore it is important that a proper structure is put around the education, formation, qualification and regulation of people doing such work. The whole impetus in seeking and obtaining a Charter was to 'elevate' the profession and raise standards to the benefit of all concerned.

The Royal Charter also allowed us to evolve as a distinct profession. We are not economists. Nor are we lawyers although, according to the Charter, a practical knowledge of the law is 'quite indispensable'. We are accurate, pragmatic people who are interested in business at the practical level. As one leading member said to me recently, the Charter recognised that all of us could, and should, be organised into an honourable profession.

All that we have and do today grew from 31 petitioners who called themselves chartered accountants. Because of the leadership of our predecessors, we now number almost 23,000 members with another 6,000 aspiring chartered accountants in their formation period. Our members are in all corners of professional practice, business and public service. When we group what we do together, our member firms are the largest employer of graduates from Irish universities and we have members in over 90 countries worldwide. I am also very proud to say that through all of the very, very difficult times we have had on this island, we have maintained a strong collegiality between all chartered accountants, north and south.

One of the reasons for commissioning and publishing this book at this time is to remind ourselves of the interesting narrative of our profession. We have developed, grown and changed with the evolution of business life on this island. It is useful to remind ourselves and the wider community about how 'what we do' fits into our broader collective story. There has been a steady development over the past 125 years of many areas of the profession, with progressive innovation to match the shifting patterns of focus in business.

This year we have had a number of events designed to reflect a reminder of that public recognition of the importance of the profession but also an acceptance by us that the existence of the Institute is there for the public benefit, not our own individual or even collective gain. Our programme for the year also contains a set of challenging questions that we must face as a profession so that we can reflect on how we will progress the Institute over the next period and further contribute to our communities.

I trust this book will appeal to as wide a readership as possible and will be read not only by our members and members of the other accountancy bodies but by the general business reader who will gain some insights into how the Institute, its members and the development of the accountancy profession generally sits within the broader context of the social, political and economic development of the island of Ireland.

Brendan Lenihan, FCA
President
Chartered Accountants Ireland

Introduction

It is natural to suppose that, as the basic structure of things is now, so it has always been. But over the long period since this book starts in 1850, the accountancy profession has adopted three quite distinct business models. These models required different organisations, different work mixes and different ways of getting new business. And it turns out that, despite the popular identification of chartered accountants with auditing, pure audit has been a much smaller aspect of the business than this identification would imply.

The first model, the one that obtained at the time of the Charter in 1888, was accountants as insolvency and liquidations practitioners and book-keepers. The relative importance of insolvency work is clear from the petition for the Charter presented to the Privy Council, which stressed 'their employment under decrees in Chancery, in the winding-up of companies, in bankruptcies or arrangements with creditors and in various positions of trust under Courts of Justice; as also in the auditing of the accounts of public companies and of partnerships and otherwise.'

Typically at this time, firms were headed by one or two accountants and employed unqualified seniors as the 'engine'. The key sources of new business were solicitors, firms and banks; so, after 'The Queen', the first toast proposed at the dinner was 'The Legal Profession'. To match their lawyer clients, accountants stressed their gentlemanly respectability.

The 1900 Companies Act, consolidated in the 1907 Act, which remained the basis of Irish company law until 1963, established the requirement for annual audits, and so heralded the second business model for the profession, accountants as auditors and book-keepers. From 1900 until perhaps 1980 the profession was primarily engaged in writing up and auditing annual accounts, while maintaining its position in the less regular insolvency field, supplying company secretarial services and tax compliance work. For most of this time few client companies were capable of creating a trial balance from their ledgers and fewer still the accounts.

So, as the then doyen of the profession, Gabriel Brock, put it in his expert testimony in *Stokes Brothers v. Featherstonhaugh* (1936), 'accountancy work must always precede audit work. We prepare and audit a/cs. In Ireland it is the rule and not the exception.' Once the accounts were prepared the firm's tax return would also be drawn up, usually by the same audit senior who had done the accounts work. Tax was almost entirely compliance-based, and in the hands of generalist partners.

Organisationally, firms evolved into confederations of generalist partners, with seniors (qualified and unqualified) and trainees as the engine. The senior partner (normally the oldest) would chair meetings and represent the firm, but there was little central management as such. The calculation of fees, for instance, was the responsibility of each partner, and there would have been only the vaguest idea of who was contributing what. Fees were very often furnished only just before the next audit was due. The firm might have several partners, but never so many that they could not meet every morning and open the post. In this quiet environment, matching the slow growth of the Irish economy, the prized virtues were discretion and steady reliability.

By the 1970s the Irish economy was opening out, and the flow of foreign investment created a range of new opportunities. Hundreds of foreign firms, notably from America, came into the country accustomed to buying a wide range of services from accountants. Opportunities in the EEC, and the strength of the foreign direct investment sector, pushed Ireland's economy (and with it the profession) into the stratosphere.

In response to the new environment, firms remodelled themselves. Thus was born the third model, accountants as suppliers of business services. John Callaghan, managing partner of Stokes Kennedy Crowley, presented this as inevitable, noting in 1987: 'whether we like it or not, the modern practising accountancy firms are in business—the business of providing a range of professional services . . . it is only if practising accountants recognise that they are in business and act like businessmen' that they will succeed. In 1992 managing partner Billy McCann told the Price Waterhouse *Newsletter*, 'we are no longer just auditors or tax consultants, but business advisors to our clients'. The new watchword was 'service'.

In order to provide this new range of services firms had to grow, so a great cascade of amalgamations and overseas connections started, until the top firms had 40 or more partners each. The old generalists were gone; now there were young, hardworking and highly competitive specialists in audit, in tax planning (and eventually in particular types of tax), in treasury management, in consultancy and in corporate reconstruction. Coordinating all this there was now an elected managing partner, with a range of sub-committees. Surprisingly quickly, the new services unseated audit from its predominance, until it soon accounted for less than half of fee income.

The core activity of the profession has from the earliest post-Famine days been the understanding and translating of the financial ambiguities of life into formats for decision-making—by clients, fellow managers, shareholders, tax inspectors, creditors and regulators. And, of course, familiarity with the numbers meant that accountants have often been able to take leadership roles. Even with computer accounting programs, translating businesses flows is not automatic: the swirling activity of the shopfloor has to be pinned down and monitored; cash flow must be attended to; tax returns must be made; shops, estates and partnerships need to be sorted out; insolvencies unravelled. Doing all this, there are thousands of accountants, especially in small and medium-sized firms and in businesses, practising their profession in ways that the signatories of the petition leading to the Charter 125 years ago would easily recognise.

Acknowledgements

My introduction to accountancy was as an articled clerk in the old City of London firm then called Ball Baker Deed, which traced its origins to a firm started in 1870 by John B. Ball. He was President of the ICAEW in 1908–9. Ball Baker Deed finally became part of Pannell Kerr Forster in 1989. My first acknowledgement therefore has to be to that firm and my principal, the senior partner William Thompson. Although I soon abandoned accountancy for book writing and publishing, what I learned in 18 months there has stood to me ever since, and not least in the writing of this book.

Sadly, very little archive material from individual Irish firms is available. As a result the bulk of the work was based on desk research and a wide range of published materials, as the source notes make clear. So I am grateful for the interviews with accounting practitioners including Paul Creedon, Emma Delaney, John Blake Dillon, Cecil Donovan, Margaret Downes, Vincent Finn, Richard Hewitt, Bruce Lyster, Trevor Morrow, Hugh O'Hare and Terence O'Rourke.

From previous research I have used inputs from Gerard O'Brien, Marie O'Connor and William Cunningham. Geoffrey Perrin made documents available, and Tom Lyons of *The Irish Times* provided materials and John Dudley Latin translation. Rebecca Hayes of Freemasons Hall allowed access to their archive.

From academia, Niamh Brennan (UCD), Peter Clarke (UCD)—who also read the text and provided valuable comments—Antoin Murphy (TCD), Philip O'Regan (UL), Brendan Walsh (UCD) and Keith Warnock (NUIG) provided many ideas.

From Chartered Accountants Ireland the book has benefited from inputs and guidance through the technical thickets by Pat Costello, Simone Doran, Daisy Downes, Brian Keegan, Aidan Lambe, Brendan Lenihan, Ben Lynch and Ronan O'Loughlin.

On the publishing side Michael Diviney of Chartered Accountants Ireland has provided major help and support, and his colleague Liam Boyle contributed largely to the finished product.

Finally, once again, I have to thank my friend Frank Litton and my partner in business and life, Anna Farmar, for stimulus, and patience.

Tony Farmar

Chapter One
The Early Days of a Young Profession: 1850–1888

Double entry book-keeping, while a science, deserves to rank among the fine arts. It challenges the admiration of lovers of the beautiful and true. It cultivates the judicial powers of the mind. It quickens and strengthens the love of justice and equity. It promotes fair dealing among men. It contributes to private and public virtue. It leads to economy and thrift in private and public affairs. Its general study and practice will reduce pauperism and crime and promote frugality and virtue.

Mayhew Practical Book-keeping Key (1884) *[1]

Professional accountancy emerged in Ireland and Britain in the 1850s, well ahead of the US or the continental countries, as part of the wave of new Victorian professions that included nursing, architecture and engineering. The development of a full-scale accountancy profession required a dense, numerate economy[2] so, as the historian of the Institute of Chartered Accountants of England and Wales put it, 'it was not until the middle of the nineteenth century that the professional accountant really saw the light of day'.[3]

Another historian of the British profession confirmed that: 'the art of accountancy was still undergoing its metamorphosis into a profession during the third quarter of the nineteenth century . . . accountancy was the last among the major techniques to develop into a profession.' And of course this emergence was not universally welcomed, for, as he continues, 'practitioners of established professions, especially when the rising new profession usurps some of their work, are bound to look uncharitably upon it'.[4]

The newness of the profession was recognised at the time; as the 'Commercial Intelligence' column of *The Irish Times* noted in August 1860, professional accountants were 'a comparatively new and important body'. The first accountancy association in Ireland, the Institute of Chartered Accountants in Ireland, received its Royal Charter in 1888.

* *Endnotes identifying the sources begin on page 247.*

The birth of double entry

Accounting, in the sense of compiling figures to measure wealth, is a very ancient discipline. Indeed, evidence of accounting or book-keeping practice of sorts appears in some of the oldest artefacts known to human history. Clay-baked shards with counts of cattle and goods from thousands of years ago have been found, and records survive from most societies of their accounting methods.

These more or less sophisticated single-entry book-keeping systems sufficed for thousands of years. As far as the West is concerned, the complex form of accounting called 'double-entry book-keeping' emerged in the Italian merchant houses in the 13th century. By no coincidence this was in the same northern Italian cities where modern banking also evolved—Florence, Venice and Genoa. The new system—for long called 'the Italian method'—slowly spread as best practice in mercantile houses throughout Europe over the following centuries. Part of its appeal was as a special 'rhetoric' or way of speaking about finance that brought simplicity, neatness, clarity, logic and objectivity into mercantile worlds that often lacked most of these virtues.[5]

In the merchant houses of north Italy in the 13th and 14th centuries, where double entry evolved, the typical business model was a short-lived venture (a trading voyage, perhaps) of two or three years, during which the capital was tied up. At the end of the period all the costs would be accumulated, income ascertained and profits distributed according to capital subscribed (perhaps in the form of goods at an agreed valuation). The partners would then be free to re-engage. So embedded was this method that famous trading companies such as the Medici, which are loosely spoken of as lasting 70 years or more, are normally found to have been in fact an elaborate series of constantly renewed contracts.

We have a very full account of the business world in which double entry emerged, that of the north Italian merchant Francesco Datini of Prato (1335–1410).[6] Starting his career in the rich Papal city of Avignon, he created trading companies in Barcelona, Genoa, Prato, Pisa, Venice, Florence, Majorca and other places, trading largely in fine cloth and other luxury goods. Most of the partnership contracts were for two years only, renewable of course, but the partners could withdraw nothing until the end of the contract. The accounts of each branch were written, on Datini's insistence, in 'the Italian method' and the first pages of each leather- or vellum-bound *Libri Grande* inscribed: 'In the name of God and of profit.' There is evidence from his papers that during his time in business he made the momentous shift from using the traditional Roman numerals in the books to the modern Arabic numbers we use today.[7]

Datini was a very modern type: a driving, remorseless man of detail. He would spend nine hours or more at his desk every day, writing copious instructions to each of his partners. And if they were separated, he would send equally detailed sets of instructions to his wife. Datini died childless, but so rich that the charity he established in his will was still in action 600 years after his death.

Double-entry book-keeping was a perfectly evolved tool to account for Datini's kind of activity, in which, crucially, there was a clear and imminent end. Many of the technical difficulties that modern accountants experience (with goodwill, depreciation, deferred taxation, accounting for leases, asset valuation, etc.) derive from the fact that double entry is now used to account for *continuing, unending* ventures. While it is certainly the best accounting technique there is, it was not quite evolved for the modern world—any more than the human body was to sit in front of a computer screen for seven hours a day. The simple process Datini and his contemporaries undertook had no need for such complications as extraordinary items, brand valuation, off balance sheet finance and consolidation, which can cause such difficulties today.

Double-entry book-keeping was well known and widespread in Italy by the time Fra Luca Pacioli described it in his famous book of 1494, *Summa de Arithmetica, Geometria, Proportioni et Proportionalita*. As the title suggests, this was an encyclopaedia of current mathematics. Its 600 big pages contain a 27-page section describing double entry, which is the first published description of the technique. Ironically, in view of his future identification with book-keeping, Pacioli was a Franciscan, an order whose founder had a particular devotion to the poor and to apostolic poverty. Pacioli did not claim to have invented double entry, any more than he claimed to have invented the other mathematics he described. Indeed, there is evidence that his observer's grasp of the finer points was somewhat wobbly—for instance, no merchant's clerk would assume that merely because the trial balance agreed, the ledger was error-free (Chapter 34), and in his description of the so-called merchandise account he includes opening but not closing stock values (Chapter 22). His grasp of the business entity concept varies also: in Chapter 22 he writes of including in the books household purchases for oil and hats and even gambling; in Chapter 23 the store is to account separately as a debtor for things supplied from the house.

Double entry in Ireland

The techniques invented in Italy took some time to percolate north. They came to south Germany first, then Spain and France, and had arrived in London in time to record the trading adventures of Queen Elizabeth I's sailors. The first publication on book-keeping/accounting published in Ireland came out in 1696.[8] Its author, S. Ammonet, described himself as an 'Accomptant' who taught book-keeping in Essex Street in Dublin. His book proved surprisingly controversial, with an attack on it published by a rival in the same year. We can assume that double-entry book-keeping was increasingly used in progressive merchant houses during the 18th century, for by the 19th century it had become a curriculum item in the hedge schools and academies of Ireland. It was often taught with commercial arithmetic, shorthand, dictation and cognate subjects. However, whether it was the Christian Brothers, teaching from their own published *Book-keeping by Both Double and Single Entry* (1867), or the national school-teachers plodding through *Elements of Book-keeping in a Series of Short Examples for the Use of Schools* (1835), it is likely that the subject was dry, theoretical and, as the Report of the Commissioners of National Education commented in 1850: 'very unskillfully taught'. And as with the actuarial studies, algebra and Latin which used to be part of the first exam syllabus of the Irish Institute, we might wonder how much ever found practical application.

Although by the 19th century double entry was usual in merchant businesses, a large proportion of general Irish businesses maintained, just like Francesco Datini's contemporaries, 'somewhat rough and ready accounts which were often little more than memorandums of entries of credit, without any record of cash transactions'.[9] But as Datini himself admitted, 'though four out of six of them have no book or inkwell and those who have ink have no pen . . . [yet] just for that reason they call things to mind better after four or five years than most men would after a month'. The image of the Irish village publican and storekeeper, with no more accounts than could be kept on a nail and yet forgetting nothing, is familiar from literature.

It was not only such simple environments that resisted double entry. As late as 1897 a witness told a commission on manual and practical education in primary schools that 'systems of book-keeping differed in commercial houses so that the system learned in a national school may not be the system used in the employer's business'.[10] Commercial people actively running their own enterprises were not much interested in regular annual accounts. They knew intimately how debtors and creditors waxed and waned, how stock and other assets were growing, and how much they took out of the enterprise. Until the business got big, or the taxation authorities became pressing, they did not need the complicated technical presentation of profit and loss to know that they had had a good or bad year. Only if there was a sleeping partner or other outside interest would the firm bother with regular profit measurement. 'Indeed', writes one historian, 'the problems we associate with the *concept* of profit and the careful calculations of *periodic* profit do not appear to have been problems worrying the early practitioners or teachers of double entry in England.'[11]

Ledgers were balanced only when the particular volume was full. It is likely that even today, if it were not for official requirements, small businesses would not bother with annual accounts. Sir Desmond Lorimer confirmed that in his early days in practice in Belfast, in the 1940s and 1950s, 'there seemed to be no great understanding of accounts and accounting. [Managers] did merely what was necessary from a legal point of view—and there would have been no auditors if the law had not required them!'[12] In Britain and Ireland (but not in continental Europe), this changed for the larger concerns with the coming of joint stock companies, although an annual audit was not technically compulsory until 1900. The newly rigorous tax regime necessitated by the unprecedented costs of the First World War reinforced the annual ritual of accounts and audit. In Germany it was not until 1931 that large public companies were obliged to have an annual audit, and private companies were later still.

Ireland after the Famine

In the 1840s Henry Brown, who survived to become the oldest of the signatories on the petition for a Royal Charter in 1888, began to advertise his services as an accountant in Pettigrew & Oulton's *Dublin Almanac* and in Thom's *Directory*. This was an interesting time in the economic and business development of the country. A series of rolling ecological, political and financial crises in Western Europe made the 1840s the hinge on which the history of the 19th century turns. The potato famine devastated Ireland, but the same blight heavily affected Belgium (where it was first imported, in June 1845, from the US), northern France, Germany and Scandinavia.[13] In addition, there was a collapse of over-hyped railway shares, causing runs on banks and a money crisis. In 1848, the so-called 'year of revolution', there were revolutionary uprisings in Austria, France, Germany, Hungary, Poland, Sicily and Venice. Even in England tens of thousands of militant Chartists, led by the Irishman Feargus O'Connor, terrified the House of Commons with a 'monster petition' calling for universal suffrage, annual parliamentary elections and other reforms. In May 1848 Prussia and Denmark began a war over the province of Schleswig–Holstein.

Although the very worst effects of the Great Irish Famine were felt in the west and the south of the country, and among the poorest agricultural populations, the ramifications had been felt severely throughout the whole economy. At its height, in August 1847, the diarist Elizabeth Smith travelled to Dublin from her Wicklow home:

> 'On getting to the suburbs of the town the melancholy evidences of the distress of the nation were to be met with—every second house to let . . . I began to count the number of shops shut up as we advanced and got to twenty-six by the time we reached the entrance to the busy part of the City. The shops are deserted. One or two we had to enter, we were alone in, few shopmen either, there being nothing for *them* to do, and they offered us their goods for anything we chose to give them.'[14]

Back in her home near Blessington she noted the commercial chaos: 'little in the papers but failures. Cattle dealers in Dublin have gone, and caused immense distress, in fact paralysed the markets. Not an offer for a beast of any sort at any of the late fairs. Banks, merchants, brokers, agents all are bankrupt in all places.'[15] These collapses caused others, in Britain particularly, as debts were progressively called in.

However, in the 30 years following the 'mighty collapse' of the Great Famine of the 1840s, Irish society recovered astonishingly well, growing into the kind of commercial environment in which accountants could make a contribution. To contemporaries there was even a kind of economic miracle. As the Registrar General, Thomas Grimshaw, put it: 'It may be that Ireland has advanced more rapidly, and recovered from a condition of almost wreck more completely than any other country would have done or ever has done.'[16]

The country's economy did not of course go back to what it had been in the 1820s and 1830s. Contrary to the traditional story, in those days

Ireland had numerous small towns (in the south of the country as well as the north) scattered with embryonic manufacturing processes, as witnesses to a British enquiry in 1884–5 reported.[17] Among these, said one, was the town of Bandon in the county Cork which had a population of 14,100 in 1824, the majority of whom were artisans employed in the manufacture of linens, woollens, corduroys, etc., which were produced by hand looms; females being employed in weaving and spinning. There were two extensive cotton mills, driven by water power, in full work for upwards of half a century until 1826, when the protective duty was removed and the country became flooded with English manufactures.[18] By 1883 the population of Bandon had sunk to 5,800.

The wool merchant, William Keating, remembered Birr, County Offaly, as it had been (with perhaps a touch of nostalgic exaggeration):

> 'They had extensive factories of tobacco, soap and candles; they also had a large production of combs, brushes and hats; they had two extensive distilleries and two breweries; they had extensive production of woollen stuff goods, both for public sale and for home consumption by farmers in the neighbourhood. Of all these industries there remains but one distillery working about half the extent it did previously and one weaver; that is all the small manufacturing in the district. Then in the neighbouring town of Roscrea in Tipperary there were 1,000 men employed as weavers and wool-combers; those 1,000 are now represented by 2.'[19]

Sir Robert Kane, the author of *The Industrial Resources of Ireland* (1845), was a key witness to the 1885 Select Committee, among other things reporting that years ago there had been 28 water-powered mills on the River Dodder: 'it was one succession of mills from the source to the mouth almost . . . most of those mills are idle now.' (The breadth and depth of the modern Dodder's river-bed, which winds through south Dublin to the sea, gives an idea of the power of the old river before waterworks in the Dublin Mountains robbed it of its force.) Alderman Cornelius Redmond told the Committee the same story in respect of Waterford: the Portlaw linen factory was down from 3,000 employees to 500; the famous glass factory brought to its knees by a strike; and shipbuilding and iron-founding had also disappeared by the 1880s.

In the 1830s the mighty Malcolmson empire of Waterford sent ships all across the world, from China to the United States, and made the city a more important shipbuilding centre than Belfast at that time. Its collapse was in this case not due to British or even Belfast competition, but the extravagance and incompetence of the second generation (building a series of elaborate mansions in Waterford, and backing the South in the American Civil War, for instance). There was, sadly, a strong tendency for Irish consumers to buy from English manufacturers, for various reasons ranging from cheapness and ease of supply to snobbery. This was reported by gun-makers, iron founders and even spade manufacturers. It was, for instance, estimated that 5–6 million pins and nails were used every day in Ireland, 'barely a tithe of which' were made in the country.

In most other cases the witnesses believed that aggressive competition from English manufacturers flowing through the new railway system was the root cause of the decline of local industry. Witnesses to the 1884 enquiry told tales of predatory behaviour by British businesses. Perhaps an extreme case occurred during a strike in a glass factory in Cork, where 'an attorney in Cork paid the wages provided by glass-makers of St Helens and Birmingham for two years'. The Cork firm was of course ruined.[20]

The focus of the 1884 enquiry was not on how to create Irish industry but how to re-establish its pre-Famine status. What most witnesses believed would be most effective was tariff protection, which they also knew *laissez-faire* England would find intellectually and politically unacceptable. As one member of the Committee put it: 'you are probably aware that State interference with industry is very much objected to . . . this is a principle and a popular principle.'[21] The Irish witnesses did know that, and were obliged to accept the position. The proceedings were followed closely in Ireland, and these opinions in favour of protection ultimately fed into the policies of the Irish nationalist movement.

The railways

The coming of the railways marked a turning point, not only in the economic history of Ireland but also in the development of the accountancy profession. The enormous amounts of capital required, and the fact that so much had to be spent before a penny could be earned, led to new demands on financial control and reporting systems that naturally involved accountants. Railways were also the drivers of the new business economy. They were the motor cars of the 19th century: they changed manners and people's opportunities; they presented severe engineering and management problems; they also enabled wars to be bloodier and more damaging (as in the American Civil War and the Franco-Prussian War of 1870); and they offered some people the opportunity to make a lot of money. They were by far the very biggest businesses of the day, having an enormous impact as navvies ripped and tore through the countryside, to the distress of tender-minded country-lovers as landscapes and vistas became reconfigured.

Because everyone interested in money could see the potential of railways, there was a great speculative boom in the 1840s. This was perhaps the first time since the South Sea Bubble of the early 18th century that ordinary people had the chance to take part in City action. Hundreds of more or less wild railway schemes were presented to Parliament (until 1844 an Act of Parliament or a Royal Charter were the only ways to establish a limited company). Shares were made available by private placement and by public subscription. Speculative activity was increased by shares being only part paid-up and the floating of low-value 'light stocks' at £1 or £2 each (ordinary shares were typically denominated as £20, £50 or even £100 each). To feed the appetite, in London in 1845 alone there were no fewer than 20 journals to track railway matters, 14 of which were weekly and two even daily. In true boom style, as stories spread of fortunes being made, the ignorant and the gullible piled in. One list, itemising the various subscribers to schemes at the height of the boom in August 1845, included barristers, bankers, earls, merchants, tradesmen and clerks. One-quarter of the members of the House of Commons were subscribers, as well as numerous clergymen, for large sums from £2,000 to £26,000.[22]

The Irish rail network had started modestly in 1834 with the Dublin and Kingstown line, which took a little time to prove its worth, but by 1846 was transporting over 2 million passengers a year and paying a steady 10 per cent dividend. Attracted by this example and no doubt by developments in England, local promoters let unfettered creativity rip. In the mid-1840s there were 47 Irish schemes struggling for Parliamentary attention, of which 26 were direct competitors; for instance, there were at least three schemes for the short run from Cork to Passage (to catch the shipping from Cobh, then called Queenstown), and five for the Cork to Fermoy route. By 1850, 700 miles of track were open or under construction, 90 per cent of which had been paid for by the public (half of the capital coming from Ireland). The Dublin to Cork and Dublin to Galway lines were among them. By 1852 it is said that the basic structure of the railway system was in place.[23] The practical gains for passengers and freight were immediate. For instance, the train took five hours and 20 minutes to go from Dublin to Belfast—the mail coach had taken 15 hours and had cost considerably more. Similar improvements in speed and cheapness were achieved across the system.

Positive indicators

The number of people living in cities and towns as opposed to the country gradually increased throughout the post-Famine period. By 1881 there were 19 towns with more than 10,000 people, holding 16 per cent of the population, compared to 10 per cent in such towns in 1851. The biggest of these was Dublin, which (if suburbs such as Rathmines and Blackrock are included) had grown by 22 per cent since 1851. Belfast had doubled in size in the same time. Emigration over the years had driven out the poorest people, so the number of families living in first- or second-class houses had gone from a just over a quarter of all families to just under a half. Pupils attending primary school had gone up by 40 per cent; the number attending universities and colleges had doubled. The Registrar General, Thomas Grimshaw, reported that most of the economic indexes were up very substantially since 1851.[24] The index of farm prices moved from 58.9 in 1850, just after the Famine, to 102.3 in 1880.[25] Crucially, rents and farm receipts were up. This followed market demand. The rapidly growing English manufacturing towns exhibited a constantly increasing demand for Irish meat and butter. In response, Irish farming had cut the area under crops and expanded the pasture. There were 37 per cent more cattle in the country than there had been in 1851, but cereals were down from 3 million acres in 1851 to 1.8 million. There was now 2 million acres under hay and clover. Agriculture accounted for half of national income, but its steadily growing prosperity spilled over into shop-keeping, building, banking and professional services.

Other indicators were positive also. The steadily growing wealth of the country was revealed in the fact that bank deposits had gone from £8 million in 1851 to £30 million in 1881; money in the humbler savings banks had gone from £1.3 million in 1851 to £3.7 million in 1881. The profits of businesses and professions (as reported for tax) increased by 65 per cent between 1854 and 1870. Shipping activity in and out of the country had more than doubled, and linen and beer production were both substantially up. Even emigration had shrunk, to the extent that the Registrar General estimated that in 1876 there had been a small increase in population for the first time in 30 years.[26]

By 1880, 2,370 miles of railway were operational across Ireland. The commercial impact was quickly felt. As the historian R. V. Comerford wrote: 'One of the prime functions of the railway was to distribute throughout the land products of the industrial age . . . the British-oriented world system into which Ireland was incorporated in these decades produced an increase in the volume of traffic of all kinds.'[27] Goods, people and, crucially, ideas in the form of publications and letters were given easy passage. In the 1850s there were three daily papers in the country—by 1870 there were 17; in 1851 there were 39 million letters delivered—by 1870 there were 65 million.

From an accounting point of view the railways presented an interesting problem. Normally, a new business such as a factory or workshop could start small and progressively expand as the sales grew; the initial capital requirements, even of mines, had been relatively insignificant. Canal and railway companies, on the other hand, needed to spend truly enormous sums before they could earn a single penny. The so-called 'double account' system, which distinguished (a) funds raised from shares and debentures and the amounts spent on fixed assets from (b) 'floating' assets and liabilities, such as debts, was devised. Its key purpose was to prevent management from placating restless investors by paying dividends out of invested capital while the building work was progressing.[28]

Railway accounts were seen as highly specialised. Certain English accountants, notably Edwin Waterhouse and William Deloitte, dominated this field of accounting. And this field was regarded as so specialised that when Waterhouse proposed his partner Samuel Price to become auditor of the huge Midland Railway he was turned down by the company as insufficiently experienced, despite his work with smaller railways.[29]

Despite this complexity, insisted on by law, as late as the 1870s most of the large Irish railway companies still had their accounts audited by fellow shareholders, who typically had no professional qualifications, but were trusted with the details of the books as 'one of us'. Thus, the Great Southern (478 miles of track, 2.2 million passengers a year) was audited by Luke McDonnell and James Haughton; the Great Northern (503 miles of track, 3.5 million passengers a year) by George Leaming and James Gildea; and the Waterford and Central Ireland (226 miles of track, 217,000 passengers a year) by John Mackesy. None of these names appear in the lists of accountants in Thom's *Directory*.

How many accountants?

The predominantly agricultural nature of the Irish economy meant that the accountancy profession was slow to emerge. The 1851 Irish census did not even have a separate employment category for accountants (as opposed to merchants, clerks, etc.). In British cities comparable to Dublin there were numbers to make the basis of a professional body: there were, for instance, 264 accountants in London, 69 in Liverpool, 52 in Manchester and 267 in Edinburgh and Glasgow, where Scottish bankruptcy legislation was different and more favourable to the evolution of the profession.[30] For Ireland, Thom's *Directory of Ireland 1861* listed a mere 43 individuals under the heading 'Accountants' (all men) and two firms in Dublin; one of the individuals doubled as a German translator. Until the Charter was gained in 1888, these men were commonly known as 'public accountants'.

The occupation tables of the 1871 Census had added a new category of 'accountants' and there were 761 people across the country who described themselves thus, six of whom were women. By contrast there were 12,365 people describing themselves as 'writing clerks', most of whom presumably worked in small business offices. In the 'Situation Wanted' columns advertisers began to make much of their 'good knowledge of book-keeping'.

Many of the self-described 'accountants' would have worked in businesses, especially banks, or were small operators like Mr Rugg in Dickens's 1857 novel *Little Dorrit,* described as 'a professional gentlemen in a very small way' who advertised his services as 'General Agent, Accountant, Debts Recovered'.[31] (The image of accountants as dull was not in Dickens; rather to the contrary—Rugg is sharp, knowing and effective.) By the 1881 Census there were 1,501 'accountants' and 11,395 'commercial clerks' out of a total population of 5.1 million recorded in the occupation tables.

One of the earliest 'public accountants' was Henry Brown who had first advertised his services in the *Dublin Almanac* in 1845.[32] His services were no doubt much the same as those offered by another 'public accountant', William Hayes, who described his activity thus in the *Dublin Almanac* of 1844:

> 'Nobody but a person who filled the department of Accountant in a mercantile house, as the advertiser did for a period of twenty years is qualified to balance accounts involving the slightest complexity . . . those therefore who are preparing to account whether to Partners or principals, or to Courts or who wish to have their Books on such a principle as will enable them to do so at any period . . . will find it in their interest to apply.'

This was the profession's first business model, with work in and around the courts featuring strongly. Public accountants' services were evidently perceived as providing occasional specialist functions, typically at moments of death or legal crisis. An important aspect of the work was to do with liquidations and with winding up of estates. Here, the work of the emerging profession was to bring order and control to all kinds of financial muddles so that they could be easily handled by the legal profession. There was very little company audit work to be had (compulsory annual auditing for general limited companies was not to be finally introduced until the 1900 Companies Act). As with the railways, most companies had quite small numbers of shareholders who would very often be known to each other and to the directors, so they found it natural to appoint one of themselves to do the audit.

Thus, in advertisements from firms later involved in the Charter, in Thom's *Directory* in 1882, N. Peterson & Co. offered 'many years' experience in matters of Accounts in the Courts of Bankruptcy and Chancery, also in opening and balancing Merchants Books, settling Partnership Accounts, Auditing, checking Rentals etc., etc.'. In the same issue Craig Gardner announced that they 'are engaged in all matters of Account in Chancery, Bankruptcy, Partnership Accounts, Rentals, etc.; also in opening the Books of Public Companies, in accordance with the provision of the Joint-Stock Companies Act, winding up estates as Liquidators, acting as Auditors, etc.'. Kevans and Kean declared that they 'have practical experience in all matters of accountancy connected with the Courts of Chancery, Admiralty and Bankruptcy, in partnerships, rent accounts etc.'. The priority given to the Courts of Bankruptcy and Chancery is clear.

Although the contemporary journalist A. M. Sullivan commented unenthusiastically that the purchasers of distressed estates in the 1850s brought into the management of their purchases 'the ledger and day-book principle',[33] to the dismay of tenants used to more elastic systems, archives show that many estate records ranged from merely incomplete to chaotic. Lists of receipts from tenants would most likely be separate, but household purchases, payments to tradespeople and all other running costs are jumbled together, with every document smelling faintly perhaps of cow dung, porter or tobacco. One such list, from the Shapland Carew estates in Wexford, throws together expenditure on: 'bleaching 22 yards sheeting, purchase of 20 wethers, turf, wages, meal, a cask of white wine', the local Rector's tithes, the purchase of some salt and pack thread, slates, a shovel and '6½d to a messenger for a bunch of grapes'.[34] Putting these messes into order was no light task. In his 1858 advertisement in Thom's *Directory*, Henry Brown quotes from an endorsement from Sir James Stewart: 'Now that you have brought to so happy an issue the Accounts between my land agents and myself of upwards of thirty years standing . . .'.

In order that executors and the courts could handle all this information, the figures had to be expressed in some standardised format. Judges regularly grumbled if this was not done: in 1863 Judge Lynch complained of the 'large class of case' coming into the court in which the poor quality of the book-keeping was such that 'it is sometimes impossible to trace the fair operations of trade'.[35] A few years later, in 1870, Judge Miller ascribed the bankruptcy of a draper to 'a want of proper book-keeping', and in another case actually penalised a would-be bankrupt for poor accounts.

The ideal that a firm of accountants' employees (typically what were later called 'unqualified seniors') took with them into the remote corners of the country was that of a well-kept, city-based merchant's set of books, clear, impeccably neat and controlled, with waste-book, journal and double-entry ledgers. Assets and liabilities were to be clearly differentiated, based on the 'separate entity' theory, so that household and personal expenses were extricated from business costs, and associated costs and income sources combined in appropriate summations. An important part of the process was an estimate of the substance and value of both assets and liabilities—elderly debts, doubtful liabilities, stocks that had deteriorated in the haggard, and so on. It was the accountant's job to mediate between the chaos of everyday life and the well-understood formats of public life. As best they could, they had to translate the muddle of trading or estate accounts, often going back over years, into a presentation that could be readily understood and expeditiously handled.

The normal process in bankruptcy cases was that a solicitor would engage an accountant to investigate the applicant trader's affairs and produce a statement of assets and liabilities, which the solicitor would then use in the Court of Bankruptcy. The role occasionally brought the accountants into conflict with the judges of the court. In 1876, for instance, the senior bankruptcy judge, Judge Miller, complained bitterly about the activities of one clerk, a member, as *The Irish Times* put it, of 'an eminent firm of accountants'. In drawing up the accounts he had omitted from the assets of the arranging trader some goods which had been burnt, presumably taking the view that they had no resale value. 'Judge Miller said that this was an assumption of a duty entirely outside the province of an accountant, as it was practically deciding matters of law.' He considered that the solicitors engaged in such cases should keep their business in their own hands and 'not allow accountants to take such matters upon themselves. He found in one case that an accountant had filed a schedule without the intervention of a solicitor at all and now he found an arrangement practically conducted without a solicitor.' He continued: 'if these gentlemen did not keep themselves in their proper place, he would control them by disallowing their expenses.'[36] These remarks echoed equally choleric comments made by Judge Quain in Bristol in 1875. He complained of accountants, debt collectors and others, 'an ignorant set of men', who were taking over the bankruptcy process in place of solicitors who (and this was the nub) were 'a respectable body, subject to the control of the court'.[37]

The partnership of Brown and Craig split up in the early 1870s and William Craig took Robert Gardner, an employee, as his new partner. A private ledger from those early days shows that in the first half-year the firm tackled 114 jobs, yielding a gross income of £1,788.[38] Three fees accounted for 20 per cent of the income, while the average was just less than £16 (about one-third the average working man's annual income). The range of clients for whom they performed book-keeping tasks is wide: two hotels, a seed merchant, a builder and timber merchant, a piano warehouse, two publishers, two charities, some drapers, a few solicitors and a stockbroker. The record does not allow us to say whether these were once-off or repeat jobs, and if the latter with what regularity. We can guess that the typical job consisted of writing up the books against a variety of vouchers and then perhaps preparation of accounts.

Perhaps the downturn in business activity initiated by the very poor harvests of the later 1870s caused a shift in the business pattern, or possibly Gardner, since 1872 the sole partner, perceived insolvency as a more profitable line, but by 1886 court-related work represented nearly half the business.

The extension of the income tax to Ireland in 1853 provided an opening for accountants, especially to people who believed they had been over-assessed, but who were loath to expose their private affairs to public gaze. Advertisers, such as C. B. Mahony of Capel Street, made a special point of this, as did another *Irish Times* advertiser, Alfred de Blois Bliss of D'Olier Street.[39] Generally though, income tax only became significant when rates were raised substantially from 1916 onwards to pay for the First World War. At a lower level was James Joyce's father, John Stanislaus Joyce, who began his career as a book-keeper/accountant in Cork in the early 1870s. His biographers speculate that he learned the craft as an unpaid apprentice to a Cork businessman, and then went out on his own providing book-keeping services. This was certainly the pattern after his short-lived job as secretary to a Dublin distillery came to an end in 1876.[40] In a more ambitious way of business was Cleary & Co. of Lower Ormond Quay who announced in *The Irish Times*: 'Accounts and Balance Sheets audited and furnished. Books posted and balanced. Errors and complications adjusted. Partnership profits ascertained and apportioned. Accounting statements and schedules for arranging debtors, bankrupts, executors, administrators and trustees prepared and vouched with skill and expedition.'[41] Neither Mahony, Bliss nor Cleary & Co. were still in business in the early 1880s, so were not involved in the Charter.

Sometimes a glimmer of light on the work can be provided by a court case in which an accountant sued for fees. Thus in 1882 the firm of Kevans and Kean was employed to prepare Chancery accounts in respect of the personal estate of one Daniel J. Fegan of Westport, and also rentals and accounts of the real estate. This was clearly a substantial task, employing four experienced men for a month or more, plus others. Kevans claimed for 14½ days at £2 2s for a principal, 100 days at 15s a day for four first-class assistants, 26 days at 10s for five second-class assistants, plus some expenses, coming to a total of £184 6s 6d. The defendant argued that the job was worth no more than £115, and produced expert witnesses to prove it. Among these were Robert Gardner and Michael Crowley of M. Crowley & Co., who later served as the first Catholic President of the Institute of Chartered Accountants in Ireland from 1912–3. Against them were witnesses from the firms of Stokes Brothers and Peterson & Co. (Six years later, all four witnesses and the plaintiff were to be signatories of the 1888 Charter.) The judge took a sympathetic view of Kevans' case, declaring that 'when persons employ accountants occupying an eminent position, they should have to pay at a rate higher than might be charged by others'. The jury duly found for the plaintiff.[42] Given the social chasm in the city between Catholics and Protestants (extending to recruitment into firms), it is worth noting that in this business matter no such divide affected things. The Catholic Kevans was supported by the Protestants Stokes and Peterson, and opposed by the Protestant Gardner and the Catholic Crowley.

Early audit work

Although audit was nothing like the central preoccupation it later became, from time to time such jobs were on offer. An event a year before this case reveals much of the business atmosphere, the relations between directors and shareholders in those early days, and incidentally exposes the Catholic/Protestant rift that had been absent in Kevans' case. At an extraordinary meeting of the Hibernian Bank in March 1881, the shareholders assembled to vote on turning the bank into a public limited company, something the directors had previously rejected. Like many other public banks the Hibernian had resisted limited liability: from conservatism, from a sense that unlimited liability engendered confidence (on the assumption that with the whole of their wealth at risk the directors would take especial care) and from a reluctance to reveal details of their balance sheets. But the spectacular collapse of the unlimited City of Glasgow Bank three years before had changed people's minds.

The collapse of the City of Glasgow Bank in 1878 bears a striking resemblance to that of Anglo-Irish Bank 130 years later. It had occurred because in a chase for growth, in this case to support its rapidly-developed 133-branch chain, the bank had greatly increased its loans in certain speculative areas. The inherent dangers of this policy were worsened by taking insufficient and inappropriate security for its loans. In the end it was discovered that '70 per cent of its advances were owed to it by four people, described subsequently by the London *Times* as "a gang of desperate adventurers"'. There were also substantial unsecured loans to directors. After the collapse the creditors ruthlessly demanded their money from the unlimited shareholders. Hundreds of cases were pursued through the courts, to the ruin of widows, small businessmen, clergy and retired persons. The contemporary law of bankruptcy left little to the debtor. Homes were sold and women and children driven to the workhouse. As one historian wrote: 'the failure dramatically demonstrated the unsuitability of unlimited liability of investors as a basis on which to organise large-scale commercial activity . . . a concept which produced such harsh results for innocent investors was unacceptable.'[43]

The 1881 EGM of the Hibernian Bank was asked to vote both on the question of limited liability and on the appointment of a public accountant to audit the accounts. At this time there was a gradual move by the small number of public companies to replace the previous shareholder auditors with public accountants. Often, as in the Hibernian case, a change in legal status was the prompt. The Chairman of the bank reported that several gentlemen had presented themselves for the post of auditor. The choice was entirely the shareholders', but the board supported the candidature of Robert Gardner of Craig Gardner, whose reputation, he said, was well known. (The directors of the bank, which had been founded in 1825, were all prominent Catholic businessmen, and included John Fitzgerald Lombard, the property developer father-in-law of William Martin Murphy.) The Chairman went on to comment that, as far as he could see, the fact that Gardner was already auditor to another bank (the Royal Bank) was not an impediment. 'On the contrary', as *The Irish Times* reported, 'it told in his favour.' He then added, perhaps with the City of Glasgow affair in mind: 'the appointment of a Government auditor appeared looming not very far in the distance, and then probably all banks would be placed in the hands of one official belonging to the Local Government Board.' Nothing of course came of this idea, which would undoubtedly have been strongly resisted by the new profession.

Then a Mr Sexton, supporting the candidature of Edward Kevans of Kevans and Kean, raised a sensitive issue:

> 'he understood that this was a bank which had been established by Roman Catholic gentlemen and they—(cries of 'Oh, oh' and confusion). The Chairman: We know nothing of religion or politics here, sir. (Hear, hear) We may be all very good on Sunday, but we come here to transact our business and not to discuss questions of religion or politics. (Hear, hear).'

The vociferous Mr Sexton declared that he thought it was 'in exceedingly bad taste' for the directors to propose their own candidate; then, returning to an earlier theme, he continued, 'this was a bank got up by Roman Catholics (cries of 'oh, oh') well, he would pass that by and would say for their own sakes and for their own interest let them be great or small they should not sustain the nominees of the board (hear, hear).' And so it turned out. The matter was put to a vote, and Kevans (described by his supporters as 'the thoroughly independent man') won by 202 votes to 189.[44] A motion passed immediately afterwards set the remuneration at £150 per annum, about three times the annual wages of a labourer.

In its report, the nationalist *Freeman's Journal* made no reference to the Catholic/Protestant issue, which indeed seemed to be against the spirit of the meeting, but criticised the heavy-handed attempt of the directors to guide the shareholders, which, it declared, had lost Craig Gardner the job. As it happened, a few years later it was discovered that one of the directors had seriously compromised the bank's liquidity, a situation made worse when a staff member ran off with £2,000. The bank survived, with some difficulty, eventually to be subsumed in the Bank of Ireland Group in 1958.

Craig Gardner were appointed auditors to Arnotts department store in 1876, and their work for Sir John Arnott in respect of the store no doubt led to their being brought in to examine the affairs of the Glanmire Mills Company. The manager of the company (who was also the Cork City Treasurer) was accused of defrauding Sir John of £300,000 after a series of disastrous speculations. John Shanks, a senior clerk from Craig Gardner (and later a signatory to the Charter petition), had examined the books and found evidence of enormous losses, which had been covered up by some quite crude book-keeping tricks: pages in the ledgers were stuck together and rewritten, references from daybooks removed, literally hundreds of erasures in the cash books and even the creation of a completely false ledger (with appropriate ageing of the leather binding).

Surprisingly, the three accused were acquitted on a technicality, and even more surprisingly Henry Brown, who had evidently been lined up as a defence witness though he was not actually called, wrote to Cork City Council claiming in the forthright way of the time that the evidence given by John Shanks and Robert Gardner was 'cruel, uncandid and unfair' and exhibited 'a determination for a legal conviction'. He claimed that they had deliberately twisted evidence of admittedly 'wretched and incorrect book-keeping' to make things appear more criminal than they had been. Members of Cork City Council suspected an animus between the parties: 'Was not that gentleman a partner in the firm of Craig and Gardner?' asked one councillor. 'I think that this is a kind of fight that is got up between them'. All this was fully reported in *The Irish Times*,[45] and cannot have increased the enthusiasm of the one-time colleagues (Gardner had been trained as a clerk in Brown and Craig) for each other.

The two economies

As we have seen, the railways enabled British manufacturers to access even the remotest parts of the country, and turned Dublin into a great transport hub, with work for professionals, office workers, retailers and general labourers, but without adequate factories for the employment of skilled workers. The rest of the south was overwhelmingly agricultural. The development of Belfast and the North was, of course, very different, to the extent that economists talk of the two economies of Ireland.[46] Starting with linen and shipbuilding, and selling largely into England, the city was poised to expand into all kinds of heavy goods: steam engines, foundry products, ropes and heating and ventilating equipment. Other manufacturers were to diversify into mineral waters, cigarettes, agricultural machinery and motor cars. Before the First World War Belfast had a population of 400,000 and it was one of the prosperous cities of the British Isles. Wages had kept pace with Britain's (and as a bonus to the household the linen works gave employment to women) and there was little unemployment.

These were to be the economic bases for the establishment of the newly chartered accountancy profession in 1888.

Chapter Two
Charter Days: 1888–1899

We trust our health to the physician; our fortune and sometimes our life and reputation to the lawyer and attorney. Such confidence should not safely be reposed in people of a very mean or low condition. Their reward must be such, therefore, as may give them that rank in the society which so important a trust requires. The long time and great expense which must be laid out in their education, when combined with this circumstance, necessarily enhance further the price of their labour.'
Adam Smith Wealth of Nations (1776)[1]

The earliest associations of accountants in Britain and Ireland were based in Scottish cities. The first was the Institute of Accountants in Edinburgh (1853); this was quickly followed by similar societies in Glasgow and Aberdeen. This pre-eminence stemmed from the fact, underlining the general importance for the profession at the time of court work, was that Scottish insolvency law was more conducive towards accountants than the law in the rest of the country. Over time, similar societies sprang up in Liverpool (1870), London (1870), Manchester (1871) and Sheffield (1872)—in 1880 these combined with the Society of Accountants in England (1872) to form the Institute of Accountants.[1]

In 1880 this Institute presented a petition for a professional charter to Queen Victoria and the Privy Council, and it was approved. By this action the Institute of Chartered Accountants of England and Wales was established, with 587 members. The professional journal the *Law Times* called this 'a step in the right direction', and it was one that the Irish profession was soon to follow. No doubt the Irish noted the comment by *The Accountant* that 'it was impossible to prevent the assumption by quacks and rogues of the designation of accountant, but that the public would, for the future, be well advised to employ only the services of members of the Institute of Chartered Accountants and to look for the initials "FCA" and "ACA" after their names.'[2] This chapter deals with the social and economic atmosphere in which this great step for the Irish profession was taken.

The best-known Irish public accountant of the day was Robert Gardner, who was by now at the head of the country's largest accountancy firm, Craig Gardner & Co.[3] In 1880 Gardner married the daughter of his neighbour, John Brown Johnston, who owned a number of bakeries around Dublin. When his father-in-law died a few years later Gardner inherited the management of the firm. He decided to amalgamate the separate businesses on a site in Ballsbridge, just across the River Dodder from the Royal Dublin Society's new show grounds (which had opened in 1881). The new premises (which in 1890 became the headquarters of the bakery firm Johnston, Mooney and O'Brien) was opened on a very hot day in July 1886. Gardner invited over 100 men to celebrate the opening with a tour of the bakery followed by a fine luncheon. The names of those invited (carefully listed in *The Irish Times*) give us a clue as to his business network and his position in Dublin society.[4]

The guests were well-connected rather than elevated. There were, for instance, no lords, no-one from the Chief Secretary's office, no judges, no senior physicians, no clergy and no members of the great business families such as the Arnotts, Pims, Bewleys, Jamesons or La Touches—and there were also no names beginning Mac or O'. On the other hand, there were two MPs, three aldermen, several Justices of the Peace and a good representation of Findlaters, relatives of Robert Gardner's wife. There were plenty of solicitors (by far the largest group, lawyers being the major source of work for accountants), and many senior managers of banks, railway companies and life assurance offices. John Fitzgerald Lombard, William Martin Murphy's father-in-law and Chairman of the Dublin Tramway Company, was there, as were both the proprietor and manager of the *Freeman's Journal*. So too were the City Architect, the auditor of the Local Government Board, the Treasury Solicitor for Ireland and the proprietor of the Theatre Royal.

During the inevitable after-luncheon speeches, Gardner thanked the assembled crowd for coming. He was, he said, 'indebted to his friends for their company here and in an atmosphere almost as hot as the political atmosphere outside'. He was referring to the fact that the month-long poll for the General Election in Britain and Ireland was in progress (single-day voting was only introduced in 1918). Gladstone's first Home Rule Bill had been defeated the month before, and he had gone to the country in the hope of a sweeping endorsement of his policy. Quite the opposite occurred. Even as Robert Gardner was speaking, it was clear that the combination of Conservatives and Liberal Unionists was going to get a majority. The only question was—how big would it be? In fact at the end of the month the new Conservative government had a majority of 116 seats. This election was to mark the beginning of a 20-year period of Tory dominance of the House of Commons, a matter of great political significance for the Irish who aspired to Home Rule. These were undoubtedly a minority, if present at all, at Robert Gardner's opening.

Gardner's reference to the political heat outside was exemplified that very night. The likely victory of the Unionist side in the United Kingdom, as a whole, was in sharp contrast to the certainty of a pro-Home Rule vote in Ireland. In protest at this disheartening result, a nationalist crowd marched up Grafton Street and down York Street, near St Stephen's Green in Dublin, where the Nationalist Club, the Conservative Workingmen's Club and the Orange Hall were based. As the crowd surged passed the Conservative Club, at No. 38, members leaned out of the windows and hissed and groaned at the sight of the green and gold nationalist flag (the club itself proudly flaunted the Union Jack). The crowd threw some stones, and windows were broken; members retaliated by hurling bottles and, as more windows were broken, astonishingly, began shooting at the people in the street. One member of the crowd died (possibly of heart attack) and several were injured. When the police eventually regained control there were 80 arrests, though virtually all were released later.[5]

The English electorate decisively rejected Home Rule for Ireland. Although the Irish had voted overwhelmingly for nationalists (who won 84 out of 97 Irish seats), the result gave the Conservatives plus Liberal Unionists a comfortable majority of over 100 seats in the House of Commons, and so the possibility of Home Rule had to be shelved for a generation. The Irish Party had lost its pivotal position. With the backstop of a House of Lords implacably opposed to Home Rule, Irish Unionists could be forgiven for being quietly optimistic—even, as Robert Gardner's joke suggests, a little complacent. This was the political background to the granting of the Irish accountants' Royal Charter.

With the benefit of hindsight, it is tempting to argue that Unionist complacency was misplaced, and that independence of some sort was historically inevitable. That is by no means how it looked at the time—or indeed as late as the Rising of 1916. For the British Empire was at its zenith, and was clearly, as the 1886 election showed, in no mood to hand away power. The Irish, it was well understood in Westminster, had their grievances, but with Land Acts and Congested Districts Boards and other innovations, the famous policy of 'killing Home Rule with kindness' would surely bring them round. (The death of Charles Stewart Parnell in 1891, and the quarrelsome eclipse of the Irish Party, made these views more sustainable.) In the meantime the Irish economy was becoming daily more closely bound to the English; for instance, as one commentator noted, 'it is fast becoming as common a sight to see the man in the tram with an English morning paper as with a Dublin one'.[6] The economy was steadily growing: by 1913 per capita income had climbed to, or was not far below, the European average.[7] There was certainly no discussion of any partition of Ireland; the very idea was deplored on all sides, and would not enter the political vocabulary for a generation.

Economic growth did not particularly benefit the once-dominant Anglo-Irish Ascendancy, whose strength had come from their landholdings. Economic and political pressure was rendering this group increasingly ineffective. The global agricultural markets on which their rents, and hence their position, depended had been completely undermined by imported meat and wheat from North and South America and from Australia and New Zealand. As happened to their peers across Europe, the economic lifestyle of the Anglo-Irish rapidly became unsustainable. Effete, if stylish, they lost the aggression and drive that had so characterised them in the 17th and 18th centuries. When the challenge of the Land War came in the 1880s, as the novelist George Moore wrote, they failed to display the one virtue they prized above all—physical courage. The best went to England or to the Empire; the less energetic stayed in Ireland, devoting themselves to hunting and reading newspapers.

In Ireland energetic middle-class Protestants dominated the largest companies (the railways, the shipbuilders and industrial concerns of the North, Guinness, Jacobs and the department stores) and the financial sector (banks and insurance companies in particular) and the professions, and it was they who gained in the new economic dispensation. This domination, far beyond the proportion of the population they represented, was to last well into the 20th century.

As the 19th-century economies grew more complex, the division of labour ensured that new economic niches emerged and new skill-sets evolved to fill them. Accountants were only one of the new sets of professionals; there were also engineers (civil, mechanical and naval), pharmacists, dentists, architects and surveyors. They took their tone as far as possible from the old professions of medicine, church and law—though not going so far as to preserve the tradition that professional work was somehow *pro bono* and payment was merely honorary.

The new professions were not automatically accorded respect. In an Anthony Trollope novel of 1870, Miss Marrable

> 'had an idea that the son of a gentleman, if he intended to maintain his rank as a gentleman, should earn his income as a clergyman, or a barrister or as a soldier or a sailor. She would not absolutely say that a physician was not a gentleman, or even a surgeon . . . but she had no doubt whatever that when a man touched trade or commerce in any way he was doing that which was not the work of a gentleman.'[8]

This was of course intended as a caricature, but caricatures only amuse if they contain some truth. Irish 'Big House' novels depicting the lives of the Anglo-Irish do not mention accountants, but often relate similarly dismissive attitudes to solicitors. With a characteristically English sensitivity to precise class ranking, in 1887 the respected Frederick Whinney, President of the English Institute, noted that accountants could not yet regard themselves 'as on a line with the old professions . . . but I think we have a perfect right to say that the exigencies of modern life have called into existence certain semi-professions, of which we form one, and that not the least distinguished.'[9] Sir Desmond Lorimer (President of the Irish Institute in 1968–9), who qualified in Belfast in 1949, detected even then a remnant of self-consciousness: the profession, he thought, 'was jealous of other older professions because it was young and felt it had never got itself to be recognised as a true profession'.[10]

The origin of the professions as a social phenomenon has been a favourite topic for sociologists, and no strong consensus as to how they established themselves or how they retained their position has been achieved. The first requirement was 'a thing that needs doing', as one scholar put it; the professionals were those who did this thing full-time and so developed a special expertise, and a knowledge of what it is to do that thing well.[11] Reaching back to monastic times, when 'profession' meant taking religious vows, professionals in the modern sense were distinguished from craftsmen by the abstract nature of their activity and its ethical content, and from ordinary business people by an ethically driven aloofness from the marketplace. The archetypes against which the new men modelled themselves were law and medicine. For a new group to achieve professional status certain strategies were typical, and these certainly can be traced in the Irish circumstances. They are:

- Attaining legitimacy, for instance by Royal Charter
- Instituting entry, written examination and training requirements
- Establishing a code of ethics
- Promoting a professional knowledge and task set
- Pursuing state support for the profession, for instance by the establishment of a Register
- Developing work standards
- Self-regulation.[12]

A profession may be seen as having an implicit social contract with the public, as follows: in exchange for certain rewards guaranteed by a quasi-monopoly, we will make sure that anyone calling themselves a doctor, a solicitor or an accountant meets high standards of respectability, knowledge and ethical behaviour. Members of the new profession benefit by securing position and respect, as well as the income to support it.[13] The public gains by being offered a solution to the problem of how to judge abstract and technical services which are otherwise almost impossible for the public to assess and for which price is not an adequate indication of quality. A qualification or a presence on a register at least ensures a minimum of technical ability and ethical awareness. How otherwise could a buyer tell the plausible charlatan from the tongue-tied genius?

We have seen that by the 1881 Census there were 1,501 people in Ireland claiming to be 'accountants' (in 1891 this was down to 1,294). Some of these would have been working in financial organisations, such as banks, rather than in public practice. Nonetheless, this was a large group, though no doubt with many at least at the fringes, far from the 'respectability' that the Institute was to demand of its trainees.

Anyone could call themselves a public accountant, and combine that with some debt- and rent-collecting, agenting of various sorts, perhaps book-keeping. As mentioned in Chapter One, James Joyce's father, John Stanislaus Joyce, was no doubt typical of many: he did some book-keeping for shops and small businesses, had a period of rent-collecting, spent some time in the Collector-General's office, canvassed for ads (like Leopold Bloom) and spent time in Smithfield working out commissions and fees for the Dublin Cattle Market. As a book-keeper, 'he would go from shop to shop or business to business, checking the tots and the receipts and making regular returns of each office's annual figures. The routine was flexible and allowed for a good deal of idle chatter and the occasional drink in shop business or bar.'[14] He was clearly a rung or two down from the 'respectable' accountants looking for business from solicitors.

The range of problems these public accountants grappled with was considerable. At this time there were, as the Students' column of the *Weekly Irish Times* (the weekly version of the daily paper) put it, 'two systems [of book-keeping] are now adopted—known respectively as single and double entry. Single entry is principally useful to smaller traders and those whose transactions are numerous but small. The system of double entry is the more perfect and is used by every large commercial firm.'[15] Earlier, the same column had detailed the elements of 'the Italian system' viz.: a *Waste Book*, in which the day's transactions were entered just as they occurred, sometimes including transactions that were not destined to go forward into the ledgers; a *Journal* in which the debit and credit of each transaction were established, this being 'the real test of the accountant's skill', correctly classifying the higgledy-piggledy events of the day; and finally the *Ledger* into which the debit and credit decisions made in the journal were transcribed, this process 'requiring little more than accuracy and neatness'. This three-stage process would have been instantly recognisable to Francesco Datini in his Prato office. However, it seems that, like the use of the phrase 'the Italian system', it was somewhat old-fashioned. In his *Commercial Handbook* (1891), leading accountant Michael Crowley, principal of M. Crowley & Co. (President of the Institute 1912–13), assumes a two-stage process, posting straight from the books of first instance into the ledger and only putting through the journal entries that need special attention.

The anonymous author of this piece in the *Weekly Irish Times* was conscious that although there are basic principles, 'if a systematic examination were made of the books of a dozen of the leading merchants of London or other large city, it would be probably found that no two were exactly alike.'[16] As a result, the public accountant's job had plenty of variety; from opening books, auditing, doing investigations and preparing Chancery accounts, to accounting for anything from family estates to factories, from shops to institutions. An extreme example was described by the well-known London accountant Gerard van der Linde, who presented a paper to a gathering of accountants in Ireland in 1893. In his *Reminiscences,* van der Linde recalled how on one occasion he was asked to change the book-keeping of a small business from single to double entry. A routine task, except that, for privacy, the single-entry books were all in cypher, with the letters of the word CUMBERLAND standing for numerals (C = 1, U = 2, M = 3, B = 4 and so on). This was a long job.

Going for the Charter

Before the 1844 Companies Act a new professional body, such as physicians, surgeons, civil engineers or architects, had two choices of incorporation: a private Act of Parliament or a Royal Charter. A Charter had better resonance than an Act of Parliament, as it signified royal approval, a certain dignity traceable to the 14th century, and an implicit acknowledgment of superiority. For Irish accountants, there was also the strong precedent of the English body chartered only a few years before. The route was to petition the Queen sitting with the Privy Council for such a Charter, addressing her via her proxy in Ireland, the Lord Lieutenant. The first step, therefore, was to draw up an acceptable petition and organise for the leaders in the profession to sign it together.

Like other professionals, accountants are holders of secrets. The ingrained habit of discretion is perhaps the reason why so few have written accounts of their lives. We will therefore never learn the inner story of the gaining in 1888 of the Royal Charter by the Institute of Chartered Accountants in Ireland. Howard Robinson, the historian of the Irish Institute, has described how Robert Stokes, who had trained in England, was originally approached by a member of the Council of the newly formed Society of Accountants and Auditors proposing a Dublin branch of their society. This route of establishing an Irish branch of a British society had been favoured by the surveyors, who had joined up with the London-based Royal Institute of Chartered Surveyors (incorporated 1837), and was to be by others, for instance the Chartered Secretaries. However, like a latter-day Nelson putting a telescope to his blind eye, Robert Stokes apparently retorted that 'they would have a Charter or nothing'.[17] It is not entirely clear why. One factor may have been an unsettling stream of new law in respect of Irish insolvency. Irish insolvency law being, as we have seen, different from English and Scottish, an association headquartered in London could hardly be expected to protect members as well as a local organisation.

The core legislation was the Irish Bankruptcy and Insolvency Act 1857, which established the Court of Bankruptcy in Dublin and generally consolidated the laws as different from those obtaining in England and Scotland. Fifteen years later came the (Irish) Bankruptcy Arrangement Act and the Debtors Act of 1872. The former conferred additional powers on the Court, the latter abolished the distinction between an insolvent trader and a non-trader and abolished imprisonment for debt (following a similar 1869 English Act). In 1886 a Bill was abortively floated by some

Irish parliamentarians proposing that a debtor could gain the assent of three-quarters of his creditors and complete the business in the offices of the Official Assignee, which would of course have cut the accountants out, to the considerable detriment of the small Irish profession. Another Act, in 1888, set up local bankruptcy courts in Belfast and Cork. For the rest of the 19th century the Council of the newly formed Irish Institute fought a series of battles against 'officialism', i.e. the transfer of company liquidations to an official liquidator, which would take the business away from the profession. One of the earliest of these activities was the establishment of a sub-committee in 1893 to fight a Bill that proposed to establish the Official Assignee in Bankruptcy as Official Liquidator under the Companies Acts.[18] Similar proposals were fought off in 1896 and in 1899.[19]

Stokes called meetings of accountants in Dublin, Belfast and Cork, and towards the end of 1887 a petition was presented to the Lord Lieutenant. Undoubtedly there were then behind-the-scenes discussions and perhaps a calling-in of favours. There would perhaps have been quiet lobbying on the edges of grand dinner parties, and casual discussions in clubs or perhaps in the hunting field (Robert Gardner followed the Ward Union staghounds in north Dublin). On the other hand, if Robert Gardner's invitees to his great opening day in Ballsbridge are a good measure, the accountants would not necessarily have had many very elevated strings to pull. As far as we know (from e.g. listings in Thom's *Directories*), accountants were not on the board of any of the public companies or financial institutions; nor were they represented on civil society institutions where leading businessmen met the Anglo-Irish Ascendancy, such as the Royal Dublin Society, the Statistical and Social Inquiry Society or the Kildare Street Club.

The religious mix of the original petitioners is another clue to their status. Of the 31 signatories, the religious affiliations of 27 have been identified.[20] Of these, only 10 were Church of Ireland, four Catholic, three each Methodist and Presbyterian, two Brethren, one each Baptist, Christian Unitarian, Christian Scientist, Episcopalian and 'No church'. In a society in which class and religion went hand in hand, this is a mixed set. We have seen in Chapter One, in the Hibernian Bank EGM of 1881, a general concern that the Catholic/Protestant divide should not be introduced into business matters. However, the contemporary academic observer Arthur Clery (a Catholic—later Professor of Law at UCD) noted the limits to that aspiration. In the city, he wrote, 'men of all religions mingle freely. They lunch together; they drink together; and in a sense they forget the religious question. Yet . . . a single shot, a blast on the bugle, a tap on the drum and they rush to take their places on the opposing firing lines.'[21] The predominantly Protestant founding fathers of the Institute would also have been conscious that Protestants were a comfortable majority in other professions. At a time when Protestants represented just 25 per cent of the population (including Ulster), the 1891 Census reported that 60 per cent of doctors, barristers and solicitors, and as many as 74 per cent of civil engineers were Protestant.[22] The 85 per cent of Protestants in the new Institute was an exceptionally high proportion.

Everyone, except perhaps the unfortunate John Shanks, was one or the other. It was he who described himself as 'No church'—we have met him before, as the senior clerk who uncovered the book-keeping problems on the Glanmire Mills case for Craig Gardner. He was evidently a bit of a contrarian, being also an active member of the Protestant Home Rule Association. Shanks was excluded from the Council of the newly founded Institute in 1889 on his becoming bankrupt, though, if his 1901 Census return is not misleading, he seems to have continued to practise. (The Christian Scientist, incidentally, was John Gardner, son of Robert.)

By far the best connected politically of the petitioners was Henry Brown, the second President of the Institute whom we have seen advertising his services in the 1840s. He was active in Dublin Conservative circles. He was a Conservative member of Dublin Corporation, a Guardian of the South Dublin Union and a member of the Dublin Chamber of Commerce. Clearly, Brown would have known well all sorts of men for whom the 1886 general election, which established the Tories in power for 20 years, was a triumph. Brown was auditor of the City and County Conservative Club (the respectable one, in Dawson Street, as opposed to the other in York Street) and was also involved in temperance associations. Both he and Robert Gardner were on the Citizens Committee for Her Majesty's Jubilee in 1887. Apart from these two, it is difficult to identify other lines of contact with power and influence. It has been asserted that Robert Stokes was 'actively involved in unionist politics',[23] and this may well be so, but his name is not traceable in *The Irish Times*' copious lists of attendance at meetings and gatherings.

Catholic and nationalist polemic then and since would lead one to assume that Freemasons were likely to be involved in conspiratorial lobbying behind the scenes. According to Fr Edward Cahill S.J., describing Ireland in 1932, Freemasons 'control very much of the economic life of the country, including the banks and the railways, and several of the more important academic and educational institutions'; in a Catholic Truth Society pamphlet written a year before, the Rev. G. Clune wrote 'the Masonic Lodges of Ireland . . . thrive on secrecy and underhand ways, plotting unfair advantage over their rivals in industry, trade and commerce'.[24] Freemasons and Jews, described by the nationalist Arthur Griffith as two of the 'three evil influences of the century', were, in certain Catholic circles, supposed to be in a mighty world combination against the Christian faith.[25] The special provision in the abortive Government of Ireland Act 1920, exempting Freemasons from the controls imposed on other secret societies, continues to be seen as proof positive of their sinister influence.[26] But the index of the order in the 1880s suggests that only two of the 31 petitioners, Edward Allworthy of Belfast and Joseph Woodworth of Dublin, were members.[27] There is no evidence of any other involvement. This respectable group of mainly Protestant men (but clearly not Ascendancy in background) from all over the island—13 from Dublin, 12 from Belfast and six from Cork—was attempting to establish something that had been established very successfully in England only a few years before. Perhaps the Conservatives' new policy of 'killing Home Rule with kindness' inclined the establishment to look kindly on the Irish petition.

Given that as many as 1,501 people were reported in the 1881 Census as practising accounting, it is striking that the initial membership was limited to the very small group of 31 men. The Institute of Chartered Accountants in England and Wales (ICAEW) had begun with nearly 600 members. It seems possible that a major consideration in the choice of early members of the Irish Institute was participation in active work in and around the courts. Here the petitioners were working, if not actually competing, with the established solicitors' profession, which was formally accredited to the court. As late as 1899, Judge Boyd of the Court of Bankruptcy produced a crotchety outburst while examining the schedules of an arranging debtor: 'I consider', he said, 'the whole system of [accounts] scheduling in the court is bad—absolutely bad. These schedules ought not to be prepared by men who merely try to make both ends meet, but by the officers of the court who have no interest but to see that justice is done between all parties. If I had my way I would have the thing altered.'[28] This was, as we have seen in Chapter One, only the latest of a series of similar judicial outbursts criticising the emerging accounting profession. The first necessity for the leaders of the new profession was how to defuse such criticisms. As *The*

Irish Times put it when the Charter was achieved, 'the object of the Charter is evidently to raise the status of the profession, and we congratulate the promoters on the success of their efforts.'[29]

In old-fashioned companies there was also some prejudice to be overcome against bringing strangers into the privacy of the accounting rooms to do an audit. At a meeting of the Royal Bank in 1868, a shareholder commented that 'the affairs of such a concern as theirs were frequently so delicate that they could not be put before auditors'. He continued: 'he could well understand men of high respectability and deep solvency being in an emergency indebted to a bank and who would be deterred from taking such a step if they knew it would of necessity be brought under the notice of auditors.'[30] In this context the appointment of a shareholder auditor ('one of us') had made sense, as did the absolute premium put on public respectability or trustworthiness by the fledgling profession.

Respectability and the marks of respectability were therefore both intrinsically desirable and a marketplace necessity. In the petition requesting that a Royal Charter be granted presented to the Lord Lieutenant at the end of 1887 it was stressed that:

> 'the functions of public accountants are of great and increasing importance in respect of their employment under decrees of Chancery, in the winding up of companies, in Bankruptcies or Arrangements with Creditors and in various positions of trust under Courts of Justice; as also in auditing the accounts of public companies and of partnerships and otherwise. . . . To the due performance of a profession such as this a liberal education is essential, and the object of the petitioners is to secure that education and to maintain the efficiency as well as the respectability of the professional body in Ireland to which they belong.'[31]

In this petition and, as we have seen in Chapter One, in advertisements in Thom's *Directory*, audit takes a clearly secondary place to insolvency work. The only direct evidence of the importance of such work comes from Craig Gardner's fee books, completed in Robert Gardner's flowing, clear, but sometimes careless hand. By 1880 much of the work consisted of 'bankruptcy, liquidation and arranging debtors' and other semi-legal work (see *Table 1*). The predominance of 'one-off' tasks gives rise to considerable fluctuations in activity. For instance, the firm charged fees on 584 jobs in 1883–4 and only on 421 in 1885–6. In 1883–4 there were 31 fees over £50 (equivalent to the annual wages of a skilled labourer at the time), but in 1885–6 only 11. Where they are described (and Robert Gardner is distinctly unsystematic in this), most of the large jobs are liquidations, chancery accounts or trust estates. The drastic drop of activity in the mid-1880s may be associated with the decline in the wave of insolvencies following the crisis years of the late 1870s and early 1880s. It is not until after 1900 that the marked fluctuations in activity changes to a much steadier pattern, as year-on-year audits gradually become common.

Table 1: *Craig Gardner Fee Book* [32]

Job mix (January 1884)	#	%
Audit	15	17
Bankruptcy, liquidation, A/D (Arranging Debtors)	23	25
Trust deeds, deceased	4	4
Miscellaneous (debt collection, stock taking, fire claims, valuation, opening books etc)	9	10
Not described	39	43
Totals	90	100

The Charter achieved

The Charter was formally approved by the Queen on 21 April 1888 and issued by the Under-Secretary in June.[33] The 31 petitioners became Fellows and established the Council of the Institute of Chartered Accountants in Ireland, as it was to be called for over 100 years. 'The first Council', writes Howard Robinson

> 'appointed by the Charter consisted of Robert Gardner (President), Henry Brown, Robert Stokes, John H. Woodworth, Edward Kevans, John Shanks and Michael Crowley of Dublin; John McCullough, William Fitzsimons, Martin Shaw and Edward Allworthy of Belfast; and William R. Atkins of Cork. Many of the names on the first Council represented firms that were to dominate the profession for the best part of a hundred years—Craig, Gardner & Co; Stokes, Brothers & Pim; Woodworth & Company; Kevans & Sons; M. Crowley & Co, John McCullough & Sons; Wright, Fitzsimons & Co, Martin Shaw, Leslie & Shaw and Atkins, Chirnside.'

The first meeting of the Council, on 19 November 1888, was held in Craig Gardner's offices in Trinity Chambers on the corner of Dame Street and Trinity Street in Dublin.

With the Charter came a crest, incorporating, as was normal, aspects of the business. Even in 1888 the images chosen must have seemed a little old-fashioned: two crossed quill pens (which had long ceased to be commonly used in offices, after the advent of metal pens in the 1820s), scales (presumably a reference to currency dealing) and a merchant sailing vessel. The motto below was '*Remque fidemque servo*' which derives from a phrase of the Latin playwright Plautus and means 'I preserve both wealth and credit'.[34]

The first formal task was to establish the bye-laws of the new Irish Institute. These were sensibly based on those of the English Institute, with some variations. There was little debate about them, since drafts had apparently been available for some time. Members were forbidden to tout for business, or to give or accept commissions from other professionals, for instance by way of a kick-back for business. They were also specifically forbidden to carry out any other business than that of a public accountant, and this was to be a regular reason why applicants for membership who did not reach this austere standard (who, for instance, did some debt collecting or, as in the early Thom's listings, business translation) were rejected. The only law on which any debate arose was that prohibiting advertising, which Martin Shaw of Belfast proposed negating. The spirit of the meeting, however, was very much against this. Chairman Robert Gardner (somewhat hypocritically, since he had up to then been a regular advertiser in Thom's *Directory*) described it as 'a discreditable system which should at once be given up'; he was supported by Joseph Woodworth, who described advertising as 'derogatory to the profession'. The law prohibiting advertising was confirmed, and the agreed bye-laws were submitted to the Privy Council in London for approval. This approval was duly delivered in February 1889.[35]

On the evening of the first meeting a tremendous dinner was held, with every single guest (as the British professional journal *The Accountant* noted) being of direct practical and daily importance to the accountants of Ireland. This was an all-male affair, ending with no fewer than 14 speeches, including a claim by the 70-year-old Henry Brown to be the Father of the new profession (thus claiming an honorary status as the oldest member, like the Father of the House of Commons). His one-time employee, Robert Gardner, now the first President of the Institute and head of the largest firm in the country, was less than generous, perhaps remembering the hard words spoken in the *Glanmire Mills* case some years before. He conceded merely that Brown was certainly 'the eldest' accountant in the gathering.

Barely a week after the inaugural dinner, on 6 December, a subcommittee began its work assessing applications for membership, of which there were two grades, Fellows being the senior established men and Associates being relatively junior. The minutes of the Council of the Institute of 7 March 1889 record that '21 applicants had been received: 4 admitted as Fellows, 9 admitted as Associates, decisions on 5 postponed pending further information and 5 applicants were deemed ineligible'. In the first two years, 19 new members were elected.

Following the example of the English Institute, the Irish insisted on trainees serving a five-year period formally apprenticed to a member, called a principal. This relationship, modelled on the legal profession, was embodied in 'articles of clerkship'. The trainee was referred to as an articled clerk. As well as working in the principal's office, articled clerks had to pass a preliminary exam and then two more exams over time (there was a three-year term of articles and a waiver from the preliminary exam for university graduates). The first man to pass through this system was Benjamin Twamley of Stokes Brothers. The preliminary exam, taken by the non-graduate majority, reflected the Institute's fulfilment of its pledge to insist on a 'liberal education' in its trainees. It included papers on such genteel subjects as Latin, Euclidian geometry, algebra and the History of England, subjects clearly favouring the small number of the population who had attended secondary schools. The barrier to entry was deliberately high: not only was there a stiff premium or fee to be paid on signing articles (very often as much as £150, or three times the annual wages of a labourer) but the period as an articled clerk was virtually unpaid, ensuring that the new clerk would have to be kept by his parents.[36] A bright young office boy, starting work at 14, could aspire to a long and reasonably well-paid life as an unqualified senior, but could not qualify as a chartered accountant and so could never expect to become a partner.

In the meantime, the work of the world went on. The general recovery of trade in the late 1880s produced an increase in the number of businesses seeking incorporation and listing on the Dublin Stock Exchange. A previous generation's fear, that limited liability was merely a declaration in advance that a company's debts might not be paid, had long faded. Many of the new companies were well-established concerns that, for a variety of reasons, were looking for the protection of limited status. In his exploration of these companies in 1901, Michael Crowley estimated that 'about half' of companies were formed to carry on the business of previously existing firms and that the balance were new businesses.[37] The market was undoubtedly attracting investors, so established concerns began to consider flotation. Sometimes it was because of the death or retirement of senior managers, sometimes the opportunity to monetise the goodwill. As the historian of the Irish Stock Exchange, put it: 'From around 50 or so registrations in the mid-eighties the number rose to 90 in the early 1890s, reaching 134 and 145 in 1896 and 1897 respectively. . . [these companies] provided a welcome diversification from dependence on government stocks, banks, railways and foreign stocks and in doing so supplied a staid and proven range of industrial investments.'[38]

The change of corporate structure often (but by no means always) led to the employment of a professional auditor. The legal position was that the current Companies Act, passed in 1862, unlike its predecessor of 1844, did not require the directors to present statements of accounts to their shareholders or for any audit to be conducted (though the model Articles and Memorandum in the Act assumed such an audit to be normal). It was not until a new Companies Act in 1900 that this actually became compulsory, as opposed to just good governance. This lack of confidence in the audit function can perhaps be ascribed to experience of the futility of the usual amateur audit by representatives elected from the body of shareholders. In practice, however, more and more companies were employing public auditors. Most companies required their annual accounts to be written up as well as audited. These so-called 'book-keeping audits', in which the auditor first draws up the accounts and then audits his or her own work, were to be a feature of the accountancy business for most of the 20th century.

It has been suggested that one of the reasons why the Institute of Chartered Accountants in Ireland was founded was because Irish businesses of the day turned to English accountants to meet their needs. Thus, the historian of the Institute, Howard Robinson, writes 'with the development of accountancy in Ireland and with the agitation for Home Rule there [was] in the twentieth century a move towards the employment of Irish firms of accountants in place of the English auditors which some of the larger companies tended to employ'.[39] A row that broke out in the first two years of the fledgling Institute has been thought of as reinforcing the proposition. In 1890 Robert Gardner brought together two other bakeries to join his already existent Johnston & Co. in Ballsbridge, thus creating Johnston, Mooney and O'Brien, a firm that was prominent in Dublin for 100 years. Fatally, he proposed that the London firm Cooper Brothers work on the prospectus and be the auditors. Gardner knew Cooper Brothers because he had worked with them on the Dublin end of two London-registered Irish companies, the Provincial Bank and the Dublin Distillers Company. The appointment was taken badly by his colleagues on the Council, however, and after a hasty meeting chaired by Henry Brown (and injudiciously without hearing any explanation from Robert Gardner) a note was circulated to the press condemning this action as 'very prejudicial to the interests of the Institute and unfair to its members'.[40] Despite efforts to row back on this, Gardner resigned from the Presidency, the Council and the Institute, and never rejoined, though he did participate in various special activities. *The Accountant* took the view that the Council had made a serious mistake in offending Gardner in this way, declaring that 'it can hardly be supposed that men capable of the short-sightedness which possessed them when they commenced kicking a lion under the idea that they were dealing with an ass, will let it be their last, though it may be their greatest error of policy.'[41]

It is not clear how far this dramatic event can be used as evidence of English penetration into the Irish accounting market. For instance, it is hard to believe that, if Gardner had been conscious of this as a motivating grievance in the establishment of the Institute, he would have been so insensitive (autocratic and impulsive as he undoubtedly was). In such a small world he was perhaps more conscious of a desire to keep his private business private; and in fact after a couple of years Craig Gardner took over the audit. We might also wonder if, after the less than cordial exchanges at the inaugural dinner and in the Glanmire affair, Henry Brown was not sorry to put Gardner on the spot. Brown succeeded Gardner as President and served four annual terms.

There was, equally, little evidence of a predatory appetite in the City of London. A modern historian of English accountancy has commented that, far from looking for expansion, 'most of the relatively big City chartered accountancy practices were remarkably slow to establish branches in the provinces, reflecting the small scale of accountancy firms generally down to the Second World War.'[42] Thus, one of the largest city firms, Price Waterhouse, only established its first UK branch in Liverpool in 1904; the next was in Newcastle, which was closed in 1920. 'A further factor seems to have been a desire to supervise personally the work undertaken . . . the policy laid down by the founders of Cooper Brothers & Co. was that the business should be conducted only from the office in London.' The use of London-based accountants by Irish firms very often stemmed from the fact that the Irish business concerned was incorporated in London. Cooper Brothers, as we have seen, had the audit of the London-incorporated Dublin Distillers Company, though in fact the monthly work for Distillers was done in Dublin by Craig Gardner, Coopers finding it too expensive to send its own people across the water. The whole audit eventually came to Craig Gardner.

A sample of the larger companies floated in Dublin in the decade from 1888 supports the idea that at least by the 1880s there was little serious incursion into the Irish market by English firms, and the suggestion of a change associated with ideas of Home Rule an illusion. It shows only three out of 25 as being audited by other than Irish firms. The rest went to Craig Gardner, Stokes Brothers, Kean & Co, Woodworth or Peterson.

Of the outliers, Dublin Brick and Tile, floated in 1890, was audited by an amateur shareholder in the old manner, as were still many of the larger railway companies and some financial institutions, such as Northern Assurance. Bolands Mills was in fact a Belfast firm, and the audit went to Hill Vellacott's Belfast office, which also had the audit of the Northern Bank (the firm of Jones Hill Vellacott being the conspicuous exception to the reluctance of City of London firms to establish offices outside the City). At the shareholders meeting assigning this audit, the Catholic Dubliner Edward Kevans was outvoted by 990 to 290. As it happened, his former partner John Kean took over the audit in 1904.

The wines and spirits firm Kinahans was audited for 20 years by the London firm Pratt & Norton (not one of the London top 20). The company got into trouble in the mid-1900s, and a shareholder proposed 'under the present circumstances they should employ one of the eminent public accountants who resided in Dublin and had local knowledge. The absence of local guidance had been one of the causes of the disasters.'[43] Nothing changed, and the firm was put into liquidation in 1910.

At the end of the 19th century there was a brief but exciting flurry on the Dublin Stock Exchange in bicycle and tyre shares, which provided prospectus and ultimately audit work. A dozen new companies were launched in 1893, and prices soared 200 or 300 per cent. Old hands were reminded of the railway boom. Dealing time had to be extended to cope with the rush, especially after the defeat of another Home Rule Bill in 1893 attracted money from London. There were eventually as many as 40 large and small companies involved, some being no more than agencies with balance sheets inflated with 'goodwill' but little working capital. Of the larger companies the first in the field was Pneumatic (auditor Stokes Brothers), followed by the 'Grappler' Pneumatic Tyre and Cycle Company (auditor Peterson), Seddon (auditor Craig Gardner) and Revolution Cycle (auditor Stokes Brothers).[44]

By now, the business community and the accountancy profession were beginning to evolve detailed understandings of the role of audit and the keeping of proper books. Furthermore, even outside the commercial world regular accounting was increasingly recognised as unavoidable. Thus so unworldly a group as the General Synod of the Church of Ireland was told by a speaker in 1887 that 'it was the fashion nowadays to ridicule book-keeping, but it was impossible to get on without it'.[45]

But things were changing. As we have seen, the shareholder bodies were still quite small: of a sample of larger companies registered in Dublin and Cork between 1888 and 1897, three-quarters had shareholder bodies of fewer than 500; only four had more than 1,000 shareholders and one of those was the speculative Grappler Pneumatic.[46] Nonetheless, only one of our sample of 25 companies launched between 1888 and 1897 was audited by a shareholder.

An unexpected advantage of the use of public accountants by a company was the gaining of a regular financial advisor with a kind of detailed knowledge that neither solicitors nor bankers could rival. Thus the fact that Craig Gardner audited most of the department stores in Dublin must have given their remarks about the accounts a special authority. These early auditors deployed a notable freedom of exploration and a robust independence of expression. They were in effect writing management letters long before the practice became general.[47] For instance, in 1891, in an attempt to identify where a drop in gross profits in McBirney's department store had come from, a Craig Gardner partner made an unprompted analysis of the gross profits of various departments. The same partner noted that the allowance for bad debts was too small and commented meaningfully: 'we have to express the hope that the collection of accounts is well looked after'.

In 1899, John Gardner was equally blunt to the directors of the Ballaghadereen general store, Monica Duff & Co.: 'the profit is equivalent to only three per cent of sales which having regard to the nature of the commodities is perfectly absurd'. Four years later they returned to the attack:

'we still entertain the opinion that dishonesty in some shape or form has been the cause of the serious deficiency shown by the Accounts.'[48] (In this case the firm evidently did not feel that it was their duty to explore the possible fraud.) In 1896 David Telford, also of Craig Gardner, took a more proactive line. Explaining to the H. Williams shareholders that he had not been satisfied with the stock sheets provided by the company, he told them: 'I got our people to examine all the more important items and to satisfy themselves that the principle on which they were valued was a correct one . . . the stock sheets have undergone considerable alteration at our hands.'[49] The practice appears to have waned. When in the 1950s Donal O'Mahony of Kennedy Crowley explained to his principal that as a young audit clerk he had provided some advice to the client on cash flow (for which they were duly grateful): 'I was met with a frosty glare and informed that we were not paid for that type of thing!'[50]

A few years later, after the decision on the leading case on auditing, *Irish Woollen Manufacturing v. Tyson* (1899), Telford might have acted differently. In this case, the auditor, Edward Kevans, was being sued (with others) for negligence. At first there was a suggestion that he was even negligent in employing clerks rather than doing the work himself—he was, after all, the man specifically chosen by the shareholders. Luckily for the development of the accountancy profession, this was shrugged off in the Court of Appeal. The case finally went against Kevans, but not before several of the judges had expanded on what they thought auditors could and should do. Lord Justice Holmes declared that the auditor:

> 'is not to assume that the officers of the company are either honest or dishonest. He had a right to see their books and to ask them for information, but he was not called on to seek information outside the company or to communicate with creditors. He was not the insurer of the company against fraud or error. There is no duty on the auditor to take stock.'

Lord Justice FitzGibbon concurred, commenting that 'the auditor was entitled to assume that the books were honest books until his suspicion was aroused, or until something occurred which ought to have aroused his suspicions'.[51]

These comments, and the better-known dictum from the *Kingston Cotton Mills* case of 1896, defining the role of an auditor as 'a watchdog rather than a bloodhound', suggested that there was a gap between what some professional auditors thought was their duty and how that duty was construed by the law. David Telford had clearly thought it his duty to explore the stock sheets on behalf of the shareholders. In practice also auditors had taken on a more actively protective role than the 'watchdog' description implied.

The mix of business was gradually shifting from predominantly court-related work with some book-keeping to predominantly audit (i.e. writing up accounts and then auditing them) with whatever insolvency work came to hand. In practice, the profession began to concentrate on protecting its client companies:

- against incompetence and fraud by employees, especially in accounts offices—until the 1950s textbooks regularly described this as the principal purpose of audit;[52]
- against over-optimism, or perhaps deliberate manipulation, by managers, with conservative treatments, e.g. of stock valuation, by closely matching expenses to revenues, and by appropriate bad debt allowance and depreciation; and
- against opportunistic shareholders and predatory trade rivals by masking the real activities of their clients with deliberately opaque accounts and active use of reserves.

And these were to remain the aims of audit, and therefore of most accountants, for a long time.

Chapter Three
Auditing Becomes the Norm: 1900–1922

The two principal reasons for which an audit may be instituted are: (a) the detection of fraud, (b) the detection of errors, and coincident with these the prevention of fraud and errors by reason of the deterrent and moral effect of the audit.

Spicer and Pegler Practical Auditing (1914)[1]

History has bathed the years up to Irish independence in 1922 in an exciting political light. But as is normal, most people heavily engaged in business life had not much to do with political agitation, nor did activists know or care much about business. In retrospect, partition, independence and all that followed might seem inevitable, but that was not so clear at the time. As a small but telling example, it was not until a meeting of February 1923, more than a year after the Anglo-Irish Treaty, that the question was raised at the Council of the Irish Institute 'as to what authority or otherwise the Institute now has in the six counties known as Northern Ireland'. The legal opinion, reported in May, was that the Institute's writ still ran in the 'Six Counties'.

Before this, however, Irish businesses, most especially in the North, generally strove to deepen and intensify their commercial connections with their nearest and best markets in Britain. Dublin thrived on import–export activity across the Irish Sea. Irish agriculture exported its produce to the hungry industrial cities such as Liverpool, Manchester and Birmingham. Indeed, during the First World War period Irish agriculture did particularly well on the British market.

At the same time nationalists worked hard to create a new image for Ireland, one in which the balance sheet, the trial balance and the cash book had a low place. Leading the van in this was Douglas Hyde with his 1892 lecture, "The Necessity for De-Anglicising Ireland". Hyde's view was that the Irish must aspire to be 'most racial, most smacking of the soil, most Gaelic, most Irish', starting with the language. He declared that, if offered, 'nine out of ten Irishmen' would reject the alternative of making

Ireland 'a land of wealth and factories . . . fat, wealthy and populous' at the expense of the Irish language and other distinguishing factors. The movement he initiated despised what it called 'Manchesterism', which started as a description of free trade liberalism but became a general term of abuse memorably characterised by W. B. Yeats as 'fumbl[ing] in a greasy till'.[2]

As well as being clearly part of the commercial world, the Irish accountancy profession (north and south) was largely Protestant, like so many in the more elevated financial and commercial sectors. Their minds and hearts were therefore inclined to support the connection with Britain. This was confirmed when the profession as a whole responded strongly to the recruitment calls on the outbreak of war. In November 1914 the Irish Institute followed the English by permitting articled clerks to proceed on active or government service without prejudice to their terms of service. Robert Walsh of Belfast, an original Fellow and signatory of the Charter petition, was President of the Institute and heartily approved: 'Belfast members agree English decision. Think patriotic resolution should be published Dublin and Belfast' he cabled to the Institute.

The response from members and their staff to recruitment calls to join the British forces was significant. Towards the end of the war it was recorded that a striking proportion of the 1914 count of 116 members and 63 students under articles had joined up, not to mention an unknown number of unqualified assistants. The mortality rate of those who enlisted, at 14.8 per cent, was only just less than that suffered by the German army during the war, and higher than the average British rate of 12.3 per cent.

A 'Salaries Book' from Stokes Brothers & Pim (a very Protestant firm, and later a core part of KPMG) identifies no fewer than 11 young men who enlisted from that firm, five of whom died. Three joined up in September 1914, all of whom were killed in action, one in the Dardanelles. The first to join up was A. E. Deane, evidently a reservist, for he was called up on 5 August 1914. Deane, who was originally employed as a typist in 1909, returned to the firm in 1919 and was still there in 1942.[3] These were staff: the partner, F. H. Pim (half-brother to the original J. Harold Pim), also joined up, serving in the Royal Army Service Corps in Egypt, France and Gallipoli.[4]

Perhaps the best known exception to the general pro-British tendency is Michael Collins, who worked briefly with Craig Gardner in early 1916.[5] There were others. In the same office was Joe McGrath, who fought near Jameson's Distillery in Marrowbone Lane in the Easter Rising of 1916, and who later became Minister for Labour and subsequently managed the Irish Hospital Sweepstakes, by a long way the greatest money-making machine of its era. (His memories of his time with Craig Gardner obviously remained happy enough for the Sweepstakes to become an important Craig Gardner audit from its beginning.) An older man, Jeremiah Buckley, qualified with Kean & Co. in Dame Street and in 1900 bought the militant nationalist paper the *Limerick Leader*. In 1902 he was briefly imprisoned for publishing anti-British leaders, and in 1919 the paper was suppressed by the authorities. Buckley became a close friend of de Valera's and was heavily involved in the foundation and development of the *Irish Press*. He died in 1937.[6]

Percy Reynolds, who later founded Reynolds McCarron, was in the Stephen's Green brigade in 1916. Both his father J.R. Reynolds, an accountant with an office in Westmoreland Street, and his sister were in the GPO. After the Rising, Reynolds, who subsequently became the first chairman of state-sponsored transport company CIÉ, was imprisoned first in Wormwood Scrubs and then in the internment camp at Frongoch.[7] Joseph Considine, whose brother had been 'out' in 1916, but who was not himself involved until 1919–21, also worked for Craig Gardner. It was rumoured that he used one of the partner's rooms for clandestine meetings, and that some inkling of this led to a Black and Tan raid on the office in 1921. (Legend said that none of the Catholic staff came in that day, having been forewarned.)

Apart from these well-known names, it is difficult to identify others involved in 'the national struggle'. (Unsurprisingly, Stokes Brothers & Pim's Salaries Book does not record any sudden or unexplained departures around Easter 1916.) At the AGM in May 1916 David Telford of Craig Gardner, then President of the Institute, made his negative feelings about the Rising quite clear. He was no doubt prompted by the fact that his son, also David, had served in France since 1914, and that his partner, Sir Robert, had recently lost a son in the Gallipoli campaign at Suvla Bay. 'None of us', he said, 'thought that when we met again we would be through the horrors of an inexcusable insurrection costly both in property and valuable lives; there is no doubt that the rising occurred at the instigation of our common enemy and it meets with the condemnation of all right-thinking Irishmen, including, I venture to say every member of this Institute.'[8] The Council of the much more numerous solicitors' profession agreed, the minutes of the Incorporated Law Society of Ireland recording its 'abhorrence and condemnation' of the Rising.[9] We might wonder what the Catholic and Irish-speaking Michael Crowley (President of the Institute 1912–3) thought of this.

Political and professional developments

As the profession developed, a strong opinion grew of the desirability of legal recognition by an official register, like that established for the medical profession in 1858. The English Institute was particularly keen on the idea, which would, as with doctors and solicitors, amount to an exclusive licence to practice. Access to public company audits, as well as tax and other government-related work was intended to be limited to those on the register.

The great difficulty was: who was to be 'in' and who 'out'—which group or groups would get this exclusive licence? The English Institute had started by answering 'our members'. This was, of course, unacceptable to other groups, such as the Society of Incorporated Accountants and, indeed, to the Institute of Chartered Accountants of Scotland and the Irish Institute. Such a register would in effect require Irish accountants wishing to complete the audit of companies registered in London (as, for instance, the National and Provincial Banks or Guinness) to join the English Institute. For this reason a Bill introduced into the House of Lords in May 1909 collapsed under attack from the Scottish and Irish accountancy bodies. Another Bill was shot down by the united clamour from several of the smaller accountancy associations that had grown up: the Central Association of Accountants, the Institute of Certified Accountants, the London Association of Accountants, the Faculty of Accountants and the Central Association of Accountants, not to mention the *Financial Times*.

We have seen that both the Irish and British Institutes deliberately set the requirements for qualification high, to exclude all but the children of prosperous middle-class families. What *The Accountant* once called 'the impecunious man of ability' was deliberately excluded.[10] This was to ensure the 'respectability' of the new profession—which was code for the ability to compete with solicitors for insolvency business, and to distinguish themselves from less refined practitioners. Unless they were university graduates, the articled clerks had to pass a rather academically oriented Preliminary exam, based on the syllabus taught by traditional secondary schools; then spend five years learning the job and being paid very little; so not only did their parents have to pay a hefty premium but also keep the trainee all the while. Two more stiff exams, with pass rates of less than 50 per cent, were focused on legal and practical parts of the profession.

From the 1880s onwards a number of societies had sprung up to provide professional status to those, who for one reason or another, were unable to meet the Institute's stringent requirements. The first of these was the Society of Accountants and Auditors, which was founded in 1885.[11] It was they who had approached Robert Stokes with an idea of forming an Irish branch. The Society admitted as members those who had served in public accountancy offices but were ineligible for membership of the ICAI (perhaps not being able to afford either premium or articles); those working in accounts in commercial and public offices; municipal treasurers and accountants in local government. By 1893 there were five members of this society in Ireland, including Edward Kevans. Later Michael Crowley, Stewart Blacker Quin and Hugh Brandon, while remaining members of the Institute, also joined.[12] The Society's enthusiasm for a formal register of accountants seems to have attracted Irish members. Edward Kevans, in particular, was convinced that only formal official registration along the lines of the Medical Register would provide proper recognition to the profession. He became, and remained for 20 years, Chairman of the Irish Branch of the Society, which was founded in 1901. In 1957, as part of a general amalgamation, members of this branch became automatically members of the Institute of Chartered Accountants in Ireland.[13]

For more than 20 years Bill after Bill was promoted in Parliament to establish registration; an attempt to rectify the consequences of the exclusivity insisted on by the original Chartered institutes in pursuit of 'respectability'. Men who could not meet their demands set up their own institutes, diffusing and so weakening the general image of the profession. The Bills failed, generally on the question of how access to the register was to be controlled. The sequence started in 1892 with a Bill promoted by the Society of Incorporated Accountants. This was countered by a Bill initiated by the English Institute. There were further Bills initiated in 1893, 1895, three in 1896, 1897, 1899, 1909 and 1911 and 1912. Most of these Bills were promoted by the English Institute or the English Society; in fact the Irish Institute played very little part, which no doubt exasperated Edward Kevans.[14] None were successful. The last attempt at a registration statute in Ireland was in 1927 and will be described in the next chapter.

The Belfast branch

The Irish Institute was founded as an all-Ireland body, initially with 13 members from Dublin, 12 from Belfast and six from Cork. But by 1906 Belfast was booming as an industrial centre and over half the members were based in the North. The great City Hall, symbol of a thriving, bustling economy with world-class shipbuilding, engineering and linen industries, was opened in that year, exuding the self-confidence of an imperial class. Michael Crowley's 1901 *Statistics and Directory of Limited Liability Companies Registered in Ireland* makes it clear that of the 1,120 companies registered in Ireland, the great majority had their head offices in Ulster.[15] This included three out of five banks (not counting the National and the Provincial Banks, which were registered in England); perhaps 115 out of the 120 linen manufacturers and merchants; eight out of 16 distilleries; nine out of 16 mineral water manufacturers; three out of five insurance companies; five out of nine tobacco companies; four out of five shipbuilders; six out of nine traction engine companies, and so on. Craig Gardner had had an office in Belfast since 1894, run by a salaried clerk called Edward Buckley. In 1901 he was made a partner in the Belfast business. Hill Vellacott, an offshoot of a British firm, was also well established.

In July 1906 a meeting was held in the offices of John McCullough & Burns to discuss the formation of a local Belfast Society of Chartered Accountants. In the chair was Martin Walsh, President of the Institute in 1894/5, and this no doubt eased the Institute's way to approving the new Society and providing an initial grant of £50 and an annual subsidy of £25. Don Anderson, the historian of the Belfast (later Ulster) Society, puts the foundation of the Society into the context of the partition that was to come 15 years later. 'The prospect of Home Rule was alarming ever more Protestants,' he writes. 'Clearly there was talk of a split in the Institute.'[16]

There is no evidence of this, however, and much to suggest that at this time neither nationalists nor unionists wanted or expected partition (which both sides would have seen as a defeat)—any more than the British then expected a Great War with Germany.[17] There is certainly no mention of anything of partition in the speeches for the inauguration in 1905 of the Ulster Unionist Council, an umbrella body uniting local unionist organisations.[18] As late as August 1912, when the veteran nationalist politician T. P. O'Connor met Lloyd George on holiday at Marienbad, he was appalled to discover that the Liberal Party was going to support partition. He looked, said his friend Michael Cox, 'the picture of despair'. At this time even

Edward Carson's muted support for partition was mostly tactical, 'aimed at causing division in the Home Rule Party'.[19] The possibility of separation would have been complicated by the Charter, which was clearly issued to Dublin, so a separate Northern Ireland Institute would have required either a new, separate Charter or affiliation under the English or Scottish Charters. The new organisation was specifically called the Belfast Society, only changing its name to the Ulster Society in the 1960s.

Since the first Chairman of the Belfast Society was Martin Shaw, one of the Charter Petitioners and first Fellows of the Institute, and the three officers and two of the committee members were all future presidents of the Institute, it is difficult to infer any deep separatist intent. It is more likely that a vigorous, serious-minded group of men got together to organise professional improvement and, as the first rule book puts it, 'to promote personal acquaintance and good feeling among members of the profession' in their home town, without having to take the train to Dublin. It was perhaps no coincidence that the first Secretary of the Belfast Society, A. H. Muir (President of the Institute 1927/8), had qualified as a member of the Edinburgh Society of Accountants.[20] However that may be, as Howard Robinson records, 'they immediately undertook an ambitious course of lectures and meetings' and soon had 33 members and 23 students on their books.[21] In Dublin John Mackie and others were impressed by this activity and founded a Dublin Society, which he headed. This flourished for a while but, unlike the Belfast Society, faded away a few years after its foundation and had to be revived some years later.

The new importance of audit

In its early days, the profession had found most of its work in the insolvency courts and, as we have seen, a wide variety of miscellaneous accounting tasks, including periodical book-keeping, stock-taking, trust estates, planning and opening books for new businesses, fire claims and audit. Now a new business model was coming to the fore, facilitated by the Companies Acts from 1900 onwards. In the space of 20 years the erratic graph of earnings from irregular insolvencies became damped by regular auditing, as happened for instance to Craig Gardner.[22] The same happened in London: in Price Waterhouse, and in the more precisely recorded City of London practice of Whinney, Smith & Whinney (a precursor firm of Ernst & Young) which had less than 10 per cent of its work from audit and accountancy in 1880 (up from 2.4 per cent in 1860), but by 1900 this figure stood at 70 per cent.[23]

As Howard Robinson put it: 'the oversight in the 1862 Act in not providing for annual audits was finally made good by the Companies Act of 1900'.[24] Although audit had been required for banks since 1879, the new Act required the shareholders of all limited companies to appoint an auditor and it was clear that a professional 'public auditor' was expected to fill the role. The auditor's job was to certify that the balance sheet showed a 'true and correct view' of the state of the company's affairs, according to the books of the company (there was no mention of a profit and loss account). Importantly, as Lord Justice Lindsay declared a few years before, the auditor 'does not discharge his duty by doing this without enquiry and without taking any trouble to see that the books themselves show the company's true position'.[25]

In the previous dispensation the important business contacts had been with those, such as banks and solicitors, who had the disposal of one-off tasks like liquidations, sorting out estates and similar work. The annual audit, supervised by one of the firm's partners, was the focus of this new business model, which would be characterised by long-continuing, but usually rather distant, one-to-one relationships between a partner and his audit clients. Not only would the client partner's colleagues know little about his accounts, but typically there would be little or no contact with the clients apart from the two or three weeks of the audit.

In 1908 a consolidating Companies Act was passed, which remained in force in Ireland until 1963, confirming the requirements of a professional audit of a company's balance sheet (but not a profit and loss account) and an auditor's report.[26] Perhaps oddly, there was, as the 1958 Irish Commission on Company Law Reform (half of whose members were practising accountants) pointed out 'no obligation on a company or on its directors to keep proper accounts, proper records or proper books of account. The result is that in many small companies the books which are kept give no information about the business of the company.'[27] This was the legal underpinning of the predominance of the need first to write up the accounts and then to audit them—the so-called 'book-keeping audit'.

The 1908 Act (which was of course designed more for British than Irish conditions) was in advance of the European norm. For instance, despite its powerful industrial sector, Germany did not require even its largest public companies to have an annual audit until 1931. The French law of 1867 prescribed an audit, but did not insist on any professional qualification, so the audit was often done by friends or relatives of directors.[28] As one historian put it: 'no knowledge of accounting was required of someone to be appointed commissionaire'.[29] The French professional association of auditors, the *Ordre des Experts Comptables*, was only created in 1945. Even in the United States the audit of public companies was not mandatory until 1933.

Section 112 of the 1908 Act declared that every company (private and public) 'shall at the annual general meeting appoint an auditor or auditors to hold office until the next annual general meeting'. Importantly, the appointment was made by the shareholders, as a body, and they fixed the remuneration. If the directors wished to change the auditor, for whatever reason, they had to give 14 days' notice before proposing such a change at an AGM. Changing auditors was rarely done, however, since it was believed to give a bad signal. The Act gave auditors the right of access to the books, accounts and vouchers of the company, as well as to explanations from the directors and officers. In theory, it was the directors' responsibility to prepare the accounts, and the auditor's to examine them. Anything the auditor disapproved of, including unsatisfactory aspects of the book-keeping, was to be reported to the shareholders.

In practice, the auditor's staff inevitably drew up the accounts themselves, and reported any problems with the system to the managers. Despite the clear intent of the 1908 Act, it was inevitable that the auditor's primary relationships were with the client's management, and no more than secondarily with the shareholders. Only in extremis would they be inclined to report any deficiencies to the latter. Occasionally, the accounting and auditing functions were split, not always happily. In 1911, a row broke out over the accounts of the ailing *Freeman's Journal*. M. Crowley & Co. did the accounts and Kean & Co. did the audit. During the annual audit Kean produced a long list of qualifications to the accounts, which Crowley attempted to rebut. Eventually a third firm, Kinnear & Co., was called in and declared that most of the objections to Crowley's accounts were not material. In due course a shareholders meeting was called, and in adjudicating the matter did not reappoint Kean & Co. as auditors.[30]

As it had been for a long time, the professional accountant's task was to translate the muddle of real life into something that could comfortably be read and acted upon. Mostly it was audit, but sometimes estate or farm books had to be written up, with the associated tax submissions. Very occasionally there might be an investigation or a company flotation. In each case there was a translation and transformation of data created in one arena to another more public and conventional one. We can compare the task to that of a newspaper editor grappling with a flow of inputs (facts, opinions, rumours, promotions and scandals) to evaluate and present these into a standard form (prose) that we can comfortably read. Just so do accountants (in numbers). Both groups at the same time provide some kind of voucher for the accuracy of the result.

An important part of the exercise was to put the information into a standard format—accounts are laid out in a conventional way, just as newspaper readers expect the main news to be on page one, readers' letters in the middle and sport at the back. It was in these years that the standard formats that were used through most of the 20th century evolved. Accountants translated the muddle of daily commercial life into a form that creditors, shareholders, lawyers, taxmen and others could use (the convention of reporting assets on the right-hand column of a balance sheet, for instance, was well established by the 1900 Act). In continental countries such as France, Belgium and Germany, standardisation went much further, with state regulation requiring one common numbered chart of accounts to be used by all. This provided a common framework for all accounts, very like the Dewey Decimal Classification system used in libraries, which enables readers to go straight to history, languages, biography, etc.[31]

How auditing was done

Auditing was the core business for the profession for most of the 20th century, so it is worth exploring in detail how audits were carried out. This is all the more so since, as personal reminiscences and the textbooks make clear, neither the office environment nor the audit techniques changed much until the 1970s.

From the beginning, the purpose of the audit was conceived as twofold: first, the detection of fraud, and secondly, the discovery of errors (including misstatements) in the accounts. This priority order was repeated by successive writers of auditing textbooks until the 1960s.[32] A typical example comes in F. R. M. De Paula's often reprinted auditing textbook where he notes that 'the main object of [the auditor's] appointment is to satisfy the shareholders that no fraud is being committed by either the directors or the employees of the business'.[33] It was only towards the end of this period that priorities shifted, until by the first edition in 1966 of Cooper's *Manual of Auditing* (the most advanced of its time) it was declared that 'the object of an audit is to ensure that the accounts on which the auditor is reporting show a true and fair view and are not misleading'.[34]

The raw material of the audit was the books of account. In his text on late 19th-century commercial practice, the first book published by an Irish chartered accountant, published in 1891, Michael Crowley of M. Crowley & Co., (uncle to Vincent Crowley, founder of Kennedy, Crowley) wrote: 'the principal and essential Books of account used are: a Cash book for cash received and paid; a Day book for goods sold on credit; an Invoice book for purchases; a Ledger to contain abstracts of the accounts in all the books; and a Stock book to contain inventories of stock on hand'. The accounting process was twofold: the initial books (cash, invoice and day books, etc.) recorded the daily activity as it happened; the data was then transferred to the multiple pages of the ledgers for analytic breakdown. 'The above', Crowley notes, 'are the books used in every day commercial life. Several others may be required to meet the needs of special businesses'.[35]

The ledgers analysing the activities of a moderately sized business, with perhaps 20 employees, might have 60 or so accounts recording assets and liabilities and so on and, depending on the kind of business, hundreds or even thousands of debtor and creditor accounts recording sales and purchases respectively. Physically, ledgers were large, stout, leather-bound objects, often with a distinctly 'used' odour. The well-thumbed sheets were ruled in light blue and red, and usually had leather index tabs. One such ledger might hold 300 accounts. So a business with 1,500 credit customers would have at least five of these 'personal' ledgers. There would also have been a private ledger, containing details of senior managers' and directors' earnings, and other financial matters such as their capital contributions. This was under the tight control of a very senior employee. Other books in a typical middle-sized system might include a wages book, a petty cash book, sales and purchases day books and stores book.

The first task on taking over a new audit was to understand how the accounts system operated, and to draw up a plan of work. Thus was established the audit notebook. F. R. M. De Paula describes how there should be set up: 'an audit programme, in which should be recorded the exact details of the work to be performed by the auditor and his staff, columns being provided in order that the persons performing each part of the checking may initial as and when they complete the same. . . . if in future years different members of the staff are engaged upon the audit they can see by reference to the programme exactly what work they are required to perform.'[36] The basic audit plan was firstly to check all or a sample of entries in the books against 'vouchers', which would ideally be invoices or statements generated by outside parties, of which the bank book was, of course, the most valuable. While this was going on a junior would be assigned to checking the adding in key books. A stream of queries would inevitably arise from the checking process, each of which had to be carefully resolved, with the help of the client's staff.

A ritual in many Irish firms was that the senior clerk in charge of the audit on the ground would attend the audit partner every Saturday morning with the week's progress noted in the book. The partner in charge of the audit could thus easily monitor progress and compare with previous years. The audit programme, once developed, was expected to continue more or less unchanged. Although obviously convenient, this tended to ossify the entire audit: one Craig Gardner partner claimed to have embarked on an audit in the 1930s and seen Michael Collins's signature from his brief employment with the firm in 1916 in previous columns of the programme! The predictability of the programme, and the regular pattern of checks signalled in the ledger by neat, multicoloured margin marks, must surely have taken some of the edge off the ability of the audit to deter fraud.

Given the high importance assigned to fraud detection, it is curious how little space was given in textbooks to how frauds might operate. Doctors, after all, studied disease in detail, and priests thought much about sin; though it was not until the quality movement from the 1970s that the detailed study of manufacturing defects and their causes became normal. In his 1914 book De Paula devotes just a single page out of over 200 to fraud, and other widely used books on auditing by once well-known authors (such as Pixley, Dicksee and Spicer and Pegler) are no more generous. Dicksee's *Advanced Accounting* (1903) does have a chapter on 'Falsified Accounts', which runs to six pages out of a total of 400. The London-based accountancy publishing firm Gee did have a title called *Fraud in Accounts* originally published in 1903, but this is a self consciously theoretical volume, omitting names and identifiable detail, because, as the author piously puts it, 'the thoughtful student of accounting will require no such extraneous stimulant to his attention'.[37] Perhaps such sordid details were felt inappropriate in a profession still self-consciously aspiring to respectability—or perhaps it was not considered a good idea to fill young heads with such tricks. If so, this remained a sensitivity: in a post-Enron US Congress inquiry in 2002, accounting professor Robert Verrechia admitted that 'many of the instructors at Wharton are sensitive to the concern that in regaling students with tales of financial reporting chicanery we may also be promoting this behaviour in our students'.[38] From the young clerk's point of view, however, an introduction to the exciting vocabulary of 'teeming and lading', 'skimming', 'kiting' and 'cheque-splitting', together with an understanding of why it was important that the Senior Cashier took his holidays or that the cash book and the ledger be in different hands, might have made the long hours of tick work pass more quickly.

The trial balance challenge

Nowadays the audit team is presented with a finished set of accounts which, thanks to computers, are fully and correctly added and balanced. In contrast, before 1970, in 99 cases out of 100 the company's book-keeping staff would not have had the technical ability to extract data from the ledger to make up accounts. So the absolutely crucial task during the audit was to extract a manual trial balance from the ledgers, a process computers have made as old-fashioned as saddle-making.

The trial balance is both a proof (as far as it goes) of the ledger and the input to the final profit and loss account and balance sheet. Once it was balanced, the final accounts could be drawn up. The great majority of audits before 1970, in Ireland as in Britain, had a more or less extensive element of accountancy.[39] They were in fact 'book-keeping audits' in which the auditor himself calculated and extracted the balances from the ledger accounts, and drew up the profit and loss account and balance sheet (sometimes, as one who qualified in the 1960s remembered, 'with the managing director peering over your shoulder to see how his bonus was working out'[40]). The process certainly gave the clerk 'a very good insight into what was happening in the business', as Professor Niamh Brennan put it.[41]

The process of 'closing the books' (as it was called) and extracting a trial balance was the addition of all the accounts with a debit balance (costs, expenses, assets) and all the accounts with a credit balance (receipts, liabilities) to confirm that they were arithmetically equal, as they ought to be by the rules of double-entry book-keeping. It is very difficult in the computer era to realise how critical for the reassurance of control a successful trial balance was, and how difficult to obtain. An old book on accounting rhapsodised thus: 'to balance a set of Books at the First Trial appears wonderful and is mentioned with astonishment; and for the same person to do so two or three years following, he is considered to possess a portion of infallibility, and is freely allowed to boast of the exploit as long as he lives—but in how few compting-houses hath this been effected!'[42] A whole year's clerical work provided a rich soil for human error (entries omitted or duplicated, misread figures, adding or posting errors, balances missed, figures mangled or transposed by tired clerks). And if anyone was tempted to say 'the account is only out by a tiny amount' (this was before the idea of 'materiality' was introduced), there was the undoubtedly exaggerated fear of 'compensating error'. This referred to the fact that an apparent misbalance of only a single penny could *theoretically* conceal errors of hundreds on one side of the account balanced by equal hundreds (less 1) on the other. This possibility obliged clerks to spend many anxious hours seeking to balance the accounts exactly—to the farthing, if need be.

Although the 'self-checking' reassurance provided by the trial balance is now seen as one of the valuable aspects of double-entry book-keeping, the sheer amount of work involved in providing this check perhaps accounts for the fact that in the early days of book-keeping, trial balances were not by any means a regular part of the accounts routine. Although Fra Pacioli had recommended closing off the books annually, he recognised that in fact a typical time to extract balances was when a ledger was full and a new one had to be started. A study of early English merchant ledgers confirms that this was often the practice.[43] Ingenious ways were devised to get the information without having to close the books. Michael Crowley describes how, by using an elaborate alphabetic code against the purchases side of the account, to be matched with the same code against payments as they came in, the state of the ledger could be monitored without the need to balance the account.[44] As we shall see, many Irish businesses went on happily without annual accounts until the Inland Revenue began to demand full accounts during the First World War.

Usually human error ensured that the initial trial balance did not in fact balance. As textbook writer Roger Carter wrote (in *Advanced Accounts*, first published in 1919 and numerous subsequent editions) 'trial balances have a very unhappy knack of not agreeing'. Nothing could be relied on, so the first step was to double-check that two sides of the trial balances were correctly added and that there genuinely was a disagreement. Then the search began back through the ledgers for the errors. In the more sophisticated environments the ledgers would be 'self-balancing' by the use of adjustment accounts (the earlier term for what are now called control accounts), and this would enable errors to be localised.[45] So frequent was this hunt, indeed, that the accountancy publisher Gee had two separate titles dealing with typical causes of trial balance errors and proposing ways of detecting them: *Errors in Balancing* (which had reached its fourth edition by 1923) and *The Handy Trial Balance Book*. During training the clerk learned all sorts of techniques for identifying differences: the normal start-point was to relook at entries exactly equalling the error, so if the trial balance was out £4 18s 6d, all sums of that amount were double-checked. If the error was divisible by 2, then perhaps half the sum (in this case £2 9s 3d) had been posted twice to one side of the account. If the trial balance was out by a factor of 10, then there was probably a casting error somewhere. An error divisible by 9 indicated the possibility of a transposition (e.g. to write 53 instead of 35 gives an error of 18). Typically, of course, there were multiple errors, each of which had to be painstakingly unravelled. In a large system with multiple clerks working with ledgers the potential for error was considerable, but all had to be hunted down.

Once the trial balance was confirmed, the senior clerk (or in a smaller office perhaps the partner) would make any adjustments (e.g. depreciation, bad debt allowance), add accruals and prepayments and draw up the accounts. In many cases the final task in the process would be to complete the company's tax return. The senior in charge of the audit then presented the final results of the vouching and accounting work (with any queries that might have arisen) to the audit partner, who would go through the accounts carefully, identifying the reasons for year-on-year variations, perhaps using ratios (gross profit per cent, stock turn and assets/liabilities) to identify any fundamental changes in activity, checking the tax return and then monitoring the results of any questions that had occurred during the audit, before signing off. Barring the formalities, the annual audit would then be finished, and all that remained was for the partner in charge to present the accounts to the client and to draw up the fee, based on the internal time sheets.

Accountants become prudent

In the late 19th century the nature of shareholder bodies began to change. In the past they had been generally small and more-or-less known to each other and the directors. At AGMs they spoke easily of 'our company' and 'such a concern as ours'. Now, as share trading evolved, the personal connection grew thinner, and too many shareholders were thought to limit their interest to dividends. 'Many companies,' declared Ernest Cooper of Cooper Brothers in 1894, 'have very few *bona fide* shareholders.'[46] Throughout the 1890s the British professional journal *The Accountant* regularly warned of the destructive impact of greedy shareholders who resisted the creation of reserves, and the ploughing back of money into the company generally, in favour of higher dividends.

Perhaps daily experience in the insolvency business had made the profession pessimistic, but accountants were very conscious of the vulnerability of companies. Evidence from the first 25 years of limited liability was that some 36 per cent of companies went into liquidation within five years of formation, one-third of these as a result of fraud or gross mismanagement amounting to fraud.[47] Men of their time and position, the profession believed that corporate longevity, in itself, was in the best interests of shareholders, employees and the economy as a whole, and acted accordingly. In 1904, the textbook writer Francis Pixley was President of the Institute of Chartered Accountants of England and Wales, and at the World Congress of Accountants in St. Louis went so far as to argue that: 'many persons consider that the duties of Auditors of companies are towards the shareholders . . . I hold the view that the duties of Auditors are to the company as an institution.'[48] To this end accounting professionals evolved 'conservative' or 'prudent' techniques that minimised profits and undervalued assets, so as to create secret reserves, and gave full value to liabilities. These understatements had become normal, even praiseworthy. That same year the *Irish Investors Guardian* commented approvingly on some accounts produced by Craig Gardner's London office, that 'they clearly did not tell the whole truth. Anyone capable of reading between the lines could see that a considerable secret reserve was being created'.[49]

As a 1936 American textbook put it, the principle of conservatism adopted by accountants was 'an attempt to offset the natural optimism of the businessman by accepting the most pessimistic of two or more possibilities'.[50] Textbook writers (such as Pixley *On Auditing*, which was recommended to the Institute's students) reacted to this optimism by stressing especially the key role of conservatism and prudence in the production of accounts. In another comment in 1904, Pixley expanded, blunt and outspoken as ever: 'It is these false statements in companies' accounts that have enabled so many flourishing institutions to exist as long as they have. I have no hesitation in saying that if the balance sheets of companies had been strictly prepared without any false statements—that is to say the assets valued up to their full value, the stocks valued up to market price in times of boom and profit—the companies that have lasted say for a hundred years . . . would not have lasted one-fifth of the time.'[51] In using such terms as 'strictly prepared' and 'false statements', Francis Pixley was quite explicit about what he believed to be the profession's responsibility.

In a 1906 law case Lord Justice Wrenbury recognised that: 'assets are often, by reason of prudence, estimated, and stated to be estimated, at less than their probable real value. The purpose of the balance sheet is to show that the financial position of the company is at least as good as there stated, not to show that it is not or may be better.'[52] There were also increasingly agreed ideas about how to handle asset valuation, depreciation and so on. As the acknowledged specialists, the profession were able to implement standards that perhaps neither the ordinary shareholders (who would no doubt generally like high profits and high dividends) nor management (the optimistic businessmen mentioned above) nor potential investors (who always want fuller, clearer and comparable information about their choices) would have preferred. Only large 'insider' shareholders would, perhaps, have approved. In another profession it might have been said: 'doctor knows best'. The Australian Professor of Accounting R. J. Chambers identified this as a pivotal moment in the history of accounting—the *realpolitik* acceptance that a set of accounts was more than a statistical artefact—the information and the way it was presented had potentially explosive significance, affecting lives, jobs and businesses.

Without this perception of corporate vulnerability, no doubt other, more statistical virtues such as truth-to-life (now called reliability) or simplicity of presentation (understandability), might have been stressed. At this time specific, open-eyed choices were made and the profession opted for a practical response to the world as they saw it, rather than a purist approach. In the event, conservatism and prudence remained key 'principles of accounting' and unquestioned watchwords for the profession long after the specific circumstantial reasons for their choice were forgotten. The profession in fact created a special technical meaning for the word 'prudence' (i.e. ensuring that gains and assets are not overstated and losses and liabilities understated), one not even now recognised by the *Oxford English Dictionary*. It was not until December 2000, with the publication of Financial Reporting Standard 18 (replacing SSAP 2), that prudence was toppled from its perch. Described as 'a potentially biased concept' it became a secondary virtue, to be invoked with caution and in special circumstances only.[53]

The new importance of tax

With no munitions or other war-supplies factories in southern Ireland, there was little opportunity for Irish accountants at home to become directly involved in the war effort. The famous Grubb telescope factory, in Rathmines, Dublin, which supplied 95 per cent of the British Navy's submarine periscopes, was moved to Hertfordshire in 1916. Harland and Wolff and other factories in Belfast were of course working flat out.[54] The Council of the Institute's minutes do record a call from the British Ministry of Munitions in November 1916 seeking the Council's assistance in recruiting chartered accountants. By contrast, the administration recruited widely from the English profession. Literally millions of pounds were saved when accountants explored the reality behind manufacturing agreements that civil servants had been persuaded to authorise. Public recognition of this service, expressed in the British way with knighthoods and other honours, established the subsequent prestige of the profession in England. It was in recognition of their contribution that accountants in Britain began to be called "business doctors" and "surgeons of industry".[55]

Perhaps conscious that Irish accountants were less employed in government service than their English counterparts, in his address to the 1916 Institute AGM President David Telford declared:

> 'An overwhelming proportion of the additional money required [to fight the war] will be obtained from income-tax and excess profits duty, and in the collection of these gigantic taxes Chartered Accountants must necessarily pay an important part. I estimate that from 80 to 90 per cent of the income tax and excess profits duty returns will be prepared by accountants. This throws a heavy duty on our profession.'

The background to this was an enormous increase in direct taxation since 1914, in particular the stunningly successful Excess Profits Duty introduced in the Westminster Budget in November 1915. In 1917 this tax alone produced more than the entire UK income tax in 1914. The Excess Profits Duty was complicated, and full of potential loop-holes and debatable areas. The taxpayer could choose as the basis the average of the most profitable of two of the three pre-war years; any profits in excess of that were taxed at rates which escalated from 50 to 80 per cent during the war. Or the tax could be calculated as 6 per cent of capital employed (with assets valued at cost, subject to a 'proper allowance for wear and tear').

It is estimated that a quarter of the enormous cost of the war was financed by the yield from this one tax.[56] This was itself a dramatic indication of how profitable for businesses wartime conditions were, though the calculation is confused by inflation, since the cost of living actually doubled between 1914 and 1918. Except tangentially, in the vexed matter of depreciation, neither accountants nor officials took this into account. (As a matter of fact, as J. Edwards, the author of *A History of Financial Accounting*, puts it, in the UK 'systematic depreciation of fixed assets did not become a wide-spread practice until after 1940'.[57])

When David Telford became a member of the Institute of Chartered Accountants in Ireland in 1889, tax had been a very minor part of an accountant's role. Rates were low. Michael Crowley's book on commercial practice records that in the 1880s the rate fluctuated between 5d and 8d in the £ (i.e. up to 3 per cent).[58] Rates had risen since to finance the Boer War of 1899–1902, but compliance was still casual. According to the 1906 Select Committee on Income Tax, the most common mode of evasion was simply failure to make a return, which was only compulsory for those who believed they owed tax. According to witnesses to the Committee, the incidence of evasion revealed national character. The Scots, being 'a methodical and businesslike' people, paid tax when it was due, to the extent that the Glasgow office 'was positively incommoded in early January by the rush to pay taxes'. Despite their much-vaunted honesty, the same could not be said of the English.[59] Witnesses were not asked about the habits of Irish taxpayers.

Before the First World War, estimates of profits crudely based on cash flow were common, and assessments by the Inland Revenue officials were not aggressively high. The remorseless need for funds to fight the war was to change that. The basic rate of income tax went from 8 to 30 per cent, and even manual wage-earners were pulled into the tax net. The unprecedented weight of these taxes can be judged by the fact that in 1906 a witness told the Select Committee on Income Tax that the very highest rate in the world at that time was the 20 per cent charged in Italy. This was set so high, explained the witness, because evasion was so rampant that a penal rate had to be charged where it could not be avoided.[60] The new wartime tax rates stimulated a predictable reaction, and for the first time it became necessary to establish measures against tax evasion, which, as Chancellor Lloyd George once said, had previously been considered 'not worthwhile'.[61]

The French experience was not different. The law introduced by Joseph Caillaux in 1914 introduced a very limited form of income tax in France, with the top marginal rate at 2 per cent. There were scanty controls on accounts. 'The [French] Code of Commerce contained only a few references requiring traders to keep books of accounts and to undertake an annual inventory. There was no structured framework of rules for the preparation of annual accounts, and particularly valuation in the balance sheet, the determination of profit being subjected to all sorts of creativity and fantasy.'[62]

It is impossible to overestimate the importance of the new demands on the accountancy profession and on business accounting generally. Suddenly all businesses had to produce a tax return every year, based on accounts drawn up according to standard professional practices. Even individuals were required to submit proper accounts. As Howard Robinson put it: 'Surveyors (Inspectors) of taxes began to call for Trading and Profits and Loss Accounts and Balance Sheets in order to verify the figures submitted by limited companies, private traders and professional men. At first it was contended that inspectors of taxes had no legal right to demand accounts of any kind, and accountants merely submitted figures of profit without showing how these had been calculated . . . the revenue authorities however ultimately forced taxpayers to produce accounts certified by their accountants by making estimated assessments at figures so high that taxpayers were forced to appeal.'[63] To help the work forward the Inland Revenue would recommend accountants, not necessarily members of the Institute. Thus, at the 1917 AGM of the Institute it was even reported that a Surveyor (as Inspectors were then called) had provided a taxpayer with a list of five potential accountants. None was a member of the Chartered Institutes.[64]

A Stokes Brothers & Pim letter-book dealing with tax matters from March 1916 (barely four months after the launch of the Excess Profits Duty) to January 1917 survives, and it confirms this sense of unprecedented demands from the Inland Revenue. In May 1916, for instance, the senior clerk dealing with the affairs of James Candon & Co. of Boyle, Co. Roscommon, sought to appease the Surveyor's wrath by pleading that:

> '(1) [Mr Candon] shared in the general ignorance (at that time) of Income Tax requirements
> (2) that having no proper books until October 1913 (when we were called in) he was unaware of the profits he was making, particularly as these profits apparently were not shown by any material increase in liquid assets but must have been largely represented by increasing book debts.'

As the letter-book makes clear, Candon was not exceptional. There was apparently no expectation of regular annual accounting among private companies. In case after case, Stokes Brothers & Pim were required to create accounts going back several years to establish the base line. For instance, acting in April 1916 on behalf of the leading coal importer, Tedcastle McCormick, the firm wrote: 'the Directors of this company have asked us to prepare the figures necessary in their case in connection with Excess Profits Duty. We enclose you therefore a statement showing Capital for the four years commencing 1st April 1912 and notes of the profits for the years ended 31st March 1912, 1913, 1914 and 1915.' And in the same month for Cleeve Bros of Limerick, 'we have pleasure in enclosing your Profit and Loss accounts of the above firm for the three years ended 31st December 1912, 1913 and 1914'.[65]

In his Presidential speech to the 1916 AGM, having underlined the huge importance of accountants' work on tax, David Telford laid down what he saw as the ethics of tax returns:

> 'I wish to impress upon you particularly that every account sent in to the Surveyor, whether it be an income tax return or an excess profits duty return bearing your signature, should not only be strictly correct but be prepared in the spirit of the income tax laws as far as we are able to interpret them. . . . In other words there must be strict disclosure. No act of ours should weaken the confidence which I have reason to believe the Revenue officials have in the members of this Institute.'

There was a threefold advantage to be achieved: the patriotic contribution to the war effort; the moral imperative; and the mutual benefit of professional collegiality. On the other hand, he conceded that

> 'honest differences of opinion may exist on such subjects as change of ownership, capital employed in the business exclusive of goodwill, depreciation, and so forth, and until decided by a Court of law, we are, in my opinion, entitled to adopt the interpretation most favourable to our clients'.

This was to be the spirit, of compliance rather than planning, in which members worked on their clients' tax returns for more than 50 years.

After the war

However absorbed in practice, no accountant in Ireland could miss the military and political events of the next few years. First, there was the ending of the Great War, the 'war to end all wars'. At the AGM of June 1918, then President of the Institute, Stewart Blacker Quin from Belfast, reported that as many as 128 members and articled clerks from the profession had joined the British Army since the commencement in 1914. Of these, 19 had died. And before there was a chance to mourn these colleagues, Ireland was caught up in the War of Independence and then the Civil War. On the very day of the outbreak of the War of Independence, in 1919, the First Dáil (those Sinn Féin members who had chosen not to take their seats in Westminster) passed a Democratic Programme affirming, among other things, 'that all private property must be subordinated to the public right and welfare'[66]—not a sentiment that many accountants then or now would support. The fierce engagements of the War of Independence finally led to partition and the establishment of two governments on the island. The Institute was still under the Presidency of Stewart Blacker Quin, who as Unionist candidate for West Belfast in 1913 no doubt had his own opinions, but it remained an all-island body.

A momentous change that took a long time to come to full fruition was the admittance of women on equal terms to membership of the Institute. The Sex Disqualification (Removal) Act was passed into law in December 1919. Clause 1 includes the ringing statement, 'a person shall not be disqualified by sex or marriage from the exercise of any public function or being appointed to any civil or judicial office or post or entering or assuming or carrying on any civil profession or vocation or from admission to any incorporated society (whether incorporated by Royal Charter or otherwise)'. In the Institute's AGM before this, in May 1919, a resolution to permit the admission of women was passed 'by a large majority'.[67] The first woman to take advantage of this, becoming a member in 1925, was Eileen Woodworth, whose grandfather had been one of the original signatories of the Charter petition. However, as we shall see in a later chapter, it was to be over 50 years before there were more than a handful of women members.

Chapter Four
In the New Dispositions: 1922–1938

'It is a little astounding, and one cannot help wondering whether those who manage big companies do not sometimes forget that the body of directors of a company are the agents and the trustees of the shareholders, that they owe them full information, subject to proper and reasonable commercial necessity, and it is their interests that they have to study.'

Lord Wright's charge to the jury in
R. v. Lord Kylsant and Another (1931)

When the Irish Free State began its formal existence in 1922, professional, financial and commercial services were disproportionately run by the minority Protestant community. This was known, and mattered, because religious allegiance remained a profoundly important social and political indicator. Protestants were strong in the accountancy, engineering, legal and (to a lesser extent) medical professions, and many of the old established financial and business companies.[1] The President and Secretary of the Institute of Chartered Accountants in Ireland and most of the Council were Protestant, as were all the partners of the two largest firms, Stokes Brothers & Pim and Craig Gardner.[2]

On the positive side, it seems likely that this fact was important in retaining the all-Ireland character of the Institute, combined with good personal relations and perhaps a pragmatic view about the potential difficulty such a separation would present to northern accountants wishing to retain the prized 'Chartered' status. (The Charter was definitely given to the Dublin-based body, so in order to retain the designation of 'Chartered' a new Ulster Institute, based on the Belfast Society, would either have to petition for its own Charter or in some way join either the Scottish or English Institutes.) Fissiparous pressure, however, must surely have been felt. At a dinner of the Belfast Society in 1921, Charter signatory and former Institute President Robert Walsh talked hotly of Northern Ireland's new self-governing status (which he in fact regretted) being forced on them to avoid 'being controlled by, and included in, a cruel civilisation modelled on the persecuting ideas of the Middle Ages'.[3] This unflattering view of the Catholic Church and its institutions, notably the Inquisition, was widely held in the North, and equally uncomplimentary views about the North circulated among Catholics in the South. Over time cooler heads prevailed, and Chartered Accountants Ireland remains an all-island institution.

The new independence for the South inevitably affected the religious minority. The *Church of Ireland Gazette* 'readily admitted that most of its readers were bewildered and frightened at the final "break with all the traditions that were dear to them".'[4] A measure of this concern came in May 1922, a few weeks after the killing of 10 Protestants in West Cork, when a Church of Ireland delegation led by Archbishop Gregg bluntly asked Michael Collins 'whether the Provisional Government desired to keep the Protestant community in Southern Ireland or expel it?' Collins's replies, said *The Irish Times* grimly, were satisfactory, or 'at least as satisfactory as any promise can be before it is fulfilled'.[5] (Though Gregg put a positive face on things in public, privately he felt, as his daughter put it, that 'he had been banished from the Garden of Eden'.[6])

Although it was generally believed in Catholic circles that Freemasons (and all middle-class Protestants were vaguely assumed to be connected with Masonry) were given to 'plotting unfair advantage over their rivals' with their 'secrecy and underhand ways',[7] we have seen in Chapter Two that Masonry played little or no discernible part in the gaining of the Institute's Charter, and it is equally difficult to see it as a source of new business in the 1920s and 1930s. There was undoubtedly a general surge in membership of the Masons in the 1920s, partly perhaps as a 'circling of the wagons' by Protestant men fearing the new regime, and partly as an attempt to recapture the male camaraderie of the war. Such may have been the case for Captain Eustace Shott, Craig Gardner partner from 1924, who joined Lodge No. 399 in 1921. The other members were a brewery foreman, a railway clerk, a civil servant, an auctioneer and a commercial traveller—none of whom were likely to have any business to put his way. Shott resigned from the Freemasons 10 years later, just as his contribution to the business-getting side of the firm began to take off.

The Catholic rivals to the Masons, the Knights of Columbanus, transferred their headquarters from Belfast to Dublin in 1922. They are described by their historian as 'a preponderance of professional men', who quickly set about righting what they perceived as 'the discrepancies encountered at every level of Irish agricultural, economic, industrial and professional life where non-Catholics were solidly entrenched in positions and occupations which depended on already accumulated capital or goodwill.'[8]

As it happened, the new Cumann na nGaedheal Government, apart from the odd quirk such as renaming Kingstown Dún Laoghaire and insisting the schools teach Irish, proved to be impeccably orthodox. And so, as the *Irish Times* journalist Brian Inglis put it in his memoir of genteel Church of Ireland life in those days:

> 'after a few years in the new Irish Free State . . . [Protestants] found that nothing sinister was going to happen to them. Their social world remained stable; like a prawn in aspic it gradually began to grow stale, but it did not disintegrate. All around them "that other Ireland" was coming into its force; but they remained almost unaware of its existence.'[9]

It was quite possible, even in the South, as a Protestant to go about daily life (at least until the 1960s) without much contact with the majority or, as Inglis put it, 'R.C.s, as we called them'.[10] To do this you could be born at home, or perhaps in the Portobello Nursing Home; be baptised in one of the cathedrals or any one of a hundred other places; go to school in England, if your parents could afford it, or St Andrew's or Alexandra or St Columba's; take a degree in Trinity or a university in England; play 'God Save the King' not 'The Soldier's Song' at the end of private dances; work in Heitons or Dockrells, or A. & L. Goodbody, or Stokes Brothers & Pim (in Limerick, Metcalf Lillburn, in Cork, Atkins Chirnside); bank with the Provincial or Bank of Ireland; read *The Irish Times* and the novels of M. J. Farrell (Molly Keane) or George Birmingham; shop in Arnotts and Findlaters; have coffee in Bewleys and celebratory meals at the Shelbourne; play tennis at the Fitzwilliam or golf at Portmarnock; sail from the Royal St George in Kingstown; take in an English play at the Gaiety or some music at the RDS; live in Malahide or Rathgar; be treated in the Meath or the Adelaide hospitals; be buried in Mount Jerome.

Since all businesses were clearly known to be either Catholic or Protestant, jobs, and particularly promotion, were related to religion. When Gerard O'Brien, who eventually became Craig Gardner's first Catholic partner in 1944, joined the firm (on the advice of his father, who was Chairman of the Revenue Commissioners) well-meaning friends said, 'you're a fool . . . you'll never get anywhere there'.[11] But as the new state evolved, it began to happen that for young Protestants, as Inglis puts it: 'there were simply not enough good jobs to go round; for by this time [the 1930s] the R.C.s were moving in, securing accounts that had been in

Protestant hands for generations.'[12]

In the affairs of the Institute, there was a careful effort to ensure that the northern and southern ends stayed together. After Robert Stokes's 10-year tenure of the presidency, the presidency rotated between Dublin and Belfast. So after David Telford, Stewart Blacker Quin from Belfast took over for three years, followed by J. Harold Pim, who was in turn followed by William Mayes again from Belfast. In 1929–31 the rhythm was broken by the election of the first Corkman, Charles Olden of Atkins Chirnside. These were all Protestants—the first Catholic since Independence was Thomas Geoghegan in 1933. John Mackie, whose firm had just amalgamated with Craig Gardner, became President in 1925, and at his first AGM he commented somewhat poignantly: 'I am in the proud position of representing an Irish body which has not been divided by partition of the country and which we hope will remain undivided … I am sure our friends from the North will be interested in the problems of their next door neighbour, who but yesterday was a member of the same family.'

The business context

The northern economy enjoyed a brief post-war boom. Although still stronger than the South, its prosperity was based on a narrow range of products (specifically linen and shipbuilding, and ancillary products such as machine tools and ropes) and a particular market, Britain. Demand for the products slumped in the early 1920s and then again after 1929; and Britain's economy itself was not doing well. As the historian Jonathan Bardon put it, 'during the interwar years, the economy of the whole region languished in profoundly altered world trading conditions'.[13] As it happened, the cabinet of the Stormont government had a markedly stronger business background than that of the Free State government. The Stormont cabinet contained at the time three successive presidents of the Belfast Chamber of Commerce, as well as the managing director of a flour-milling concern and two heads of linen firms.[14] The nearest thing to such business experience in W. T. Cosgrave's executive committee in the Free State was Joe McGrath, later of the Irish Sweepstake and numerous other companies, but whose business career at this time consisted of a few years working with Craig Gardner. Unfortunately the northern cabinet's combined talents failed to address the region's fundamental problem: that it had committed itself to two specialised products (ships and linen) which had done spectacularly well up to the First World War, but now were being undermined by international competition. The result was that unemployment was at a quarter of the workforce for the whole interwar period—and would have been worse if emigration had not been an option.

When the Fianna Fáil party, with the aid of Labour, took power in the Free State in early 1932, they immediately set about establishing a great wall of tariffs, a protective shell inside which, so the theory went, nascent Irish industry would be able to grow. In a matter of years the Irish State went from being one of the most open economies in the world to being one of the most protected. The timing of this radical policy, however, was unfortunate, coinciding as it did with a world-wide slump and an economic war between Ireland and its best customer, Britain.[15] Writing of 1930 and 1931, the historian Joe Lee observes:

> 'The value of [Irish Free State] exports fell nearly 25 per cent in those two years. Invisible [earnings] fell sharply with the decline in dividends from overseas investments and emigrants' remittances with the steep fall in emigration due to contracting opportunities overseas. Industrialisation would have to occur in the context of an already shrinking home market.'[16]

To compound the problems, he continued, 'there was a lack of detailed forward planning' as to how the policy of protection might work on the ground. Faced with tough overseas markets, 'lack of competition on the home market inevitably led to profiteering. Critics claimed that pricing policies in many firms amounted to a conspiracy between employers and workers to exploit consumers.'[17] By the 1950s it was brutally clear that the policy of developing Irish industry inside a protective shell had not worked and a new departure was necessary.

To prevent British firms bypassing the tariffs by simply setting up subsidiaries in Ireland, the Control of Manufactures Acts (1932 and 1934) were passed, requiring the majority ownership of Irish companies be limited to Irish citizens. At this, some old, established firms, notably Guinness, moved their headquarters to London.[18] The Industrial Credit Corporation was established in 1933 to underwrite long-term capital issues for new industries. It was a tense time. At the annual dinner of the Irish branch of the Society of Incorporated Accountants and Auditors (which amalgamated with the Institute in 1957) in December 1933, Seán Lemass, the tough-minded Minister for Industry and Commerce, explained that the economic war was the least of their troubles. 'To solve the problem of how prosperity may be achieved, it was necessary', he told the assembled members and their guests, 'that the old order should be destroyed.'[19]

Allocating audits

One way in which the biases of the old order were to be redressed was in the allocation of state audit work. For whatever reason, the flow of business in the 1920s and 1930s from official sources to both Craig Gardner and Stokes, which between them audited the majority of companies quoted on the Stock Exchange, was disproportionately small. The audit of the first state-sponsored body, the Agricultural Credit Corporation, went in 1927 to the Catholic Thomas Geoghegan; the ESB went to Kennedy Crowley, as did Irish Life Assurance. The Irish Sugar Company went to Kean & Co.; Reynolds McCarron got Aer Lingus; and Purtill's (who had taken over Michael Crowley's business) got the Turf Development Board (later Bord na Móna). The first state-sponsored body of any size that Craig Gardner got was Coras Iompair Éireann (CIÉ) in 1944, helped no doubt by the fact that the Assistant General Manager Frank Lemass (brother of Seán) had qualified with Craig Gardner.[20]

The placing of the audits of companies sponsored by the Industrial Credit Corporation shows a similar pattern of preference to Catholic firms. Of the first 20 or so, seven went to Kennedy Crowley, four to Kean, two each to Cooper & Kenny, Stokes and Craig Gardner and the balance to other firms such as Purtill and Thomas Geoghegan. The ICC itself was audited by Kevans.[21]

This positive discrimination against the old Protestant firms had an effect on the earnings in the period of both Craig Gardner and Stokes Brothers & Pim. Luckily for them, companies only changed auditors in exceptional circumstances, so most of the audits they had, they kept. A typical change circumstance was the Craig Gardner client Williams & Woods, which was taken over in 1927 by the British firm Crosse & Blackwell. Initially, the audit was done by their own auditor, Cooper Brothers from London, before being taken over by Stokes. But this kind of thing did not happen often. At the same time the banks were still largely managed by Protestants, so there was a regular flow of liquidation business from that source.

Both Stokes' and Craig Gardner's earnings were under pressure in the 1930s. Stokes' 'Salary Book' records that in May 1933 a 10–15 per cent salary reduction was imposed on all staff. In March a newly qualified man was given notice 'owing to reduction in staff'. (He was No. 65 in the Salaries Book; for privacy reasons all staff will be referred to only by their staff number.) Another man (No. 73) similarly 'left on completion of articles, no opening in office'. Craig Gardner's normal fees in the 1930s (excluding the windfall income from the Hospital Sweepstakes) bumped along for the whole decade at an annual average of £30,000, varying only a small amount up or down. Salaries rose somewhat towards the end of the decade, from 50 per cent of gross fees to 58 per cent (and by steady progression were to reach 64 per cent in 1955). The profit per partner barely changed in the 1930s, averaging £2,810. Not all of this went to the partners, but they were likely to have been among the wealthiest men in the country. Top civil servants started the decade on £1,500 a year, and the Revenue Commissioners reported that only 1,500 people paid surtax, which started at £2,000 a year. A mere 28 people reported a taxable income of over £20,000 in 1932. Craig Gardner's peak earning per partner, at £3,600, in 1932 was, ironically, the very year in which de Valera declared on the hustings that no man was worth more than £1,000 a year to the State and, having won the election, reduced ministerial and civil service salaries accordingly.

Accountancy services under the new regimes

In 1922 there were 143 members of the Institute, a great increase on the 55 recorded in 1900. The majority of members worked in Belfast, which had 87 professional firms as against 54 in Dublin.[22] But the steadily growing market for accountancy services, combined with a lack of regulation, led to a rich variety of other accountancy professionals and an even richer variety of individuals offering book-keeping, tax and other services without the encumbrance of professional qualifications. The first Irish Free State Census of 1926 reported 382 practising accountants in the South (as index of the position of the profession, this was considerably fewer than the 1,356 barristers and solicitors, the 987 civil engineers or even the 567 journalists and authors). Although the census described the accountants as 'chartered', this was by no means universally so; the membership of the Institute was only 197, of whom many were based in the North.[23] The 1921 Thom's *Directory* lists Dublin accountants under several headings, such as:

- Institute of Chartered Accountants in Ireland (26 names, mostly of firms);
- Institute of Chartered Accountants in England and Wales (six names, most also included in the ICAI list, but not all);
- Society of Incorporated Accountants and Auditors (30 names, often with associated firm);
- Corporate Accountants (45 names);
- London Association of Accountants (six names);

- Central Association of Accountants (10 names);
- Accountants and Auditors (52 names, including some such as Michael Crowley, listed in the ICAI list, but the majority not).

For potential clients these multiple listings must have been confusing. What subtle differences were there between Irish and English Chartered Accountants practising in Ireland? Or between a Corporate and an Incorporated accountant? Or between the London Association and the Central Association? What was the uninitiated reader to make of Kennedy, Crowley, one of whose principals was listed with the Irish Institute, another with 'Accountants and Auditors'? (Vincent Crowley, the dynamic founder of the firm, perhaps the most successful accountant of his day, was famously not formally qualified.) Some members of the Society of Incorporated Accountants and Auditors were evidently in public practice on their own, some as members of accountancy firms (such as F. J. Cahill of Kevans and T. H. Robinson of Stokes Brothers & Pim) and others again were in business (such as D. R. Mack of the Royal Bank and Walter Philips of Guinness).

This potential confusion had been, of course, one motivating factor in the struggle to establish a statutory register of accountants akin to the medical register. In the absence of registration, as the Commission on Vocational Organisation reported, 'there are no restrictions on the use of or qualifications for the title' of accountant, and 'even custom and usage do not assign a certain and precise demarcation to the profession'.[24] This was still the case in the early 21st century.

The last attempt at registration

In Ireland in 1927 there occurred another attempt to establish a statutory register of accountants, through the Oireachtas. John Mackie, then President of the Institute, committed himself strongly to the cause, declaring to the 1926 AGM that 'the desirability of registration [was] now generally admitted', though he agreed that it was not likely to benefit 'members of the two premier bodies' as such, the status and professionalism of the Institute and the Society of Incorporated Accountants and Auditors being assumed. Nonetheless, as the minutes of the Council record, he recommended 'going to considerable trouble and expense to ensure that all persons holding themselves out as accountants and auditors shall be subject to the discipline of a statutory authority'.

The debate on the Registered Accountants Bill exposed many current attitudes to the profession. Accountancy was still a great mystery to ordinary people. The story of the audit clerk arriving at a country audit was often told: after a few cheery pleasantries he asks: 'Well, how have you been doing this year?' only to be answered: 'We are waiting for you tell us that.' In the Seanad debate, on the second reading Senator Oliver St John Gogarty, with a wrongheaded wit worthy of George Bernard Shaw, opposed the idea.[25] To begin with, as he put it, he 'did not think that [accountants] were sufficiently disreputable to deserve all this regulation of their conduct'. His main opposition, however, was on the grounds of handing over a monopoly to a task in which 'hundreds of men who every week in their lives act as accountants without knowing it or without acquiring professional status'. He added, 'accountants may have a certain sort of definition of accountancy, but it really amounts to anyone who can add up legibly and correctly.' Industry Minister Patrick McGilligan, exercising his right of address in the Seanad under the Constitution, agreed, scouting the analogy with the technical knowledge required to be a doctor or dentist; 'a man with a good education and a certain type of experience can acquire competency as an accountant'. Others, such as Senator P. J. Brady, took a more respectful view, declaring that 'accountancy is a highly technical art, requiring experienced training, and that it is a very dangerous thing for a person not well versed in accountancy to venture on the production of balance sheets'.

In the end, the Registered Accountants Bill was lost, mainly because of the senators' reluctance to establish a closed shop, with, as McGilligan put it, 'a council consisting entirely of members of the profession with powers to select members of the profession and to regulate at their own sweet will'. Also, as so often before in the various British attempts to establish a register, the legislators were disconcerted by disagreements between the professional bodies concerned. On this occasion, the Irish-based members of the London Association of Accountants circulated a memorandum opposing the Bill and accusing its sponsors of self-interested motives. The Bill was lost by 18 votes to 11.

A similar vagueness as to accounts and accountancy was demonstrated by James Joyce in his great fiction *Ulysses* (published in 1922). In the 'Circe' or brothel episode the mistress of the house bemoans: 'bytheby Guinness's preference shares are at sixteen three quarters. Curse me for a fool that I didn't buy that lot Craig and Gardner told me about.'[26] The image of the partners of Craig Gardner providing investment advice to brothel-keepers is unlikely, but not quite impossible (though the image of articled clerks popping down to the brothel to do the year-end books is even less likely). Joyce's understanding of the profession was probably based largely on his knowledge of his father's career, who was just the sort of unqualified practitioner to combine investment and tax advice with a little book-keeping. In the 'Ithaca' section of *Ulysses*, the lengthy, catechism-style, question-and-answer chapter, there is a two-column 'Budget' detailing Bloom's income and expenditure during the day.[27] In this debits and credits are transposed, duplicating the appearance of a bank pass book, the nearest most ordinary people got to accounts. Furthermore, though described as a budget, this is clearly a record of actual, not prospective, expenditure. In his detailed analysis Keith Warnock points out also that the expenditure record is incomplete, perhaps deliberately.[28]

Public interest in accountancy

During the late 1920s and early 1930s a number of financial scandals focused public interest on the profession's activities. The controls erected to rein in the greed of opportunistic shareholders proved less useful when confronted with powerful senior managers determined to get their way. Clarence Hatry's pyramid of interconnected companies collapsed in September 1929 (one trigger point, some think, for the October 1929 US crash). He got 14 years' penal servitude. The chairman of Ner-Sag Mattresses got four years for issuing a false balance sheet. The managing director of Blue Bird Oil got seven years in 1930 for accounts irregularities.

The 1932 UK *Royal Mail* case, however, created a scandal in the wider world that exposed the deliberate opaqueness of current balance sheet practices. At the centre of the case was the Royal Mail shipping company, which had made handsome profits during the First World War. They had paid substantial amounts of excess profits duty on account and had created a reserve for their estimated future liability. Then the Government changed the rules, by allowing shipping companies retrospectively to charge a special obsolescence allowance. Some of the tax was repaid, and the reserves were no longer required.

However the 1920s were not good years for international shipping, and Royal Mail began to make losses. As was normal practice, the even flow of dividends was maintained by transfers from the tax reserves. For the 1925 accounts, the auditor, Harold J. Morland, the assigned partner from Price Waterhouse, decided to give some indication that dividends were not being entirely paid out of profits. So he inserted the deliberately ambiguous phrase 'balance for the year . . . after adjustment of taxation reserves, less depreciation of the fleet etc'. The size or even direction of the 'adjustment of taxation reserves' was not indicated.

In 1927, a prospectus seeking funds declared 'the audited accounts of the company show that the average balance available . . . has been sufficient to pay interest on the present issue more than five times over'. When later the Royal Mail's finances deteriorated to the point of requiring a government bail-out, critical public attention began to be drawn to these expressions. It was decided in 1931 that the Chairman of Royal Mail, Lord Kylsant (who was also Chairman of Harland and Wolff), and the auditor Harold Morland should be charged with the criminal offence of publishing false information.

Harold Morland, a Quaker, was undoubtedly a clever man, with a first class degree in mathematics, but he was, as one of his partners put it, 'bone idle'. He displayed throughout the trial in the Old Bailey complete confidence in his professional position. His barrister, Sir Patrick Hastings, admitted later that he found Morland's refusal to admit the grave position he was in 'a little trying'. Asked afterwards how he had coped with the ordeal of the trial, Morland replied, 'they treated Christ much worse'.[29]

During cross-examination he was asked:[30]

> 'You would not concern yourself with the effect which the company's reports are having on the public mind?
> —That has nothing to do with the auditor.
> It is very important for a shareholder to know, among other things, what current earning his company is making?
> —I do not see why.
> Do you agree that one of the most material circumstances which every shareholder has a right to know is the earning capacity of the company?
> —Of course I do not agree with that.
> If the shareholders had realised what the true position of the company was, and what it had expended from 1921 to 1927, do you think they would have been seriously disturbed?
> —That is not an easy question to answer. I should doubt if they would. The chief thing a shareholder wants is regular dividends and that he had all the time.'

Though these views now seem perverse, they were defended by the great and good of the British profession, including the President of the ICAEW, the President of the Society of Accountants and Auditors, and others, such as the best-known accountant of his day, Lord Plender of Deloitte. This weight of professional evidence, explaining that what Morland had done was perfectly normal and was understood as such by City men, encouraged the jury to acquit both him and Lord Kylsant of false accounting. However, they found that the prospectus (with which Morland was not involved) was false and intended to mislead, and so Kylsant on his own was sentenced to 12 months in prison in the privileged second division. His acquittal came as a surprise to Morland's defence team. The story goes that when the accountant's wife rang up on the last day of the trial to ask 'would he be late for dinner?' a member of the team answered 'about twelve months, I should think'.

In England, the public controversy caused by such palpable manipulation, which the trial judge called 'incredible' and 'astounding', did not die down, and the accountancy profession was obliged to address the issues. Frederick De Paula later described the effect of the Royal Mail case as 'like an atom bomb, [which] profoundly disturbed the industrial and accountancy worlds'.[31] Another authority declared that 'the criticism aroused by the case probably had a greater impact on the quality of published data than all the Companies Acts passed up to that date'.[32]

Back-duty cases

One area in which the wide variety of people offering accounting services was visible was in the so-called back-duty cases. We saw in the previous chapter how the new rigour of tax collecting stimulated by the First World War forced companies and individuals to turn to accountants to prepare their returns. This was continued in the new State. David Telford had estimated that 80 or 90 per cent of businesses and individuals used accountants to prepare their returns, and in its discussion of the profession, the Commission on Vocational Organisation confirmed that: 'nowadays not merely all companies but even persons of modest means and practically all who pay income tax or estate duty find it advisable to employ an accountant to prepare their accounts for submission to the revenue authorities.'[33] (This was, of course, long before PAYE.)

In the troubled years prior to Independence many taxpayers had patriotically withheld their taxes from the British. They were now dismayed to discover that the newly founded Revenue Commissioners was looking for those payments.[34] Although *Reade's Case* in the Supreme Court had in 1926 confirmed that the tax was indeed due, taxpayers were no more enthusiastic than they are now. The historian of the Revenue Commissioners tells a familiar-sounding story of a recalcitrant taxpayer who produced a bank manager's certificate proving that he had no deposit account. Later it emerged that 'he had withdrawn money that was on deposit in that particular bank, had held the cash until after the hearing and then re-lodged it. He had, later enquiries disclosed, both a deposit account and a current account in every bank in the town. Also he had deposits in the names of his wife and daughter.'[35]

Collection of back tax was not helped by the IRA's wholesale destruction of local tax offices and the burning in May 1921 of the Custom House, the repository for a considerable number of tax returns. Despite lobbying by the ICAI the Revenue refused to pay for the accountancy work involved in resubmissions. The process of collecting the back duty went on throughout the 1920s and delivered a substantial dividend. The Limerick firm of Metcalf Lilburn was not the only one who found these cases an introduction to all sorts of follow-up business: 'it was the back-duty cases that really built the firm', as one of its partners put it.[36] The scale of back-duty cases was impressive, in effect doubling the income tax receipts. In 1926 the Minister for Finance Ernest Blythe reported to the Dáil that although some £5 million had already been collected, there was, he estimated, a further £700,000 or so potentially available in back duty. By comparison, in 1928–9, when the yield of back tax was described as 'small', the total income tax receipts amounted to just £4.3 million.

Inevitably there were more than qualified accountants processing these claims. In July 1921, the Council of the Institute considered a complaint that some local banks were taking on income tax work, but, as the minutes record, 'it was decided that nothing could be done in this matter as they apparently only undertook this class of work for their own customers and the Institute could not interfere with them any more than they could with the numerous Income Tax Repayment Agencies throughout the country'. And it was not always necessary to employ a professional, as Senator P. J. Brady (a solicitor) told the Seanad in 1927: 'a small trader down the country . . . very often goes to a school teacher or a local stationmaster, a man who has a knowledge of making up returns. These men make up his accounts for him.'[37]

The Revenue's zealous collection of back tax was widely resented: in the Dáil Deputy William Magennis, a UCD professor of metaphysics, declared that the Revenue 'is notorious and had always been notorious for the tyrannical spirit and the unreasonable spirit that has animated its meanest official'.[38] One of the few Protestant TDs, Jasper Wolfe of West Cork, also by profession a solicitor, spoke of a large employer whose tax affairs were unresolved. At the end, 'when the departed soul should be left to commune with its Maker, around that deathbed there floated the Income Tax fiends, following that man into eternity'. According to him, another constituent of his had apparently been imprisoned 'not for any money legally due, but to put the fear of God into other Income Tax payers'.[39]

The annual audit

Notwithstanding the contribution made by tax compliance work and secretarial assignments (dealing with the share registers, writing minutes, running trade associations, etc.), the typical work of the profession remained the audit of small businesses. This usually required writing up the books as a preliminary. Members of the Institute and the Society of Incorporated Accountants and Auditors would very occasionally have grander audits with ready-calculated accounts; members of other associations and mere 'accountants and auditors' would find more work writing up the books of local traders. The annual audit was an occasion: the story is told of how the new partner arrives for his first visit to a country audit (it always *is* a country audit in these stories). He, a teetotaller, is startled to see a tray with whiskey glasses and a decanter produced: 'Of course,' he is told, 'the Craig Gardner audit always begins this way!'

In 1936 a journal specifically relating to Irish accountancy began publication. The *Irish Accountant and Secretary* (two business functions which were often combined at this time) joined numerous other professional and trade journals of the day, including *Irish Law Times*, *Irish Investors Guardian*, *Dublin Medical Press* and a surprising range of specialist trade journals, the best known of which is *Irish Builder*, but which included *Irish Draper*, *Irish Ironmonger*, *Irish Leather Trades*, *Irish Oil and Colour*, *Irish Printer*, and *Irish Tobacco Trade*.[40] *Irish Accountant and Secretary* was published and edited by G. Ivan Morris. He was not a chartered accountant, but obviously a close and knowledgeable observer of the whole scene, so his journal is more than a members' bulletin of a particular body. Morris was also managing director of Fodhla Printing, a company founded by two anti-Treaty Civil War veterans, Oscar Traynor and Frank Henderson, and retaining connections to the Republican movement. His journal, which ceased publication in 1969 (the year *Accountancy Ireland* began publication), was for over 30 years the only published voice of the profession in Ireland. Many professionals would of course have subscribed to the long-running British journal *The Accountant.*

The first issue of the *Irish Accountant and Secretary* recorded a memory of an audit in a very rural district in the West:

> 'In addition to selling almost everything which man requires on this earth (including cradles and coffins) the client also financed migratory farm labourers, advanced passage money to intending emigrants, took the collection from the parish church every Sunday (giving the [parish priest] a quarterly cheque in exchange), paid with his own cheques the land annuities and rates for several small farmers in the district, receiving cash from them in return, and held for safe-keeping various small sums of money belonging to poor people around who drew on these sums as they required the money. To record these multifarious transactions, he kept:
> A cash book, the debit side of which he could never distinguish from the credit side when entering items,
> A debtors ledger into which the goods were entered direct, there being no credit sales books,
> An iron spike four and a half feet high embellished with a hook on the top and a disk of wood for a base, on which he impaled all invoices, receipts, letters etc for four and half years,
> His bank pass book and paid cheques.
> Any suggestion of improving the system was met with the final reply that the system which was good enough for his father, and his father's father, was good enough for him and would not be altered in his lifetime.'[41]

The annual audit usually began with the senior clerk (who, until the 1970s, was often unqualified and assigned to the same audits for years) and two or so articled clerks sallying forth from the office, having signed the attendance book there. Once in the client's office, and the pleasantries concluded, the audit team was usually placed in the corner of an accounts office, frequently on desks and chairs that for good reasons the staff did not use; sometimes the audit clerks were put into a board room or in an unused office. The accommodation of the audit team was always temporary and often inconvenient. David Rowe, who qualified in 1942, has contributed a memorable description of what he called 'auditing in the good days', in the Irish Rabbit Skin company:

> 'Upstairs, in a long loft, the skins hung around braziers to dry out. The air was warm, heavy, malodorous, moist—an ideal breeding ground for maggots. The floorboards were rough and ill-fitting. Directly beneath the den was the small and dingy main office where we worked. Papers were everywhere, ancient ledgers, spike files and grubby invoices. There a little creative accounting

> was needed to balance the debtors control and the 'advances to staff' was an endless delight of detection. Every now and then a maggot dropped on the working papers, and after a while we hung the newspaper over our heads for protection.'[42]

The audit team faced three basic tasks:

- to check entries against whatever vouchers (invoices, receipts, credit notes, etc.) were available to confirm that the entry was correctly inserted into the initial book (day book or journal);
- to check that the 'casting' (addition) was correct;
- to check that the manual posting from the first stage books to the ledger was correctly done.

Only when these tasks were complete could the senior set about producing the accounts. As William Cunningham, later senior partner of Craig Gardner, who joined the firm in the 1920s, put it: 'The usual audit started from more or less good records—very, very rarely did you get accounts made up for you. One often had to write up the books from scratch.'[43]

Vouching (the confirmation of entries with some external document) was, as De Paula wrote in his textbook, 'the very essence of auditing' because it went behind the details in books of account to the sources, such as receipts, invoices, wages time sheets and so on. In the course of vouching, discrepancies of amounts, descriptions, dates would arise. These had to be conscientiously noted in a 'Notes and Queries' list to be sorted out with the accounts staff later. The most important single external source of verification was the company's bank account records. The Bank Pass Book contained a copy from the bank's ledgers of the customer's account. Michael Crowley recommended: 'once a fortnight, or more often as occasion requires, the Bank Pass Book should be sent to the Bank to be written up, and then compared with your own account and reconciled with it.'[44] By the 1940s, the physical pass books had been replaced by machine-generated account statements on loose sheets, though pass books were often retained for deposit accounts.

A task often given to the most junior clerk was the 'casting-off' of the cash book. There were no computers and generally no adding machines, so this involved manually adding up the long columns of figures to confirm that they were correctly totalled—which they virtually always were. Eric McDowell (partner in Deloitte, Belfast, and President of the Institute 1974–5) remembered his first job: 'I was tasked to check the tots in a day book of 800 pages, with 40 lines to a page . . . and remember that was in three columns—pounds, shillings and pence.'[45] With practice, clerks effectively memorised combinations of numbers and so adding became almost unconscious and both accurate and extremely quick. Eric McDowell remembered 'there were some who could tot all three columns at once, but I never could do that'.[46]

Because every single entry in every book throughout the year was made by hand, the inevitability of human error required detailed checking that the figures in the first stage books, such as sales and purchases books or the cash book, had been correctly transferred ('posted') to the final stage ledgers. 'In the case of small businesses, where there is practically no internal check', wrote De Paula (and this was the case with the typical Irish audit), 'the whole of the castings and postings should be checked'.[47] The availability of numerous very lowly paid articled clerks and a relatively small number of transactions made checking to this level of detail possible. It is also certain that the exhaustive checking was done by juniors only.

Charles Kohler recalls: 'a more absorbing job was the "posting" or "calling-over" of figures. This was team work, not individual work. Two of us had to make certain that figures were copied correctly from one book—say the Cash Book—into another book—say the Private Ledger. If there was a mistake in transcription then the accounts would not balance. This exercise of "calling-over" could go on and on.'[48] De Paula confirmed that 'the routine checking in an audit is apt to become very monotonous and, consequently, somniferous'.[49] To liven the tedium, games were played—for instance the reader might score a point for the same numerals duplicated entry after entry and more where the pounds, the shillings and the pence were the same (e.g. £10 10s 10d); after a fixed time reader and checker would turn about. Each firm had its own conventional tick marks to record checks; different ticks would record correct vouching, correct posting, confirmed addition, and so on; sometimes different colours were used. All ticks were in ink to prevent subsequent manipulation.

A great compensation for hours spent checking postings was the variety of businesses and establishments to which the audit team was sent. A clerk might spend only a week or two with one client, a solicitor perhaps, before moving to another, perhaps a cement factory, a cigar importer or a large department store. Occasionally, there would be perks: in a hotel audit free food, in Player's free cigarettes, and Gordon Lambert, later MD of Jacobs, who did his articles with Stokes Brothers & Pim, remembered 'on an audit at Jameson's Bow Street Distillery there was a tradition of a ball of malt in the tasting room at the end of the week'.[50] The process of exploring so many varied transactions certainly gave a unique insight into how a range of businesses worked, and was the origin of the idea that an accountancy qualification was as good a business education as could be got. In each case, however, the view was from the accounts department, for no clerk was expected to go near the operative side of the business, not even to count the stock, which was not usually done in those early days. (As we have seen in Chapter Two, the *Irish Woollen Manufacturing* case had made it clear that an auditor was perfectly entitled to accept stock listings and valuations from the client.) De Paula suggests that on starting an audit the partner should be escorted around the factory or plant to get a physical sense of the transactions recorded in the books. This was not proposed for the clerks who were actually to do the work.

Occasionally, more interesting tasks arose. Charles Kohler remembers being assigned to the quarterly check of the hall porter's float in a hotel. After nervously counting and recounting the coins, he came to 19 pounds.

> '"Nineteen pounds. Nineteen pounds exactly," I said. 'You appear to be one pound short—the float should be twenty pounds." With no hesitation the porter put his hand in his pocket, withdrew a pound note and placed it in the box. "Right?" he barked.'

This was a vivid introduction to what modern fraud analysts call the difference between the prescribed and the actual system, and young Charles Kohler was baffled. 'I locked the box, returned the key and said nothing about the incident. I feared disclosure might lose the man his job . . . whether I did right or not I still do not know.'[51]

The staff who did the work

The kind of staff who carried out these tasks can be identified, for one firm at least, from Stokes Brothers & Pim's 'Salaries Book' covering 1921 to 1942. The firm started the period with four partners: J. Harold Pim (who died in 1932), his half-brother Francis Pim, R. Stanley Stokes and Francis Klinger. A total of 144 staff is recorded in the Salaries Book, some being employed for the whole period, some lasting only a few months.

The backbone of the firm was the group of senior men, some qualified and some not, with a regular pattern of accountancy/audit work year after year. Then there were the articled clerks, limited by the Institute to a maximum of two per partner. With them would be a number of office juniors, some of whom could reasonably expect to evolve into unqualified seniors, and perhaps become members of one of the associations of accountants that, as we have seen, did not require articles or a premium. There were also typists (some male, some female) and cleaners and porters.

The staff arriving in 1924 and 1925 give a sense of the activity. The first (No. 51), who joined in February 1924, had been in the British Army, so was relatively old for an articled clerk, at 23. He left after only a few months to join stockbrokers Perry & Cairns. No. 52 entered as an office boy aged 14. At first his salary advanced from the initial 7s 6d per week to 12s 6d, but then he was given six months' notice (no reason stated) and left. No. 53 started on £120 a year and she left nine years later to get married. Her salary suggests that she was a typist. The text recorded against No. 54, a probably unqualified male senior, is characteristic:

Date	*Particulars*	*Salary*
26 May 1924	Entered office. Late of Craig Gardner & Co. Engaged by interviews and correspondence. Age 30. Presbyterian.	£250-0-0
1 December 1924	Salary increased to (at his request)	£270-0-0
1 Sept 1925	Do	£280-0-0
1 Sept 1927	Do	£300-0-0
1 Sept 1929	Do	£320-0-0
Sept 1930	Given 3 months' notice to expire on 31 Dec 1930, extended to 31-3-31	
Left end of January 1931 to take up position with Messrs Kennedy Crowley & Co.		

We have seen the great importance attached to religion at the time. Stokes Brothers & Pim apparently assumed that staff were Church of Ireland, and only exceptions to that rule were noted. What seems strange to a modern eye is that this is recorded, while success or otherwise in exams is not. Thus No. 55 was an articled clerk who entered aged 18, and 'P' is marked on his record, which we might guess denotes Presbyterian. As was normal, he was paid nothing for the first year, £10 for the second, £15 for the third, £20 for the fourth and £25 for the fifth. A Christmas bonus of £5 was also given every year. No. 55 worked for two years after (presumably) qualifying and then left. Stokes Brothers & Pim do not record the size of the premium, which varied across the profession. In his autobiography the one-time Chairman of Bord na Móna and CIÉ, Todd Andrews, describes the apprenticeship fee for accountants as £200. Craig Gardner's standard premium in the 1930s was £150.[52] Margaret Downes recalls that her parents paid as much as 300 guineas in the 1950s for her articles to Henry Murphy & Co.[53]

The low wages and other aspects of the articled clerk's employment were adduced by Senator J. T. O'Farrell (a trade union official) in the 1927 debate on statutory registration as a reason for resisting the idea: 'if you want to get proper slave drivers especially in the clerical profession you have to go to the offices of chartered accountants. They pay the most scandalous salaries and drive their employees to an extent that is not equalled in any other profession.'[54]

No. 56 was a three-year graduate articled clerk who similarly stayed two years after qualification. No. 57 had served his articles with John Mackie and was now 24 (and recorded as 'RC'). He started on £120 a year with the promise of a rise to £180 when he passed his finals. This he evidently managed by June, and his income had reached £230 by May 1927 when he gave in his notice, saying he had a job in Deloitte in London. This evidently did not work out, for by April 1928 he was back. Later that year his salary was increased to £300, but he was evidently a restless soul, for in early 1929 he left again, this time to join Marwick Mitchell in Paris. One wonders what became of him (as the citizen of a neutral state) if he was still in Paris in 1940.

The next recruit, No. 58, entered as a 14½-year-old office boy on 7s 6d a week. Over the next 13 years his responsibilities and his salary increased until, when he left for a job with Industrial Vehicles, Athy, he was on £200 a year. In May 1925, No. 59 is also recruited as an office boy (also on the advice of Canon Wilson, until 1925 Rector of Donnybrook, then of St Patrick's Cathedral—the source, background and contacts are frequently recorded). He did not do quite as well as No. 58, reaching only £104 per year before he left to take up a position with the client A. Millar, a wine importer, at the age of 21.

No. 60, who had previously worked with the Gaiety Theatre, came in at £3 a week, but did not last. He was given a month's notice in January 1928. No. 61 lasted even less time; she entered as a typist, with experience from Craig Gardner and W. & R. Jacobs, on a starting salary of £110 a year. She was 35, and against her name is again the cabalistic 'P'. She was given her notice in June after only six months with the firm.

No. 62 came in as an articled clerk at the age of 17. After his articles (presumably he was by then a qualified man) his income rose to £200 a year before he left for a job with Crosse & Blackwell (as several Stokes' people did in this period). There were 27 articled clerks in the 20-year period; mostly on a standard five-year term. They usually stayed on for some years before leaving, usually for employment in a business. Only one, Alan Warnock (No. 88), became a partner in the period, at the age of 29, having qualified four years before.

There was no ruthless hire-and-fire practice in Stokes Brothers & Pim, but they were not sentimentalists either. No. 85, a 14-year old, was hired at 7s 6d a week in November 1932 after a recommendation from Archdeacon Stewart of St Stephen's (the pepper-canister church) and an interview by Stanley Stokes—and barely five weeks later, on 16 December, 'left, after ten days' notice, as he was unsuitable' as the record states. Others were simply 'dismissed' (No. 90) or 'not suited to accountancy work' (No. 94). Typically, men left to join local businesses; two senior men became Company Secretary respectively of the Irish Times (No. 71) and the Educational Company (No. 32). Some went abroad, to an impressive range of destinations: Australia (No. 13), London (several), Paris (No. 57), Penang (No. 23), Kenya (No. 65), Canada (No. 67) and Glasgow (No. 84). Sometimes they went to other professional firms such as Kennedy Crowley or Haskins and Sells in London (later combined with Deloitte).

Professionally, the most interesting destination was that of No. 68, who joined at age 16, completed his exams and articles and left three years later 'to take up a position with the Dunlop Rubber Co.' in 1936. At Dunlop's headquarters F. R. M. De Paula (whom we have met previously as a textbook writer) was pioneering new and informative presentations of consolidated accounts, including technical innovations as well as round pound reporting and display of comparative figures. The 1933 accounts were reviewed in *The Accountant,* who found it 'impossible to find sufficient praise with which to acclaim the new standard in company accounting set'.[55] With an eye to contemporary controversy, the journal went on: 'these accounts answer all the present-day criticism regarding the obscurity that is possible in the earnings and assets of subsidiary companies when accounts are presented in the manner allowed by law'.

More drastic reasons for severance were also recorded: No. 12 for drunkenness, No. 49 for 'defalcations in petty cash' and Nos. 109 and 116 for 'dishonesty'. Since women were not expected to work outside the home, 'left to get married' occurred from time to time, though not for men. Less often was death given as a cause of severance, though two men died in traffic accidents, and a couple of the older men retired through ill-health. One who had been with the firm more than 30 years was paid a pension of £100 a year (the staff partner carefully notes that half of this is to be paid to him and half to his wife). No. 16 joined in January 1916 before being 'called to the colours' in March; he was discharged in 1919 and returning to the firm became an unqualified senior, earning £320 a year before finally dying in 1940 of bronchial pneumonia.

Working towards qualification

In the very early days of the Institute, as we have seen, candidates in practice were interviewed by a committee and accepted or not. Following the British Institute, written examinations for young aspirants were part of the original intention. So much taken for granted now, it is unexpected how relatively new the idea of examinations was in 1888. Although written examinations had been part of cultural life in China from the 7th century, as a way of identifying middle-class talent, in the West they were a much more recent phenomenon. Even in universities such as Oxford, not to mention Yale, Harvard and Trinity College, Dublin, written examinations only superseded *viva voce* quizzing in the 1830s. The British and Irish Civil Service was only regulated by examinations from the 1850s. Irish solicitors sat written exams from 1860, and barristers from 1872.[56]

Once having demonstrated the requisite degree of liberal education by passing the 'Preliminary', an articled clerk aspiring to membership of the Institute faced two further exams, the Intermediate and the Final. In theory the clerk's principal was supposed to supervise the education; in practice, as Gerard O'Brien recalled of his experience with Craig Gardner, 'the partners would help you with a job, but not with training as such'.[57] We have seen that Stokes Brothers & Pim did not record exam success or otherwise in the Salaries Book.

Up to 1920, the Intermediate exam addressed five subjects: book-keeping; auditing; executorship accounts; powers and duties of liquidators; and advanced algebra. The Final had seven: commercial accounts; auditing and audit law; probate legacy and executorship accounts; powers and duties of liquidators; principles of law of bankruptcy; law of partnership, joint stock companies, etc.; and actuarial science, including probabilities. No doubt reflecting the current business mix of firms when the list was drawn up, at least 40 per cent of the papers were on insolvency issues. The syllabus largely followed that of the English Institute, though it substituted papers on mathematics for mercantile and arbitration law.[58] Actuarial science is supposed to have been a particular hobby-horse of Robert Gardner's. As things turned out, this mathematical expertise was perhaps rarely brought into real life, even in sampling for audit checks.

In 1921 a new syllabus reduced somewhat the emphasis on insolvency and introduced new papers on economics and statistics, and the theory of finance. As the Institute's historian noted, 'the most significant feature of the 1921 syllabus was that income tax and cost accounts were introduced merely as part of the two accounts papers in the final examination'.[59] In 1939 the syllabus was revised again, this time replacing the papers on economics and the theory of finance with 'general commercial knowledge' and commercial law. Bankruptcy and executorship law still loomed large.

Although the Institute was in the process of compiling a library, and a third and successful attempt to establish a Dublin Students Society had begun in 1927, on the model of the Belfast Society, there was little help given to students until, as we shall see, the acceptance of the *Derryhale Report* in the 1970s changed the Institute's approach. Perhaps as a consequence, the failure rate at both Intermediate and Final exams was high. In 1926 the then President of the Institute, John Mackie, reported to the AGM that only 28 per cent of candidates had passed the Final exam; he blamed simple lack of adequate preparation. Howard Robinson reported that the Technical Schools, and particularly the one in Rathmines, Dublin, provided lectures and classes for Irish accountancy students and, as he put it, 'it is from these and their correspondence courses that the articled clerks learnt the theories and principles of their profession'.[60]

This was misleading. In practice, both the lectures and the correspondence courses (notably those of Spicer and Pegler and H. Foulks Lynch of London) were remorselessly dry and practical. There was no interest then, nor would there be for a long time, in providing a theoretical or principled basis for accounting. As one academic accounting expert claimed in 1950, 'as soon as we pass from the elementary and technical parts of our subject, we are confronted with countless difficult points of principle—indeed, almost every important branch of accounting still lacks an adequate theoretical basis. Our textbooks never call attention to this intellectual poverty.'[61] As a case in point, the well-known textbook *Advanced Accounting* (first published in 1903 and reprinted numerous times since) by Lawrence Robert Dicksee, Professor of Accounting at the University of Birmingham, wastes no time with the ideas that occupy the early studies of modern students, such as materiality, the entity concept, the going concern assumption and the implications of other generally accepted accounting principles.[62] He plunges straight into the distinction between capital and revenue expenditure and moves quickly on to discuss how a set of accounts ledgers should be organised.

How the work was priced

As was true of other professionals, accountants were not especially money-minded. They lived well, but not grandly, and were often casual about submitting fees. Like the leading solicitor Arthur Cox, many of them, while being properly conscious of their own worth, 'were not interested in money per se'.[63] It was common then among the professional class to feel, or affect, a slight disdain for money. Thus an American journalist wrote of the famous contemporary banker Montague Norman (Governor of the Bank of England 1920–44), 'like many great bankers, he is not much interested in money personally, and he is by no means a rich man, money and its mechanism is rather a fascinating problem to him as a diplomat, a mathematician, almost a creative artist.'[64] Evidently, as with attitudes to other major life elements (notably sex and religion), there have been substantive changes in recent decades.

Fees were calculated on the basis of time sheets submitted to a designated clerk. The filling-in of time sheets was often casual, and certainly nothing like as tightly controlled as it has since become. The actual amount charged to the client was at the discretion of the partner concerned. The standard charge-out rates for a seven-hour day recommended by the Institute in the 1920s were as follows:

Principal	£4 4s 0d
Managing clerk	£2 12s 6d
Senior assistant	£2 12s 6d
First class assistant	£2 2s 0d
Second class assistant	£1 11s 6d
Junior clerk	£1 1s 0d

The principal, of course, was charged in the old-fashioned style in guineas. Until a few years after decimalisation of the coinage, this pricing unit, representing £1 1s (the coin itself had ceased to be minted in 1816) was principally used to add a gloss to upmarket items such as fine art, fur coats, and fees for medical consultants and prize bulls.

At these rates a senior assistant being paid £350 a year working a full 5½ days a week would cover his salary in 25 weeks. Such calculations were of course complicated by holidays and non-earning time. A contemporary description of accountants' costs assumes that most employees would be able to charge to clients a maximum of 80 per cent of the time spent in work, and also notes a considerable seasonal variation in workload. The two normal company year-ends were December and March, so the summer months could be slack. Chargeable hours, especially in August, might dip to below 60 per cent of hours available.[65] For the clerks there would be days spent in the office, supposedly filing or studying, but typically employed in, as Anthony Brophy remembered of the early 1960s, 'extravagant games of battleships. More vigorous pursuits included shove ha'penny [and] cricket (requiring waste paper basket, ruler and ball of Sellotaped paper)'.[66] For articled clerks at least, idle days cost the firm little.

Thomas Geoghegan on the accountancy profession

The first Catholic President of the Institute since Independence was Thomas Geoghegan, who served from 1933 to 1935, with Hugh Boyd of Atkinson & Boyd, Belfast, as his Vice-President. Geoghegan was born in 1875 and educated at Clongowes Wood College and the old Royal University, which was dissolved in 1909 when the new National University of Ireland took over its functions. Geoghegan qualified in the last year of the 19th century, and his world view was formed in another world. He was 26 when Queen Victoria died, and nearly 50 when Irish independence was achieved. He survived to be the senior member of the profession before his death in 1964. We have seen that his firm Thomas Geoghegan & Co. was awarded the audit of the first state-sponsored body, the ACC. He was on the boards of various companies, including the National Bank and the Patriotic Assurance Company.

During his presidency the Institute decided to hold its annual dinner in 1934 in Belfast (the first time, incidentally, in the 46 years since the Charter was awarded). In his speech to the assembled guests proposing the health of King George V (who was still head of state in both jurisdictions), Geoghegan gave an insight into how he saw the standing of the profession in Ireland. In his opinion, the profession had some way to go toward making its proper contribution. The public vagueness as to the significance of professional audit services had been underlined at the 1926 AGM of the Institute, where it was reported that the shareholders of the Great Southern Railway had replaced a professional by an old-fashioned shareholder-auditor, who had absolutely no accountancy experience. Thomas Geoghegan expressed his opinion that the business community was not really using accountants to best advantage. For instance, he noted that the profession still had to do an abnormal amount of accountancy and book-keeping for clients, as opposed to audit.

Perhaps surprisingly, given the prominence of the back-duty cases a few years before, Geoghegan also believed that it was not sufficiently known in the community that chartered accountants were persons fully qualified to deal with all cases concerning income tax. Despite this information gap, the President was adamant that neither touting nor advertising were appropriate to the profession.[67] On a more positive note, he said that there were now three times as many members of the Institute than there had been in 1916, and at least among the young, the opportunities of the trainee accountant to gain an insight into the workings of so many businesses was increasingly appreciated.[68]

The new role of accountancy training as an ideal business education was beginning to gain ground.

Chapter Five
War and Peace: 1938–1958

That a Catholic is not required under the moral law to make a complete income-tax return is a commonplace of Catholic teaching. The reason lies in the realistic approach of the Church to all problems. Every Government knows that a considerable number of people who are liable will be able to avoid paying income tax either in whole or in part, and in consequence the rate is fixed at a higher figure than it would be if everybody paid his or her just share. The man who pays up is entitled in strict justice to take cognisance of this device; he should not be penalised for the evasion practised by others, and he is morally entitled to hold back part of his income in fairness to himself.

Letter to *The Irish Times* 23 May 1953[1]

Significant political change can happen alarmingly quickly—as for instance when in a few short years the First World War destroyed European political arrangements that had lasted for a century, or the mere 12 years which Hitler and his cohorts took to cause so much destruction across the world. The Irish experience of 1916–22 was a less drastic case. But in any case a change of ideas and opinion takes longer. In many areas of Irish business life in the South, it took a generation for attitudes to change from the traditional pre-independence customs. Institutions such as the Royal Dublin Society (whose first Catholic President was elected in 1941) and the Royal College of Physicians (whose first president from University College Dublin was elected in 1952) and Trinity College (the toast to 'The King' was finally dropped at TCD occasions in 1945) took long to assimilate. (Others took longer still—*The Irish Times* appointed its first Catholic editor in 1986, and the Rotunda Hospital its first Catholic master in 1995.) In 1936 the President and Vice-President (Hugh Boyd from Belfast and Gabriel Brock from Dublin) had sent a telegram of sympathy on behalf of the members to the new King Edward VIII, on the death of his father George V.[2] The acknowledgement was routed via the Free State's Department of External Affairs.

Gabriel Brock

The Presbyterian Gabriel Brock, a partner in Craig Gardner, was later described as 'one of the outstanding members of the Institute'.[3] He was born in 1886, and so was in his mid-thirties when Irish independence was declared. Brock acted as Honorary Secretary and Treasurer of the Institute from 1920 to 1934, and his reputation and long contribution to the Institute were recognised when two of his colleagues, Stanley Stokes and John Sedgwick, who in the ordinary way would have preceded him in the chair, stood aside and allowed him to preside as President over the celebrations commemorating the 50th Jubilee of the Charter in 1938. He represented the Institute at the World Congresses of Accountants in New York in September 1929, in London in 1933, in Berlin in 1938, and in London again in 1952. He was an active contributor to public life, serving on two government committees, the Bankruptcy Law Commission in 1927 and the Company Law Reform Committee in 1951. Director of several public companies, he was the first accountant to serve as President of the Dublin Chamber of Commerce. A lifelong bachelor, Brock served for a long time on the board of St Andrew's College, now in Blackrock, County Dublin. He was described in his *Irish Times* appreciation as 'setting himself high, sometimes it might be thought, austere standards'.[4]

Brock, of Scottish origin, had been educated at the newly founded St Andrew's, then based in St Stephen's Green, and articled to John Mackie. A gold medal winner in his exams, he quickly became a partner in Mackie & Co., and later in Craig Gardner after the two firms amalgamated in 1924. It was said that it was he, rather than senior partner John Mackie, who attracted Craig Gardner's senior partner, David Telford, to the amalgamation.

As one of the leading accountants of the day, Brock had been called as expert witness in the case of *Leech v. Stokes*.[5] The facts of this case were that in the early 1930s Stokes Brothers & Pim had agreed to prepare tax returns based on the books, such as they were, of a solicitor's firm. The books were admitted on all sides to be in 'rotten' condition. As the solicitor's statement of affairs put it, before Stokes Brothers & Pim started work there had been 'neither Cash Book nor Ledger of any kind kept'. Nonetheless the returns were prepared as best as could be. Unfortunately, the poor condition of the accounting records hid a long-lasting defalcation by the solicitor's clerk. When this could no longer be concealed, another firm, John Sedgwick & Co., was asked to carry out an extensive investigation, which revealed that the clerk had got away with at least £3,750. The solicitor sued Stokes Brothers for recompense on the grounds that they ought to have found the deficiency. Brock's notes on the case make it clear that he believed that the solicitor, a Mr Fetherstonhaugh, 'knew or suspected that things were hopelessly wrong in the office' and that was why he asked Stokes simply to prepare the return without exploring the underlying condition of the books.

In the end, to the relief of the profession, the judge found no actionable negligence on the part of Stokes Brothers & Pim. A persuasive factor was that their fee was a mere £4 4s, as opposed to the £300 that Sedgwick charged. As was argued, if you pay the doctor to bandage your knee, you can hardly blame him if he fails to discover intestinal cancer. Nonetheless, a distinct shadow was cast over such partial work. Indeed Brock noted, in words that could have been used as a motto for the profession, that 'accountancy work must always precede audit work. We *prepare* and *audit* accounts. In Ireland it is the rule and not the exception'. He told the Court that he believed that his own firm would not have gone on with the job in the conditions.[6]

As time went on, external activities took more and more of Gabriel Brock's time, and he retired from Craig Gardner in 1949. He had by then been co-opted on to the board of the Provincial Bank (later one of the constituents of AIB), where he became Chairman in 1946. He served on the board of the Meath Hospital from 1942 to 1965, being one of the Protestant members temporarily unseated by the sensational coup organised by members of the Knights of St Columbanus. In 1949 some Knights had identified that membership of the managing committee of the hospital, one well-known for only recruiting graduates of Trinity College as doctors, could in effect be bought for the cost of a subscription. This was done, swiftly and without notice. The coup was a complete surprise and success, and a new Catholic-led committee was installed. The sitting members, including Gabriel Brock, were displaced. Soon the new committee began to replace Protestant with Catholic doctors, removing among others the world-famous urologist Dr T. J. Lane. Eventually, after some lobbying, a Bill went through the Oireachtas in 1951 to reinstate matters.[7]

In his later years Brock took up angling—as his obituarist wrote, 'no days were ever happier for him than those fishing holidays in the west of Ireland'. No doubt the same could have been written of many of his professional colleagues. He died in December 1967.

Berlin 1938

One of the World Congresses in which Brock represented the Institute was held in Berlin in September 1938. Other members of the Institute, including Arthur Muir from Belfast and Thomas Geoghegan, attended; with them was William Butler of the Irish branch of the Corporation of Accountants (later ACCA).

The Fifth International Conference on Accounting was part of the campaign, notably including the 1936 Olympics, to present Nazi Germany to the world as a respectable regime.[8] In fact the German profession was in an interesting state. It was only in 1931 (a long time after the British Act of 1900) that large public companies were required to have an annual audit, with private companies following some years later. At the same time the State (pre-Hitler) had combined the various small organisations of book-keepers, consulting economists and accounting companies that provided such services into an official *Institut der Wirtschaftsprüfer*. Official registration, which had completely eluded the British and Irish Institutes, was achieved at a stroke. The new *Institut* provided standardised accounts protocols, uniform authorisation and a stiff six-year qualification process. However, before it had a chance to establish any kind of professional ethos or self-reliance it ran into Hitler's programme of Nazification. The general meeting was dissolved in 1934 in favour of a single '*führer*' who was, of course, a Nazi Party member; new candidates had to prove their Aryan heritage; Jews steadily had their membership revoked. Although only 38 per cent of the profession were members of the Party, and there were still 55 Jewish members, these changes were apparently accepted by a vote of 612 to 0, with two abstentions.[9]

As a result of German threats to Czechoslovakia in late 1938—Hitler noisily alleging 'the oppression of three-and-a-half million' Germans in that country—an international crisis flared. *The Irish Times* considered that Europe was 'closer to war than at any time since 1914'.[10] The accountants at the conference were thus in the strange position of discussing their professional concerns, largely auditing, while the world held its breath in fear of war. Finally, the British Prime Minister Neville Chamberlain flew (twice) to Germany to ensure 'peace in our time'. Not everyone was convinced, certainly not No. 121 in the Stokes Brothers & Pim Salaries Book, who, as soon as he turned 16 in March 1939, left 'to go into training for the Air Force'. He was not alone: at least seven staff members had left to join the British forces before 1942, when the record ceases.

In the conference hall lavishly decorated with Nazi insignia, the delegates were welcomed by *Reichswirtschaftsminister* (Economics Minister) Walther Funk, who was later sentenced to life imprisonment for war crimes. The organising committee made sure that the delegates experienced nothing but lavish hospitality and smiling German friendship. In his presidential address to the Institute's AGM in May 1939, Brock complimented the Germans on their efficiency and generous hospitality, though he complained that the interpreters' grasp of the technical issues raised in the many papers in French, German and Italian was often inadequate. He did not comment on the political situation, and nor did William Butler in his description of the conference.

After such a smooth experience, the delegates must have been considerably surprised when *The Irish Times* reported in November 1938, a few weeks after their return, what was called *Kristallnacht*—'FIRE AND WRECKING IN GERMANY: JEWS' DAY OF TRIAL' as one headline put it.[11] In a supposedly spontaneous response to the murder in Paris of a junior German diplomat by a Jewish student, thousands of Nazi supporters gathered in towns and cities throughout Germany and smashed the windows of Jewish-owned houses, looted and set fire to Jewish shops, synagogues and commercial premises and beat any Jewish people they could find in the street. Mostly, the police were either absent or joined in the attacks; fire brigades stood by merely to ensure that fires did not spread to Aryan premises. (In Leipzig the Jewish owners of two department stores were arrested on the grounds that they had set the fires themselves as an insurance swindle.) The Jews arrested, so *The Irish Times* reported, were despatched to the newly founded Mauthausen concentration camp in Austria. *Irish Times* editor Bertie Smyllie was incensed: 'the appalling scenes of Wednesday night ought to have been impossible in a modern state . . . The nations have learned to tolerate many things since the Great War but it is hard to see how they could tolerate this reversion to the jungle.' A year later Germany invaded Poland and the world was at war. It was the start of a grim decade for the world and for Ireland.

In neutral Ireland

That the South, or Ireland (Éire) as it was named under the 1937 Constitution, would be neutral had long been expected, but it was clear where the sympathies of the members of the Institute lay: in 1941 the AGM minutes recorded that President R. Stanley Stokes announced 53 members and students had joined the British forces, and 'several students' (but no members) had joined 'the Éire forces'. By the end of the war some 75 members were listed as serving in various (British) units. This was a substantial proportion of the 348 members recorded in 1938 as working on the island of Ireland, and the policy of waiving membership fees 'for the duration' caused some cash-flow problems to the Institute. The Department of the Taoiseach refused to authorise some proposed changes to the Institute's bye-laws allowing concessions to members serving in the (British) armed forces, on the grounds that to do so would encourage non-neutral behaviour.

Although the South was partly prepared for the isolation of neutrality, especially since the tariff barriers and the control of industrial investment by the various Control of Manufactures Acts had been established since 1932, there were many commodities that could not be produced at home. Notable among these were fuels of all sorts, from petrol to coal; fertilizer; tea and sugar; raw materials for industry and building; and a host of daily consumables from tobacco (and matches) to clothing.

The experience of the war in Northern Ireland was markedly different. There were for instance the horrific air raids on Belfast in April and May of 1941 (and, in the context of the frigid political climate between Dublin and Belfast, de Valera's striking decision to dispatch volunteer Dublin firemen to help); there was the influx of American military, which before the Normandy landings in 1944 reached 120,000; and there was the gearing of the productive economy to wartime demands. At Harland and Wolff the workforce rose to 30,000—the yard turned out 170 Admiralty and merchant ships between 1939 and 1945; other factories across the region produced fuselages, tanks, field artillery, shells, bomb parts, grenades, radar equipment and flax fabric items such as parachutes, wagon covers, tents and machine gun belts.[12] Ominously for the future, it was found that Northern Ireland's productivity levels were consistently lower than any other regions of the UK. 'There was', as Jonathan Bardon puts it, 'abundant evidence of incompetent and high-handed management and low worker morale resulting in defective work, high absenteeism and poor time-keeping.' A report from the Ministry of Aircraft Production claimed that Short and Harland, which employed 23,000 people making planes, 'was not working at more than 65 per cent efficiency'.[13]

Twenty-six-county Ireland was still a deeply rural country, with just over 3,000 registered companies, of which 225 were in the food, drink and tobacco category and 1,150 described as 'trading' (such as large retail establishments and importers).[14] The economy was dominated by small companies employing 20 people or fewer.[15] Corporation profits tax amounted to a mere £600,000, a little more than the excise duty on imported sugar. Nearly 90 per cent of exports were either live cattle or food and drink, and half of the workforce worked on the land. Three-quarters of the population lived in towns, villages and hamlets of fewer than 10,000 people. As the 1946 census revealed, the sanitary conditions in rural Ireland were not good. Four out of five farm dwellings had no fixed toilet, running water or bath. Modesty and lack of facilities combined to inhibit washing, and lice infection was common. This was not unique in Europe: urban French people were shocked to learn from their 1954 Census that three-quarters of French homes had no indoor toilets, and a mere 10 per cent had a fixed bathtub or shower.[16]

Varieties of accountants

It is perhaps not surprising that such an agricultural economy needed only the 673 accountants that the 1936 Free State Census reported. There were 155 members of the Institute working in the South and 193 in the North at this time. This suggests that about a quarter of working accountants in the South were chartered, so that, though by general acceptance the Institute was the premier body, it was by no means dominant in the profession.[17] In 1944, after 56 years, the Institute issued its 1,000th membership certificate, to George Stuart of Dublin. Following the common path we have seen from the Stokes Brothers & Pim employees, Stuart later became company secretary to Jefferson Smurfit. (The relative scales of then and now can be seen in the fact that in the 2000s membership of the Institute rose from 12,000 to 15,000 in just a few years.)

Only about a quarter of people describing themselves as 'accountants' in the 1936 Census were members of the Institute of Chartered Accountants in Ireland. There was a confusing set of professional alternatives, most of whose rationale was to provide professional qualifications without the exacting financial and exam requirements of the Institute, such as the premium, the demand for years of virtually unpaid apprenticeship and an exam syllabus that resulted in failure rates of more than 50 per cent. Their names are strikingly similar. There was:

- the Society of Incorporated Accountants;
- the Irish Association of Accountants;
- the Irish Association of Corporate Accountants;

- the Corporation of Accountants; and
- the Irish branch of the London Association of Accountants.

These bodies all had members in Ireland. They all set exams and typically accepted proof of 'satisfactory professional experience' in a commercial office, without articles or a formal mentor, as sufficient practical background. In December 1938, the *Irish Accountant and Secretary* announced the 'sensational amalgamation' of the London offices of the Corporation of Accountants and the London Association, giving the new Association of Certified and Corporate Accountants 6,000 members and 5,000 students. After receiving a Charter in 1974, this became the current Association of Chartered Certified Accountants. The next such merger was in 1957 when the Institute and the Society of Incorporated Accountants (both dating from the 1880s and each requiring its students to serve articles) came together, and membership of the Irish Institute jumped from 984 to 1,340.[18]

In 1956 the Irish Independent *Guide to Careers* noted that the old rule that one required wealthy parents to become a chartered accountant was no longer automatically true: 'today many articles are entered into without premiums and there is often a small progressive salary'. This was confirmed at the Institute's AGM in 1957 when the President, Frank Cleland of Wilson, Hennessy & Crawford in Belfast, noted a drop in the number of articled clerks. They were deterred by the costs and, he guessed, by the persistently low pass rates in the final exams. He urged members to abandon the premium system and to improve the salaries paid to clerks. The low pass rate had been a regular presidential complaint since the 1920s, though not one the Institute had felt required to do anything about. Many students were convinced (on absolutely no evidence) that the low pass rate was the result of a deliberate policy of rationing entry to the profession.

Until the great wave of amalgamations of firms began in the late 1960s, the old firms at the top of the profession from the beginning tended to remain there. Howard Robinson commented in 1963 that the names of the first Fellows of the Institute still 'survive in firm names that are familiar to all Irish accountants'.[19] It was hard for newcomers to establish themselves. Reynolds McCarron, Oliver Freaney and Haughey Boland are notable exceptions to that rule, since they were able to develop existing political and sporting contacts as the basis of a client list. A similar strategy of developing an established connection was carried out by the small Dublin firm of Forsyth & Co. Harry Forsyth and his associate Gerry Wheeler, who had been a clerk in the Revenue Commissioner's income tax department, were the principals. Wheeler had a wide connection with the Jewish community, then at the peak of its numbers and prosperity, so the backbone of the practice for many years was small Jewish businesses.[20]

Young practitioners wishing to start up on their own might have been excused for finding it difficult to break into private practice. The professional ethics demanded by the Institute tightly controlled market conditions, so that advertising, 'touting' (defined by the *Oxford English Dictionary* as 'to look out busily for customers, soliciting') and even competitive bidding were forbidden. Another control was stressed in the Institute's 1943 AGM when it was confirmed that it was not merely prudent but a matter of professional ethics for a firm taking on a new job to contact the predecessors.

The first accounting machines

By the late 1930s the introduction of accounting machines began to change the technical conditions of work in commercial offices, and so affected the audit task. This was the first step on the path to the all-computerised accounting of the present. Sophisticated multi-functional machines began to appear in Irish offices, with significant knock-on effects both for the control and consistency of accounts information (by removing sources of human error) and for new opportunities for women in office work. As Reginald Knight, general manager of the wholesale druggist Hugh Moore and Alexander, put it: 'owing to the introduction of mechanized accounting, office staffs have been reduced to a minimum. Girls now operate these machines and have replaced the male clerks of previous generations.'[21] In practice, his remarks probably applied only to the most advanced companies. 'Girls' were of course cheaper to employ than men, and after a few months training in the specialised schools that sprung up to provide such training were well able for the complicated machines. However, only in smaller companies was there any opportunity to stay on once they got married, and in the case of an office romance, however respectable, the young woman would usually be asked to leave.

Accounting machines were mechanical and marvellously complex; their bulky frames might combine typewriter functions with calculations, tabulations and extensions, and output into the accounts system. They performed several tasks in one operation, and without the nagging human error of manual systems. A billing machine, for instance, could create the invoice, multiply and extend the total, calculate discounts and prepare posting slips. Sets of cards began to replace the old-fashioned leather-bound ledgers. The simpler 'comptometer', with eight or nine columns of nine keys, was used for all arithmetical functions but mainly for very fast, accurate addition. For the accountancy profession, auditing data produced by these machines presented a new challenge, akin to that of 40 years later when computers came on the scene.

During the war (called in Ireland the 'Emergency') sophisticated accounting machines were difficult to import, but by 1954 *Irish Accountant and Secretary* confirmed that

> 'as a class [male] clerks are fast disappearing. The days of the high stool and the brass-railed desk have gone. Only in a few old-fashioned offices do we find ledger-clerks laboriously writing up their books by pen. The accounting-machine has changed all that, and today a girl can do the work of several ledger clerks as she sits at her machine. Girls are now doing the work formerly done by male office-workers and they are turning out records faster and more accurately because they have machines to help them.'[22]

The 1956 Irish Independent *Guide to Careers* confirmed this new opportunity for young women, reporting:

> 'another office job which has come into prominence in recent years is that of accounting machine operator or comptometer operator. This is an operation for which a girl must be specially trained, but the training is not difficult and does not take more than three or four months at the most.'

Professional life in the 1940s

By 1941, the cumulative effects of wartime shortages were beginning to bite. Large numbers of men, especially from the building and engineering trades, emigrated to Britain; house-building virtually stopped. As the Department of Supplies tightened its grip, many accountants found themselves kept busy meeting its requirements. Distributors and manufacturers wishing to use rationed goods had to produce an auditor's certificate of their actual usage. Thus, Craig Gardner had to certify, for instance, the usage of sugar by Scott's jam factory by carefully comparing the output of jam with the recipe.[23] In the country, firms such as Limerick-based Metcalf Lilburn & Enright, with an extensive practice across seven counties, struggled to maintain their service to clients in the light of transport restrictions. Without cars, as partner Stewart Lilburn remembered, bicycles came into their own: 'I recall arriving at Lord Dunraven's estate office in Adare to do the audit with my assistant on a tandem. Newport, Co Tipperary could also conveniently (or otherwise) be reached by bicycle. It was a long lonely road.'[24]

But life for a professional man was not hard. With no managers or other intermediaries between the front line clerks and themselves, and very little specialisation, the generalist partners were much more directly involved than their modern counterparts with all the minutiae of the client's book-keeping, audit and tax affairs, for all of which they would be directly responsible. Their lives would have been full of intense attention to the details of this and that company's affairs, details which are now covered at the manager or senior level or in the hands of specialists.

The ethos of all professions was of control, discretion and integrity. Accountants, like solicitors and stockbrokers, were expected to be reliable but perhaps dull. They were not expected to 'set any rivers on fire', as the contemporary expression had it. It is notable that it was an exceptional solicitor, Arthur Cox, who led the way with schemes to circumvent the Control of Manufactures Acts. At this time relatively few members of the Institute worked in business, and the focus of the Institute's activities was very much on members in practice. Indeed, a contemporary book discussing the professions argued that 'the extent to which a professional ethic can be said to exist among employed persons is limited'. The essence of the professional life was the independence which the employee necessarily lacked. 'The key is the difference between the relationship between professional and client and the relationship between employer and employee.'[25]

Professionals, in common with others such as civil servants and business people generally, worked considerably fewer hours than their modern counterparts. Contrasting the 46-hour week of the American professional accountant with what G. Ivan Morris claimed was the 27½ hours worked in Dublin, he sarcastically described in *Irish Accountant and Secretary* an accountant's typical day: 'he reaches his office at say 10 am, and slips out for coffee at 11 am for half an hour. Away to lunch at 1 pm to 2.30 pm. Out again for tea at 4 pm (another half-hour). Leaves the office at 5.30. On Saturdays his hours are from 10 am to 1pm, less the coffee half-hour.'[26] In another mood, however, Morris was not so censorious—in his little book *In Dublin's Fair City* he positively revelled in the laid back attitude: 'should Ireland become money-minded, she will be ruined. The temperament of her people makes her susceptible to this chaotic lust . . . . She will slip down to the bottom of the scale and take her place as just another money-grubbing holiday resort.'[27]

Seán O'Faoláin's literary magazine *The Bell* described in 1943 how a typical young professional lived on about £800 a year. This is junior partner level; in 1942 the top unqualified seniors in Stokes Brothers & Pim had £350–£400.[28] He lived in Clontarf in a relatively new house (10 years old); he employed a maid, and a gardener who came in once a week. He had three children, a car, some books, a radiogram and a set of golf clubs. He came home from the office only at the end of the day, taking lunch in town. He did not drink any wine, except sherry, but he always had a spot of Irish in the decanter. As befitted his professional status he dressed carefully, was home-loving, liked opera, and occasionally went to the Gaiety Theatre, but did not care for the cinema. He had an egg every day for his breakfast, either with bacon or poached; for dinner he ate two or three courses.[29]

Gordon Lambert, later the managing director of W. & R. Jacobs (widely known for his role in the Jacobs TV and radio awards) and a famous art collector, recalled his time in articles with Stokes Brothers & Pim (No. 125 in their 1921–42 Salaries Book). He joined in 1940 as a three-year (graduate) clerk, initially with no pay and then moving to first £30 a year and then £40.

> 'Shortages of everything predominated. I remember that part of a junior clerk's duties was dampening the coal slack in order to mould it into briquettes with newspapers in the hope that some kind of fire could be lit to heat the large office room in College Green in arctic conditions . . . One bicycled everywhere, even to the Zoo dance with one's partner in formal dress on the crossbar—trams were a luxury. Perks were like gold dust—on an audit at Jameson's Bow Street Distillery there was a tradition of 'a ball of malt' in the tasting room at the end of the week and although I was in training for various sports I was warned to accept such a generous gesture for fear of spoiling it for future clerks. Player's cigarette audit was even more popular.'[30]

In the 1950s, as Donal O'Mahony recalled, 'if you had gone into Bewley's in Westmorland Street on any working morning you would have found a cluster of budding accountants, surrounded by an assortment of briefcases, quaffing coffees and discussing the chances of making a few bob on the nags that day. There was more chance of scoring that way than relying on Kennedy Crowley's to fill the coffers.'[31]

In the North the business community generally was completely dominated by Protestants, and that certainly applied to the accountancy profession. So when young Hugh O'Hare wanted to become an accountant after his Catholic education, he thought he had a bit of luck since his father knew a partner in one of the grandest firms, Hill, Vellacott & Bailey.[32] Hugh's father was a farmer, and John Bailey (President of the Institute 1943–5) had often shot over his land and had even leased a cottage from him for holidays. So when Hugh O'Hare and his father came into the Hill, Vellacott & Bailey office there was a long and pleasant exchange, largely about shooting, lubricated by glasses of Powers Gold Label. Finally, Hugh O'Hare's father explained why they were there, and asked 'when can the lad start?'. After some hesitation Bailey stopped the conversation with: 'I'm sorry, Pat, but we don't employ Roman Catholics in this office.'

Hugh O'Hare's father, who had assumed that they were two sensible middle-class people together, never got over the shock caused by this rebuff (and humiliatingly in front of his young son). In 1950, O'Hare joined a Catholic firm of Incorporated Accountants, serving a six-year articles and supplying a premium of 150 guineas. The partner in charge had a large connection to the Catholic Hierarchy, but was an autocratic man who did not treat his clerks well, for instance refusing them study leave. The relationship with the principal was critical, since the Society of Incorporated Accountants, which was well represented in Belfast, required, even after the completion of articles and examinations, a statement of good behaviour. This was not necessarily a formality. O'Hare remembered one dreadful occasion when a principal actually refused to provide such a certificate and the unfortunate clerk had to leave unqualified after six years' work and passing all his exams. The Society eventually amalgamated with the Institute in 1957, and Hugh O'Hare became a chartered accountant.

The profession in public life

The tradition of reticence and professional confidentiality was strong. Indeed, one of the reasons clients in the country came to the larger city firms was to ensure privacy—Gerard O'Brien, who in 1944 had become Craig Gardner's first Catholic partner, recalled one country client asking for correspondence to be sent in plain brown envelopes to reduce the temptations for postmen and other carriers.[33] Even on a normal audit, clerks were not supposed to reveal to outsiders where they were going. Being Protestant was an added bonus—it was said the country people assumed that Protestants would always tell the truth.[34]

Perhaps it was this traditional reticence that the *Irish Accountant and Secretary* was identifying when, in 1952, it complained that 'little has been heard from official accountancy circles on the Budget and its possible effects on trade and industry'. If the editor had the Institute in his sights, he made no allowance for the real difficulty of the Belfast-based President (Herbert Addy, partner in Muir & Addy with A. H. Muir) of a 32-county institution commenting on the Republic's affairs.[35]

Irish accountants generally were more inclined to spend their out-of-hours time administering sports clubs than contributing much to public or professional debate. Sir Desmond Lorimer, later, among other things, first chairman of the Northern Ireland Housing Executive and President of the Institute 1967–8, recalled his early days in the profession with the old-established Belfast firm of Hugh Smylie & Co.: 'The profession in the late forties and early fifties was fairly stagnant. It was a nice old-boy network, certainly nice if you were a partner. The top people really ran it for themselves and it had not really evolved.'[36]

Later in 1952 *Irish Accountant and Secretary* commented on the fact that, once again, no Irish paper had been delivered at the recent International Congress. 'It is a remarkable fact', the editor noted grimly, 'that very little has been written by members of the Profession in Ireland on accountancy and allied subjects. We have a feeling that mental laziness has something to do with the dearth of writing by Irish accountants.'[37] Certainly contributions to his own journal from accountants working in Ireland (of any association) were uncommon. Most of the copy was made up of pieces taken from the *Financial Times* and accountancy publications from America, Australia, India, Canada, etc. In fact, other Irish professionals, such as solicitors, chemists or engineers, were not inclined to be any more publicly vocal. Leading businessmen allowed themselves more freedom, and the *Irish Accountant and Secretary* quoted several, such as the chairmen of Switzers, Johnston, Mooney & O'Brien, Williams & Woods, and Independent Newspapers, and later Findlaters and Arklow Potteries (none of whom were accountants), who all took the opportunity of annual general meetings to criticise government tax policy.[38]

A typical accountant's obituary in *The Irish Times* was that of February 1952, which noted the death of T. J. Morrison, who had been at St Andrew's College with Gabriel Brock and who had established the long-lasting firm of Peterson Morrison (which merged with Cooper Brothers in 1968). He was a former president of the Clontarf Yacht Club, and like Robert Gardner was a keen follower of the Ward Union Hunt. The President of the Irish Rugby Football Union in the late 1950s was Ernest Crawford, famous as a full-back who played for Ireland 30 times, half of them as captain. He had qualified as a chartered accountant in June 1914, just before the war. Most of his professional career was spent as City Treasurer of Belfast.[39] Many such obituary articles note the accountant subject's enthusiasm for the middle-class urban games such as rugby, tennis and golf (it is perhaps not a coincidence that, with the Institute, among the few organisations that retained a 32-county remit after 1922 were those dealing with the so-called 'garrison games' of rugby, hockey and cricket). Thus, William White, senior partner of the Cork firm of Atkins Chirnside, who died in 1952, was treasurer of Cork County Cricket Club and also involved in Munster hockey. Thomas Bell, senior partner of Kinnear & Co., who died in 1949, had been President of the Leinster Branch of the Irish Rugby Football Union. An exception is Oliver Freaney, noted as a powerful forward in the triumphant Leinster side that won the inter provincial Railway Cup football final at Croke Park four years in succession in the early 1950s.[40] Oliver Freaney & Co. was founded in 1958 and became the fourth largest firm in the country before finally merging with the UK-based Smith & Williamson in 2008. Less well known was Dr John Fitzpatrick, who was elected President of the Federation of Irish Manufacturers at the age of 42. A member of two golf clubs and a tennis club, he qualified in between the wars and finally retired from practice in 1976 when he began to promote employee participation in companies and founded the Irish Profit Share Foundation.[41]

Perhaps the best-known accountant of the day was Percy Reynolds who, with his friend Eamon McCarron, founded Reynolds McCarron in 1926. Reynolds McCarron eventually amalgamated with Ernst & Whinney in 1987. We have seen that Reynolds fought in the Stephen's Green brigade in 1916, though he appears not to have taken part in any action in the War of Independence after his return from internment in Frongoch. Reynolds came to national prominence when, following the liquidation of a bus company subsequently acquired by the Dublin United Tramways Company, he became managing director of that company and in 1944 whole-time Chairman of the newly formed Coras Iompair Éireann (which combined DUTC and the Great Southern Railways Company).

Immediately a political row broke out, as commentators noticed a flurry of share dealing in advance, indicating leaks of information. An inquiry exonerated Reynolds, implicating an official in the Department of Industry and a group of his friends connected to Milltown Golf Club. The inquiry did, however, criticise Reynolds for (characteristically of his time) having taken it on himself to inform in advance Archbishop McQuaid, the Bank of Ireland and the Representative Church Body, all as trustees holding large stocks of Great Southern shares. Reynolds explained this as 'an act of courtesy' to such large holders of shares. The revelations were timed for the Friday before a Monday general release, after the Dublin stock exchange had closed for the day.[42]

During his time with CIÉ, Reynolds became something of a household name, with Myles na Gopaleen noting in his column in *The Irish Times* that 'as I was travelling on one of Percy Reynolds' buses . . .' and the 'Irishman's Diary' making similar references. He was also well-known as a horse breeder, having bought in 1948 a large estate in north county Dublin for a stud. The stables at Abbeville, Kinsealy, were designed by architect Michael Scott's office, which also designed Busáras, CIÉ's new bus station behind the Custom House.

Abbeville was bought in 1969 by an even better known accountant, the then newly appointed Minister for Finance, Charles Haughey. Reynolds had only been with CIÉ for a few years when he put forward a proposal that, in light of the continuing decline of the railway, CIÉ should invest in diesel engines and cut down on unprofitable lines. The coalition Government rejected his proposal and he was replaced. Six years later his successor introduced diesel locomotives, and major surgery of the railway operations was presided over by Todd Andrews, starting with the closure of the Harcourt Street line in 1959.[43]

Behind the scenes a notable contribution to national life came from a chartered accountant in a detailed memo proposing the establishment of the Industrial Development Authority. This was sent to the Government in 1948 by Eustace Shott of Craig Gardner. Shott was best known nationally for his 1940 liquidation of Clery's department store. His quick acceptance of an offer from well-known retailer Denis Guiney, based on an apparently casual walk-round valuation of the store, was challenged in court. Shott's method of establishing valuations was described by the judge as 'very informal indeed', even 'unorthodox', but the challenge was rejected, mainly on the grounds that no one had offered anything more.[44]

In an interview given long after he retired, former Taoiseach John A. Costello said 'one of the most important contributions [of my Government] was the establishment of the Industrial Development Authority . . . the idea came from an economist, a Mr Shott.'[45] It is a confirmation of Sir Desmond Lorimer's opinion of the public image of the profession as 'not really evolved' that though as a lawyer Costello would have known well the difference between an economist and an accountant, he seems unconsciously to have assumed that such an idea must have come from the former.

A few grim years

The end of the war in 1945 brought little relief from austerity: '[1946] was a curious year', wrote *The Irish Times*, 'in which luxuries were plentiful enough, while the essentials of life remained scarce'.[46] By luxuries, the writer meant bananas, nylons and sport, including the Horse Show, back in full gallop after seven years; by essentials, bread and fuel. Rain and gales throughout the early summer forced dramatic radio appeals from the Taoiseach and the Minister for Agriculture, calling for help with the harvest in a potentially disastrous situation. No wheat meant no bread—a dangerous prospect for so many of Dublin's poor, for whom bread was the centre of the diet. The country was alarmingly close to food shortages. There was no chance of assistance from overseas, since the rest of Europe was teetering on the edge of famine and was in no position to help. So thousands of volunteers were driven from their offices in army trucks to the fields of Cork, Meath and Tipperary to do what they could. In the end, some 80 per cent of the harvest was saved.

The time, said the ever-forceful Minister of Industry Seán Lemass, was opportune for economic expansion. In an attempt to stimulate industrial leaders, he declared: 'it is now or never'. Gabriel Brock, speaking this time as President of the Dublin Chamber of Commerce, was more prosaic: 'Our hopes for the future', he said in February, 'are on the whole bright, but we must keep our feet on the ground. We must reduce taxation and costs and prices . . . hard, well-directed work will in my opinion mean prosperity to Ireland.'[47]

The long winter of 1946–7, combined with an acute shortage of fuel, brought industry to a standstill.

> 'The opening months [of 1947] were marked by continual blizzards, gales and heavy snow and rain storms which beat all records for fifty years . . . snow-storms caused the complete cessation of coal exports from Great Britain and fuel supplies in Dublin dwindled to a stream and then dried up altogether . . . in the city men and women queued to buy wet turf.'[48]

Bread was rationed. With the population lower than at any time since the late 18th century, at just under three million, this was probably the

Republic's lowest point since the Great Famine a hundred years before.

The final years of protectionism

The Republic's economy just marked time, and international connections and trade were at a minimum. As the editor of *The Irish Times* put it in 1951:

> 'We who live in the Republic are just as much out of the stream of current affairs as ever we were. In fact in some ways our little backwater has become yet stiller than it was . . . ever since the end of the war we have been behaving as if our island were really on another planet.'[49]

It was believed on all sides that 'Ireland is essentially an agricultural country and to be prosperous should expand agriculture both in volume and the number of people working in it.'[50] Nearly half a million people (40 per cent of the working population) worked on the land, compared to 16 per cent in manufacturing industry.[51] Four-fifths of the transportable goods firms employed fewer than 50 people and so lacked the muscle to engage in effective exporting, research or even capital investment. It was also a land of small shops. The Irish Census of Distribution in 1951 recorded that there were some 31,400 retail establishments, of which a third had annual sales of less than £20 a week. In the grocery sector, over 40 per cent of outlets were in this meagre category.

Although the policy of protection had driven up industrial production, the number of accountants in the country seemed hardly sustainable. G. Ivan Morris, the editor of the *Irish Accountant and Secretary*, sadly stated in August 1952: 'our profession is overcrowded to such an extent that emigration has become necessary'. The editor returned to the theme six months later, saying that there was 'no scope in Ireland' for a young professional. 'The blunt fact', he wrote gloomily in March 1953, 'is that there are already too many qualified accountants competing for too few jobs.'

In December 1956 Morris recorded that

> 'many people will be glad to see the end of 1956: it has been a hard year in business and the accountancy profession is feeling the repercussions. The future as far as we can foresee is grim-looking, with the continual drain on our population by emigration and the increasing difficulties facing the industrial and business community. One of the most disturbing features of our present slump condition is the number of large concerns which are closing down and going into liquidation.'[52]

Things seemed better in the North: since 1945 '42,000 jobs had been created in various industries, including Courtauld's viscose rayon factory in Carrickfergus in 1950, AEI's turbine factory in Larne in 1956, Chemstrand's Acrilan plant at Coleraine in 1959, Du Pont's synthetic rubber factory in south Antrim in 1960, and Standard Telephone and Cables also in south Antrim in 1962.'[53] Less hopeful was the state of the linen industry, which lost 26,000 jobs between 1951 and 1958 and now 'the industry was in a state of near-terminal decline'.[54] The other great mainstay of the Ulster economy, shipbuilding, did well in the 1950s and the Belfast dockyards boomed. But by the end of the decade they were facing stiff international competition based on new, less labour-intensive construction techniques from Japan, Germany and Sweden.

In his *Irish Review* economic summary of the year 1956, future Taoiseach Garret FitzGerald noted that in an attempt to stimulate demand for local manufactures, the Government had imposed a series of import levies, 'but the impact of these levies upon imported raw materials outweighed the benefits of added protection'.[55] The customs duties payable on all sorts of imports made a bizarre impediment to business. An importer would be charged 75 per cent *ad valorem* on ready-made garments, handkerchiefs and hats, but only 60 per cent on zip fasteners; school satchels attracted 20 per cent duty, unless they were made wholly of leather, in which case it was 40 per cent, which was also the rate charged for leather dog collars and whips; office desks were 75 per cent, while typewriter ribbons were only 50 per cent; on holiday, your hooks and fishing flies were 50 per cent, other fishing tackle 15 per cent, while the boat's sails were 33⅓ per cent and the ropes 60 per cent. All of these rates were echoed by preferential rates, usually about half, which were sometimes applicable only to the UK and sometimes to the Commonwealth.[56] This dense network was to be swept away after the *First Programme for Economic Expansion* and various international trade agreements.

It was reported that over 200,000 people (equivalent to 1 in 14 of the population) had left the Republic between 1951 and 1956. The political system was characterised, said the 1957 Irish Times *Irish Review and Annual,* by 'quietness and lack of thrust' from both the Fianna Fáil Government and the Opposition. It appeared almost to have given up on the big problems of production and emigration, to the extent that, as Alex Newman of *The Irish Times* put it in dismay, 'the suggestion is commonplace that the natural destiny of the Irish people is to emigrate, and that our sensible course would be to let the population run down to something like two millions.'[57] Exactly the attitude he deplored was expressed at the Annual Dinner of the Association of Certified and Corporate Accountants when Frank Peard (then senior accountant at Guinness and later MD of Guinness Ireland) robustly told members 'our surplus population was readily absorbed by the industrial areas of Britain and the US'. As he saw it, the challenge was not to take 'a narrow nationalistic viewpoint', but to equip potential emigrants with appropriate educational tools.[58]

Professionally, however, things were opening out, as companies increasingly began to think of employing accountants as such, rather than as company secretaries. Perhaps pessimistically, the *Financial Times* reckoned that 'a few hundred employees' was the lower limit of size for the employment of a full-time accountant.[59] Unfortunately, according to the analysis in *Economic Development,* there were only about 100 such firms in the Republic.[60] In common with the profession as a whole, the 1956 Independent Newspapers *Guide to Careers* clearly still saw the work of the accountant in practice rather than in business as the norm:

> 'the work he does for his clients includes accounting, auditing, costing, taxation and liquidations and he may act as a financial advisor to large and small businesses . . . the accountant in commerce or industry is a full-time official, but his work will be on the same lines as that of the public accountant.'

Nonetheless, there were increasing opportunities for the aspiring practitioner to act as part-time secretary and book-keeper to smaller companies and to offer income tax work for business concerns and private clients, as well as providing advice, and assistance with the completion of government forms. In March 1956, the *Financial Times* detailed three reasons why there was such a demand for accountants in industry. First, it noted the level and increasing complexity of tax (and, he might have mentioned, numerous other government requirements, such as import licence requests and statistical returns); secondly, the general level of economic activity generating more transactions; and thirdly, the increased use of management accounting, budgeting and costing in businesses.

However, this last could by no means be relied on. As a striking indication of the innumeracy of British management at the time, the writer obviously felt that *Financial Times* readers would be vague about what budgeting entailed—and we can certainly suppose a similar vagueness among business readers of *The Irish Times* and the *Cork Examiner*. The journalist elaborately explained that a budget

> 'involves setting up for a given future period (which may be a year or a quarter)

a plan setting out in figures expected sales, costs, raw material consumption, changes in balance sheet positions, profits, productive capacity needed and labour requirements. One of the principal uses of a budget is that daily and weekly records can then be drawn up and compared with the planned figures. The mere setting-out of these facts can often help to eradicate impractical or inconsistent projects.'[61]

It was clear that the appetite for figures of the employed accountant's colleagues could certainly not be taken for granted. 'Many executives', wrote G. Ivan Morris in 1957, 'seem to have an inherent horror of figures, they mistrust them, and do not fully understand their implications.'[62]

Despite the efforts of the new Irish Management Institute (founded in 1952) business people generally saw 'experience' as incomparably more valuable than anything academia could contribute. In 1952, Sir Hugh Beaver, the Managing Director of Guinness and Chairman of the British Institute of Management, had depressed an early meeting of the IMI by saying that there was in England no acceptance that 'business management contained a sufficiently high intellectual content to justify . . . the conferring of a specific degree on the subject'.[63] Nonetheless, there was a persistent feeling that American industrial success stemmed largely from 'management'—a mysterious term not always clearly defined.

Under the auspices of the Marshall Plan, groups of Irish engineers, businessmen and farmers visited the US to study industrial practice. Edmond Grace, ACA—one of only 14 men and women to gain honours (75 per cent or more) in his finals in the 40 years between 1924 and 1963—was in the party, and on his return boiled 'the essentials of management' down to (1) set work standards, (2) record, (3) compare results and (4) 'take appropriate action'.[64] That an intelligent commentator should think such a simplistic analysis useful is a measure of how little management thinking there was in Ireland at the time—or in Britain, if the *Financial Times* article quoted above is a good guide. Nonetheless the first three of his tasks at least were obviously tasks which trained accountants could do. Gradually people began to think of the professional accounting qualification, which exposed articled clerks to so many different environments, as providing an ideal practical business training. The public success of men such as Percy Reynolds, Jerry Dempsey of Aer Lingus (ex Peterson, Morrison and four years in Kennedy Crowley's secretarial department) and Frank Lemass of CIÉ (ex Craig Gardner) no doubt contributed.

The professional market in the 1950s

Economic historians have distinguished between familial capitalism, where the interests of the controlling family have a strong priority, and managerial capitalism, where the priorities of the firm and its professional managers take precedence over those of the family. In the 1950s, Irish business life was very clearly at the familial stage. A study of the share registers of 66 leading publicly quoted firms of the time (including such companies as Beamish & Crawford, Irish Glass Bottle, Jacobs, Roadstone) revealed that 70 per cent were family-controlled and 88 per cent controlled by a combination of family and institutional interests. (This was of course not unique to Ireland. Norway, Sweden, France, Germany and Italy, not to mention Japan, would have shown similar characteristics.) These were by and large old firms, two-thirds of which were founded before 1922, and most had a strong family presence on their boards. Furthermore, as Professor Kelleher, who undertook the study, reported, interlocking and overlapping directorships and shareholdings meant that 'the Irish corporate structure of the 1950s was controlled by prominent identifiable families'. A very small, tight group was in control. 'The Irish business elite of the 1950s consisted of 107 prominent families.'[65]

Perhaps as a result, the audit market was stable. At the end of the 1950s the two old-established Protestant firms Craig Gardner and Stokes Brothers & Pim still dominated the audits of Stock Exchange-quoted companies. Apart from state-sponsored bodies, these were by definition the larger companies and the most sophisticated audits. Of the 105 companies where auditors are recorded in a standard business directory, 32 were audited by Craig Gardner and 17 by Stokes Brothers & Pim. Of other firms, Kennedy Crowley had six, Kean five and Cooper & Kenny four. The spread of such work is wide by modern standards, for of the 36 firms with Stock Exchange-listed clients, 28 had only one or two audits.[66] There was little re-assignment of audits. 'I cannot recall', as Noel Stewart of the Ulster firm of Rawlinson Allen & White put it, 'any real competitiveness among accounting firms. New work came in by reputation, connections, friends and recommendation from existing clients.'[67]

According to the Institute's *List of Members* there were nearly 200 firms of chartered accountants in Belfast and Dublin: 84 in Belfast and 111 in Dublin. Other centres with four or more firms included Ballymena, Coleraine, Cork, Galway, Limerick, Derry, Portadown and Waterford. As was perhaps appropriate to the undeveloped state of the economy in the Republic, half of firms were sole practitioners, with a slightly higher proportion of sole practitioners in Dublin. Only two firms, Craig Gardner and Cooper & Kenny, both in Dublin, had more than five partners. Fully 30 years after the first woman qualified, the membership listed only nine women, three in Belfast and six in Dublin, one of whom was a future President of the Institute, Margaret Downes (née Gavin). She was then working in London, having completed her articles with Henry Murphy & Co.[68] Another was the only married woman, Ellen Fannon, an assistant with Kevans & Sons, who had qualified 20 years before. (The so-called 'ban' on married women working only applied to the public service and businesses that modelled their personnel practices on such.)

A spectacular liquidation

To the ordinary newspaper reader, the best-known accountants of the day, apart from a few high-profile managers, were the liquidators. Audited accounts, like bridges, are only of public interest when they fail, and the most spectacular failure of the 1950s was undoubtedly that of Shanahan's Stamp Auctions. The background was the bizarre attempt to turn Ireland into a world hub of the stamp-collecting business.[69]

In 1954 Dr Paul Singer, an Austrian by birth, approached a small family auctioneering business in Dun Laoghaire called Shanahan's and proposed they set up a stamp auction company. He was persuasive, knowledgeable and full of drive. Hunting for investment cash, he set up a publication called *Green I.S.L.E. Philately* which began to drum up money from all over the world to invest in international stamp collections. With the classic scam promise of 'the probability of an outstandingly large profit within four months with full safeguard for your capital' on investments of as little as £10, by 1958 Shanahan's was receiving money at the rate of £5.2 million a year from America, Europe and Ireland. In court it was revealed that the majority of investors were Irish and 30 per cent of investments were in the £500–£1,000 range—a married National School teacher earned £800 a year at this time. Ninety staff handled a hectic programme of auctions. *The Irish Times* reported that 'the company claims to have earned for investors capital gains amounting to a net return of from 35 per cent to 50 per cent on the capital invested.'[70]

Brought in to audit the 1958 accounts, Reynolds McCarron came to a different view: they reported that of the apparent sales of £883,000 in the year, only £197,000 had actually been purchased by outsiders, the rest being 'bought-in on behalf of subsequent investors' at rates inflated to provide existing investors with a notional profit. 'In our opinion the result of this procedure is that investors are being paid out of subsequent investments coming in.'[71] After disagreement with the directors, Reynolds McCarron suggested that another firm be brought in; they were not going to propose themselves for re-election. Of course there were neither enough stamp collections in the world, nor enough buyers to sell them to. Nonetheless, by the Ponzi techniques of huge positive publicity (members of the staff were driven to the airport so they could sing 'For he's a jolly good fellow' when Singer returned from one of his stamp-hunting trips) and lavishly paying early subscribers with recent cash, Singer staved off disaster until May 1959, when the firm suffered a mysterious robbery. A large, recently bought collection of stamps, variously valued at between £100,000 and £460,000, was apparently lost. Questions began to be asked about the operation, and a panic set in, with people besieging the office seeking their money back. Two weeks after the robbery, solicitors Arthur Cox announced the firm was going into liquidation.

Gerard O'Brien of Craig Gardner was appointed liquidator and immediately attended the offices, accompanied by Des Hally, later Professor of Accountancy at UCD. Hally recalled how they were shown up to Singer's flamboyant office with its large desk and multiple telephones. Singer got up to greet the liquidator and his staff in his usual extravagant way and began showing them the office. By the time he turned round, O'Brien, a small, tough man, was seated behind the desk, in Singer's chair. It was, as Hally remembered, as neat a demonstration of the new power relationship as could be devised.[72] O'Brien quickly discovered that there was nothing like enough assets to cover liabilities, and after a court hearing he was appointed Official Liquidator. Singer and his fellow directors were eventually prosecuted for fraud, but they managed to muddy the waters sufficiently to be acquitted.

Planning Ireland's future

In September 1957 the humorous magazine *Dublin Opinion* printed a cover showing Hibernia visiting a fortune teller and asking: 'Is there any future for me?' In later years T. K. Whitaker, at the time Secretary of the Department of Finance, described this as the immediate stimulus to his path-breaking study of the Irish economy, although since work had already begun earlier in the year, it was more probably a confirmatory stimulus than an initiation.[73] However that may be, the major analysis of the economy called *Economic Development* was published in November 1958, and with it a White Paper, the *First Programme for Economic Expansion.* Between them these documents have attained an almost legendary status as initiating a major shift in economic policy away from the protectionist approach that had been the orthodoxy since 1932. Eamon de Valera, the Republic's dominant political figure, was coming to the end of his career, and his approach, that there were so many more important things than the economy (specifically, he gave priority to the Irish language and the integrity of the national territory), had frankly not carried the people with him. In 1959 he left practical politics altogether to become President.

The economist Peter Neary of UCD wrote that

> 'economic planning may be said to have started in Ireland in 1958, with the publication of the *First Programme for Economic Expansion.* This document was a landmark in Irish economic history; for the first time the government set out a comprehensive statement of its policies and objectives, not just for one year ahead but for the following five years. The Programme was also a landmark in that it explicitly admitted that self-sufficiency had failed.'[74]

At the time the Irish Times' *Irish Review and Annual* commented that 'the White Paper reflects, perhaps, a fundamental revolution in Irish economic thinking, not merely at official level but at every level of society'.[75] With neat symbolism, this was also the year that saw the beginning of Aer Lingus' service to America, via Shannon. Accountant J. F. Dempsey, Aer Lingus' General Manager, was certainly pleased, boasting of 'a spectacular improvement', with passenger traffic up 13 per cent and cargo up 17 per cent.[76] The coming tide may not have lifted equally all boats, as was promised, but it certainly was going to make an enormous difference to the accounting profession.

Chapter Six
Economic Development in the 'Super Sixties': 1958–1969

By 1959 'self-reliance' had come to mean for Lemass not self-sufficiency, his once favoured slogan, but an economy sufficiently viable to enable all the Irish to live in their own country. How did he propose to mobilise the sceptical or obstructive adherents of the possessor principle including many businessmen, trade unionists, professional people and civil servants, not to mention farmers, in pursuit of that apparently impossible dream?

J. J. Lee Ireland 1912–1985: Politics and Society (1989)

There was a quick and remarkable response to the new economic policy initiatives in the *Programme for Economic Expansion* in November 1958 preceded by, as some have argued, the Export Sales Relief introduced in December 1956.[1] By 1960 the *Irish Review and Annual* was able to list 39 new companies established since January 1959 and a further 20 in the pipeline. Among those already in operation were firms with American, Belgian, British, Dutch, German, Japanese and Swedish backgrounds. Importantly, only a few were established in Dublin: others were in Cork, Killarney, Kinsale, Dundalk, Limerick and several in Shannon Airport. Products included everything from cranes (Liebherr) to greeting cards (Hallmark) and radios (Sony).

It was as if someone had pressed a national starter motor, firing new initiatives across the country. The surge in industrial production, up 35 per cent in five years, meant that there was more to spend in the wages packets and, importantly, the confidence to spend it. In January 1961 the *Irish Review and Annual* reported that hire purchase for cars, household equipment, furniture and clothing had risen by 35 per cent in 12 months. By 1963 (when the Institute celebrated its 75th anniversary) all sorts of indicators were cheerfully breaking bounds: motor car sales were up 11 per cent on the previous year; electricity usage was up 50 per cent on the 1958 baseline; over the same period the stock exchange had shot from an index figure of 94 to a high of 252. Even the population, which, apart from war times, had been declining steadily since the Famine, showed a small increase. This was caused by a one-third drop in emigration.

Under the headline 'Super Living in the Super Sixties', journalist Caroline Mitchell enthused: 'this country is on the way up. We are going up financially, industrially and artistically . . . the first whiffs of outside air have been stimulating, enabling us to see ourselves more clearly as others see us, and in many cases for the first time'.[2] Others noticed the same. In Shannon, Michael Viney commented on 'the sweet tang of optimism . . . like an aura of aftershave applied freshly each morning.'[3] There was, wrote a returned emigrant, 'an unaccustomed briskness about the way Dubliners moved, and a freshness of complexion that I had not noticed before . . . even the grumbles were indicative. There were complaints about all the money being spent on airlines and luxury hotels, and it was annoying that the upsurge in car ownership meant that the Irish would now have to take examinations for driving licences.'[4]

Despite these changes, the Catholic Church retained much of its traditional high esteem. In research done in 1963–4, over 90 per cent of people agreed with the statement that 'the Church is the greatest force for good in Ireland today'. One priestly respondent told the researcher, an American Jesuit called Fr Bruce Biever: 'no one questions our authority. How can they? We have more education, thank God, and with that education comes responsibility to lead.'[5] And Catholics practised their religion, whatever their belief: as Taoiseach Lemass's biographer put it 'not to do so would have been politically unwise, and perhaps bad manners'.[6] And the same applied to business people. As one businessman told Fr Biever, 'there is nothing like attending Mass with your wife and kids, making sure to be seen of course, to help the business.'

The old attitudes were, however, in the process of revision, particularly as the new medium of television applied its levelling acid (Telefís Éireann began broadcasting at the very end of 1961). The famous chat show *The Late Late Show* in particular gave people a new sense of how the world worked, of what mattered; and after watching, people would never feel quite the same about politicians, about the rich, about the clergy. You might, for instance, see a real live Communist (who turned out not to have horns, despite what the parish priest had implied); you might hear a woman describing what she wore on her honeymoon night (very little by all accounts); or a Trinity student calling a bishop a 'moron'!

The Second Vatican Council (1962–5) was to energise clergy and lay people alike. The old repressive, defensive ways of thought that had first been established in the 16th century at the Council of Trent were, it was hoped, gone forever. At the same time the airs and noises of 'swinging London', from across the water and on many a TV screen, were both exciting and disturbing. They undermined, so felt *Hibernia* magazine (then published for the Knights of St. Columbanus), 'the strong moral tradition of the country . . . [which had] so many corrupting forces in direct competition with it.'[7] It was not only clergymen who felt that some kind of genie had been let out of the bottle. In the business world, religious background was progressively less important. *Irish Times* journalist Michael Viney noted 'the day of the identifiably "Protestant" or "Catholic" firm is passing, as family ownership is progressively diluted or bought out . . . the old myths of working behaviour which prejudiced Protestant and Catholic employers are all but extinct.'[8] When an old-style Protestant building firm asked its accountants, Craig Gardner, to recommend a company secretary/accountant, a name was proposed. With some diffidence, however, the Craig Gardner partner felt obliged to point out that the candidate 'dug with the other foot', as the phrase was. 'Oh that's nothing', said the client, 'as long as he can do the job'.[9]

Economically, the Republic was merely catching up with the North, which had between 1950 and 1960 'enjoyed the most sustained improvement in living standards since 1922'.[10] Industrial production in Northern Ireland had risen by 40 per cent in the same period, with new factories being built by industrial giants such as Courtaulds (Carrickfergus 1950), AEI (Larne 1956), Du Pont (County Londonderry 1960) and Standard Telephone and Cables (south Antrim 1962). However, although GDP of Northern Ireland rose by 2.6 per cent per annum in the 1950s, this was weak compared to Denmark's 3.5 per cent and West Germany's sustained 9.3 per cent. Only when compared to the Republic did the North's performance seem something to be complacent about.

Throughout the 1960s, Ireland's economy did change, as the numbers employed in agriculture declined and the numbers of manufacturing workers, office workers and professionals increased. Thus, those employed in 'Professional and Technical Occupations' went up 50 per cent, from 26,000 in 1961 to 40,000 in 1971.[11] The Republic's Census of 1971 reported that there were 3,400 men and women practising accountancy in the South, nearly nine times the number reported in 1926 (see *Table 1*).

Table 1: *Numbers in certain professions in the Republic of Ireland*

Census	*Lawyers**	*Accountants*	*Engineers*	*Architects*
1926	1,356	382	987	199
1936	1,759	673	1,047	279
1946	1,849	1,414	1,765	380
1951	1,909	1,446	2,126	507
1961	1,863	2,378	2,744	1,050
1971	1,963	3,418	3,985	1,935
Growth multiple 1926–1971	1.45	8.95	4.04	9.72

* Includes judges, barristers and solicitors
Source: occupational tables of relevant census

At this time most accountancy practices, North and South, were small. For instance, of the 116 practices based in Dublin, 93 had only one or two partners. The very largest, Craig Gardner, had only 10 partners. However, it was becoming clear that, as Howard Robinson put it in 1963, 'with the increasing complexity of a professional practice it is well-nigh impossible for a single man to acquaint himself with, and retain, the width of knowledge required to conduct a well-balanced practice. To face this difficulty it is necessary either to become a member of a large partnership or to restrict one's practice to specialist work of some kind.'[12] The general practitioner accountants, who could and did turn their hands to anything from tax and book-keeping to liquidation and investigations became much less common and the stage was set for a 20-year period of increasing amalgamations.

The quality of reporting on publicly quoted companies was extremely variable. A 'leader' in *The Irish Times* in August 1957 endorsed a recent letter writer by noting how 'the reports and accounts presented by too many concerns seem to be too often designed and presented to conceal information than to reveal it'.[13] *The Irish Times* was inclined to wonder if the poor quality of information explained 'the reluctance of the Irish public to invest its money in domestic issues'. In September 1962 Howard Robinson delivered an outspoken paper to the New York Congress of Accountants, which he introduced by commenting that the Irish 'tend to be as old-fashioned in our accounts as we are in many other aspects of life'. He could not decide whether the poor quality of Irish financial reporting was due to 'natural conservatism, a love of secrecy or pure laziness'.[14] Comparing published accounts of Irish Stock Exchange-quoted companies (which operated under stricter rules than unquoted companies) he applied 10 tests derived from the recommendations of the 1957 Company Law Reform Committee. In every single test, a half to a third of companies opted for the least helpful and informative presentation—as for instance in one case a single figure for 'trade debtors, bank balance, prepayments less allowance for bad and doubtful debts', or in another, lumping together 'sundry creditors, bills payable, bank overdraft, taxation, contingencies and other accounts'.

Considering who was responsible, Robinson noted that 'some of the most obsolete forms of accounts are audited by firms of accountants who are also responsible for the audit of companies who produce their statements in accordance with the most modern practice'. The general practice in the Irish profession was to accept the accounts prepared by in-house accountants and management, whether 'old-fashioned', as he put it, by which he meant obscure and unhelpful, or 'modern'. Firms were clearly not inclined to impose a generally agreed best practice.

Despite economic change, the South was dominated by small business units, which meant that it was difficult to get the scale to develop a professional practice. There were some 3,000 firms in the transportable goods industries, more than half of which employed fewer than 20 people and owed their existence to government measures of the 1930s and 1940s. Two-thirds of businesses were family owned.[15] In this protected environment productivity was not a high priority.

There was also a serious problem with the country's infrastructure. In June 1963, for instance, *The Irish Times* reported that two elderly people died when their house in Bolton Street, Dublin, simply collapsed; 10 days later two little girls were killed when two four-storey tenement houses smashed across the pavement in Fenian Street. The Corporation had to evacuate over 500 families from similarly dangerous houses. These disasters, combined with the explosion of financial energy, presented opportunities for a new breed of businessman. There were fortunes to be made in a booming economy, particularly in the property and construction sectors.[16] (To meet demand, there was a four-fold increase in the number of architects practising in the South between 1951 and 1971 – see *Table 1* above.) These entrepreneurs argued that not only did Georgian Dublin represent the bad old colonial regime but that its fabric was fundamentally rotten. 'Georgian buildings', declared the leading architect Sam Stephenson, whose first big job was the notorious Electricity Supply Board's office on Fitzwilliam Street, 'were never intended to last more than a lifetime'.[17]

Fianna Fáil, by far the largest political party in the Republic, now established 'an increasingly close relationship . . . with the emerging business elite'.[18] The new men in charge had ceased to stress the original policy objectives of national unity and the development of the Irish language, in favour of industry and enterprise. This shift became identified with the best-known chartered accountant of the day, Charles J. Haughey of Haughey Boland, successively Minister for Justice, Agriculture and Finance. He was also closely associated with the new Fianna Fáil fundraising group called Taca, which specifically targeted the business sector. Haughey Boland was closely involved with the Taca group, with Harry Boland sitting on the organising committee and partner Des Traynor, who had been articled to Charles Haughey in 1951, also involved. Many of the Taca circle came to employ the services of Haughey Boland, which grew mightily. Taca's first fund-raising dinner was in early 1967. Since the press were excluded from this £100-a-plate event, it is impossible to be precise who was present, but Kevin Boland (brother to Haughey's one-time partner in Haughey Boland) reported afterwards that 'we were all organised by Haughey and sent to different tables around the room. The extraordinary thing about my table was that everybody was in some way or other connected with the construction industry.'[19]

Property was at the heart of a remarkable spate of British take-over activity in the late 1950s and early 1960s. Generated by once well-known names such as Sir Hugh Fraser, Harold Samuel and Charles Clore, these hard-fought buy-outs were of particular interest to the profession because the predators' key tactic was made possible by the longstanding accounting conventions that significantly understated asset values. Despite the change in commercial conditions in Britain, notably a rapidly rising property market, accountants were reluctant to depart from traditional practices of 'prudence' and 'conservatism' and revalue, for instance, property assets. Managements, on their side, were generally happy to have their efforts judged against a low asset base. The accounting conventions originally adopted to restrain greedy shareholders now provided an opening for predatory bidders. It was easy for them to dazzle shareholders with offers of much more than the shares were worth on paper, secure in the knowledge that buildings valued at, say, £75,000 on the balance sheet could now be sold for £200,000.[20]

The introduction of PAYE

In 1959 the Revenue Commissioners decided to introduce a Pay As You Earn scheme for the collection of income tax, to replace the previous once-a-year process. This was part of a general policy by the Revenue to move to direct taxation as far as possible, following the recommendations of the Commission on Income Taxation 1957–62. (The single accountancy representative, incidentally, on this commission was Francis N. Kelly of W. A. Deevy & Co., Waterford, one of those who had recently become members of the Institute with the amalgamation of the Institute and the Society of Incorporated Accountants in 1957.) The Institute made a submission to the Commission proposing an extensive shift of the taxation burden from direct to indirect taxation. Among its recommendations was an abolition of income tax for those earning less than £750 a year and a substantial sales tax to replace the lost revenue. At that time income tax began to be charged on earnings of £350 pa for a single person and £600 pa for a married man. Rates were not high: a married man earning £600 paid £20 of tax. The average industrial wage in 1957 was £370.[21]

The new scheme was based on one successfully introduced in Britain in 1944. The transference of responsibility for the collection of tax to employers caused some accountants, who were, after all, intimately familiar with the workings of many business accounts departments, to fear that they would not cope. As Gerry Wheeler (a partner in Forsyth & Co., who had begun his working life with the Revenue) pointed out to the Dublin Rotary Club, 16,900 of the 18,000 employers in the country had fewer than 30 taxpayers on the staff, so the system was likely to become a huge burden on small firms who were, as he put it, 'ill-equipped to deal with such a complicated and technical matter'. He also ruefully admitted that the introduction of this scheme did away with the possibility of abolishing income tax altogether, which had remained a remote dream since its introduction to England as a temporary war measure during the Napoleonic wars.[22]

Others were less pessimistic, notably those, such as R. G. Wilkinson of the Belfast branch of the Association of Certified and Corporate Accountants, who had had considerable practical experience of the British system.[23] In the event, PAYE was introduced to the Republic from October 1960. In practice, the transition, which effectively took a lot of small tax compliance jobs out of the accountants' market, was surprisingly trouble-free.

Opportunities for self-expression

The lure of business was being felt, both in the difficulties of recruiting articled clerks and in the immediate disappearance from the profession of newly qualified people. Trying to stem the flow, President Alfred Dawson (of John Sedgwick, Dublin) urged young men to consider 'the opportunities for self-expression and service found in public practice in greater measure than elsewhere', especially in light of the new emphasis on specialisation inside professional offices.[24]

In 1960 the then President of the Institute David Watson (of Craig Gardner) had proposed that the image of the profession needed to be raised. In Howard Robinson's Presidency (1965–6) this took the agreeable form of a series of dinners at Jammet's famous French restaurant. As he told the AGM in 1966, 'some fifty outstanding men, Ministers, judges, civil servants, bankers and leaders of industry have been entertained, and the image of the Institute as a progressive and important body has, we hope, been projected.' Other initiatives at this time included a new library (opened in October 1965 and for which an elaborate catalogue was drawn up by a Trinity librarian), a prize for research papers and a new focus on post-qualification training, notably in the fields of computers and operational research and other management techniques.[25]

The economic changes of the early 1960s forced the leaders of the profession to look closely at the way new entrants were trained. The days of the unqualified seniors, who used to be the backbone of many firms, were more or less gone, but now the Irish Institute had to face the fact that (with the English Institute) it was almost alone among national accountancy bodies in not linking in in some way professional with university training.[26] In 1960 a new syllabus was introduced with five parts, so that the normal five-year, non-graduate clerk had now to do an examination every year. The failure rate, however, remained high, with more than 60 per cent failing the final part. In 1963 the President, Rollo McClure of Rawlinson Allen & White, Belfast, reported that Council was seriously considering proposals that would mean that all future entrants would take a degree while serving articles.

As part of this scrutiny a Director of Studies, Barry Hanly (a qualified company secretary and barrister), was appointed in 1962, but as Howard Robinson recorded, 'the experiment was not a particularly successful one; it may be that he was given an impossible task, or one not sufficiently defined and on his resignation two years later he was not replaced'.[27] Not immediately, anyway; as we shall see in the next chapter, in the 1970s, following the influential *Derryhale Report*, the Institute began its engagement with education in earnest.

For the profession a major impact of the 1960s was in a new emphasis on youth, which led to ever younger people being considered for partnerships (the extreme example was perhaps in Craig Gardner, where Bruce Lyster was listed as such before he had even qualified[28]). One factor that enabled this was the general abolition of the necessity for incoming partners to purchase 'goodwill' from the existing partners. As Margaret Downes explained,

> 'in the old days when you joined as a partner you paid goodwill to the existing partners' (that is you might pay £1,500 for goodwill, which they divided among themselves). This was not credited to your account; it was just a kind of key money. [Afterwards] over time a new partner built up capital because some of your profit share was paid into a capital account in your name. The charging of goodwill stopped in Peterson, Morrison certainly before Coopers came on in 1968.'[29]

This tendency to recruit younger partners gave the profession as a whole an important edge against the solicitors' firms which, for a while at least, held on to more conservative recruitment practices.

There was also a growing awareness among accountants such as Don Carroll of cigarette manufacturer P. J. Carroll & Co. (elected Governor of the Bank of Ireland in 1964) that accounts structures could be used creatively to build up businesses, such as the amalgamation of Powers, Jameson, Cork Gin and Paddy, into Irish Distillers in 1966. In a speech to a two-day conference marking the 75th anniversary of the Institute's Charter, Taoiseach Seán Lemass, in a generous recognition of the profession stimulated no doubt by the occasion, noted in particular how the State was 'much indebted to the members of the Institute. Many of them engaged in public practice have been prominently associated with our economic development. They it was who, in many instances, arranged to bring together foreign expertise and Irish capital and enterprise into effective and harmonious partnership which led to successful Irish industries and other development projects.' He went on to 'convey publicly the Government's appreciation of the advice tendered by the Institute in the course of the long discussions which had been proceeding on the new Companies Bill.'[30] This was a reference to a sub-committee of the Institute, consisting of Alfred Dawson of John Sedgwick, Niall Hogan of Reynolds McCarron, John Love of Cooper & Kenny (who had been Secretary of the Irish Branch of the Incorporated Accountants until amalgamation in 1957) and Howard Robinson of Polden, Robinson, which submitted a series of recommendations, many of which were incorporated into the 1963 Companies Act.[31]

In 1963 the very large new Companies Act was passed, finally rendering the 1908 Act obsolete. Many of the suggestions of the Company Law Reform Committee were incorporated into the 190 pages and 94 pages of Schedules. This Act remains, at the time of writing, a pillar of company law in Ireland. Among the innovations of this Act was the introduction of the phrase 'true and fair view' into the audit report, following the 1948 British Act. The justification for the change from the previous 'true and correct' was that it was intended to be less stringent. As *The Accountant* put it when the British Act was passed: 'the word "correct" has always been too strong, because it implies that there is one view that is "correct" as against all others which are incorrect.'[32] However, the contrast between the precision of 'true' and the latitude deliberately implicit in 'fair' troubled thinking accountants. What exactly was meant by 'fair' remained problematic, since it raised the question 'fair' *to* whom, or *as between* whom? (In the letter columns of *The Irish Times* the main issue for correspondents on this massive piece of legislation was the necessity, or not, of translating various Schedules into Irish.)

Howard Robinson

Howard Robinson, the Institute's historian, who became President of the Institute in 1965, was one of the most prominent accountants of the day, with a wide range of interests—as he typically put it, he was 'more at home in a wine cellar than a golf course'.[33] After a distinguished career at Trinity (first class degrees in law, arts and commerce[34] before he was 19) and in the Institute's exams (first place in the Intermediate and second in the Final), he worked with Craig Gardner for seven years and, when it seemed clear he was not going to be offered a partnership, he moved for a while to John Sedgwick before setting up his own practice as Polden, Robinson. He became a director of numerous companies, including *The Irish Times* and Brown Thomas, was involved in various Church of Ireland bodies, but his most outstanding achievement was the foundation of the City of Dublin Bank in 1964, built up out of a hire-purchase company.[35] City of Dublin became the third Irish bank to be floated on the Dublin Stock Exchange in 1971 (after Bank of Ireland and Allied Irish Banks, established in 1966).

In 1978 City of Dublin Bank bought a very small bank called Anglo-Irish, and in 1986 changed its name to Anglo-Irish Bank Corporation. Approximately at the same time Robinson stepped down from the board.[36]

With European integration on the horizon (though Ireland's first two applications, in 1960 and 1967, were rejected), Robinson reported from the 1964 European Congress of Accountants on how widely diverse were the different countries' attitudes to accounting. The French, Belgians, Swiss, Austrians and Italians were 'largely concerned with the development of accounting as a means of expressing economic developments' and as an instrument of planning. The second group, the Scandinavians, Dutch and Germans, were more concerned with accountancy rather than economics, but were seeking for a standard form of accounts. Finally, the British and the Irish group retained a resolute resistance to intellectualising: they had, as Robinson put it, 'little or no interest in economic theories and tend to oppose any standardisation of forms of accounts and to mistrust national planning'. (This was 10 years or more before problems with the old *laissez-faire* approach forced the English-speaking accountancy world to grapple with standards.) There was a marked difference between the pragmatism of the Irish and British contributions and what Robinson described as 'the rather rarefied atmosphere of the other theoretical contributions'. A small indicator of difference was the large stress one English speaker put 'to the term "true and fair"'. Neither the speaker nor Robinson was evidently aware that although the word 'fair' is a familiar part of English-speaking culture from the playground, it is unfamiliar and awkward to translate into many European languages.[37]

Enter management consultancy

Slowly the perception grew that managers needed to learn to manage through numbers, and it was natural that the profession should see a leadership role in this. As finance expert and writer Ciaran Walsh put it:

> 'prior to the 1950s, accounting was a statutory function: the accountant recorded all financial transactions and reported them to the fiscal authorities once a year. That changed with the introduction of "management accounting" in the US after the war. The accountant now had an additional responsibility—providing current, real information in a way that was useful to the company's management. The first IMI course on finance helped to consolidate that change in Ireland. It was not until the 1960s, when the IMI pioneered extended courses in management accounting, that the strategic value of the finance function was recognised and the accountant moved from the backroom to the boardroom.'[38]

As an indication of the future, it was noted that in Britain by 1971 two thirds of companies had an accountant-director, up from 19 per cent in 1931.[39]

There was certainly scope for such an evolution in Ireland. A study organised by the Irish Management Institute and published in 1966 showed that except for the tiny number of firms with 500 or more employees there was a marked dearth of quantification in Irish industry[40]:

- *In marketing*: 80 per cent of firms 'rarely' analysed contributions to profit or overhead by product; and 58 per cent of firms with fewer than 500 employees 'never' analysed sales costs; 78 per cent 'never' carried out a formal market survey or a study of market characteristics; 87 per cent had no long-range market forecasts and more than half never made an annual sales plan.
- *In production:* only one in 10 firms had a production control function; 90 per cent kept no machine loading records or work study figures.
- *In financial management:* 60 per cent of firms did not have cost accounts by product line; 80 per cent had no budgetary control system; few firms used standard costing methods or produced anything more than annual profit analysis or drew up capital requirements forecasts.

One comment in particular was significant from the profession's point of view: the study found that 'firms with over 100 employees which employ a finance executive with management training or which have used consultants are more likely than other firms of similar size to use standard costs'.[41]

From the Institute's twice-yearly *Members' Bulletin*[42] it is clear that there was an evolving idea of what accountants could and should do in this respect. At the AGM of the Institute in May 1961, for instance, President G. E. Cameron (soon to be the principal Belfast partner of Ernst & Whinney) although not suggesting that 'all chartered accountants are competent to advise management on all its problems', nonetheless thought it essential that they keep in touch with developments, not least what he described as 'the comparatively new' idea of management accounting.[43] The experience of running manufacturing concerns under pressure during the Second World War in America and Britain had led to greater involvement in work study, organisational methods and descendants of Frederick Taylor's scientific management techniques. Developments in costing and statistical quality control techniques were other aspects of this trend. Few of these techniques were in use in Irish firms.

The sociologist Andrew Abbott has written that 'each profession has its activities under various kinds of jurisdiction . . . jurisdictional boundaries are perpetually in dispute' with other established or would-be professionals; furthermore, 'it is the history of jurisdictional disputes that is the real, the determining history of the professions'.[44] In its very earliest days the new accountancy profession had to carve out a niche for itself in respect of bankruptcy, despite the legal profession's misgivings. Now an upcoming profession of management consultants 'invaded', as Howard Robinson astringently put it, the accountants' field of operations. 'Many of them', he continued, describing the situation as he saw it in the early 1960s, 'were able and conscientious firms, but others displayed greater gifts for gaining employment at very high fees than for justifying the payment of those fees.'[45]

Faced with this uninhibited competition, younger members of the accountancy profession began to wonder whether the old rules of behaviour (such as the rules against touting or advertising) were still appropriate. The Institute's Council however had no doubts. It forbade firms to call themselves 'management consultants' on letterheads and announcements in addition to 'Chartered Accountants'. It also turned down a request from Craig Gardner to be allowed to insert a change of address notice into the newspapers (as amounting to advertising) when they moved offices to Ballsbridge in 1968.[46] In 1969 there came a small move in the opposite direction when Council approved a motion allowing chartered accountants to appear on TV or radio in their own names, as opposed to being merely described as 'a chartered accountant'; they were still not permitted to mention the name of their firm, however.

Most Irish accountancy firms were too small to be able to offer consultancy services; furthermore, the vast majority of Irish companies were also small, and so unlikely to feel that such was for them. There may also have been a consciousness that the profession's own management was not particularly sophisticated. This was exemplified in what were often quite lax billing processes. Multi-partner firms typically operated as a loose coalition of general practitioners, each dealing with the range of their clients' needs, and billing practices were equally variable. Cash control was often lax. Tightening this, to the great improvement of profitability, was one of the contributions of Alex Spain (President of the Institute 1975–6) to his first firm Forsyth & Co. and then to Stokes Kennedy Crowley. Spain, son of the former master of the National Maternity Hospital, Holles Street, qualified and after some London experience returned to become the junior partner in Forsyth & Co. in 1961. As another partner, David Rowe (who we have seen enjoying the audit of the Irish Rabbit Skin Company in the 1940s) remembers, 'like many similar sized practices there was little real audit. Most of the work would have been compiling financial statements for clients—quite often from incomplete records.' When he became a partner Alex Spain

> 'introduced a degree of management and discipline which had not existed before. Neither Harry [Forsyth], Gerry [Wheeler] nor I had any idea about making money. Many fees, for example, were collected before the start of the *next* year's audit; and of course there was serious undercharging. In one year Alex lifted the profit by a factor of four. He insisted that we charge properly, and that we collect fees on completion of jobs, or in the case of larger jobs on a fees-on-account basis. He introduced our first essay into audit programming and into proper time control.'[47]

Trevor Morrow, a partner in the Limerick firm of Metcalf Lilburn, confirmed that a similarly casual attitude to billing pertained in his firm, and they were not alone.[48] Past-president Noel Stewart trained in the 1950s in Rawlinson, Allen & White, Enniskillen (later Cooper Brothers). He remembered

> 'in many cases firms did not send out bills until many months after they had completed the work. Clients only paid last year's bill at the commencement of next year's work. Payments on account were unheard of and bad debts were rare. Clients never asked what the costs would be and generally agreed the eventual bill without question.'[49]

Spain's new rigour of internal management was a major attraction for Kennedy Crowley when the idea of amalgamation of the two firms was mooted in 1968.

Nonetheless, it was clear that there was a growing demand for management advisory services, and accountants could usefully contribute. In 1959, the largest firm in Ireland, Craig Gardner, had asked one of its newly qualified men, Noel MacMahon, to specialise in this area. He went to Price Waterhouse for six months in 1960 and when he came back submitted a paper outlining how the area might develop. Given his six-month immersion in London, the extreme caution of his approach is notable. In his proposal the sole focus of the new consultancy service is to be the accounts department of the client. Advice could be offered to that department and only that department on accounting systems, clerical methods, management accounting and administrative organisation. Specifically ruled out were production efficiency surveys, time study rate setting, recruitment, job evaluation, market research proposals and operational research.

Another example of jurisdictional possibilities was highlighted by Thomas Kenny FCA at a meeting of the Dublin Society of Chartered Accountants in March 1966. Commenting on the retention of merchant banks in the current spate of merger activity, especially in London, he noted

> 'accountants could have fulfilled the role, had the Chartered Institutes been more forward-looking when setting educational standards. They were imprisoned by their own rules which ought to be under surveillance and altered to meet the new spheres in which Chartered Accountants must practice.'[50]

Beginning the practice amalgamation process

In 1961, the British accountant Henry Benson had been appointed by the Northern Ireland Government to report on the future of its railway system. Benson, who later became Lord Benson, was one of the most dynamic accountants in Britain at the time. Originally from South Africa, he joined Cooper Brothers, his uncle's accountancy practice in London, a couple of months after his 17th birthday in 1926.[51] Benson qualified in 1932 and became a partner in Cooper Brothers in 1934. He joined the Grenadier Guards on the outbreak of war in 1939, one of his earliest duties being to patrol the terrace in Windsor Castle outside where the young princesses Elizabeth and Margaret slept. After a spell in the Special Operations Executive he put his accountancy background to good use as accounts director of the Royal Ordnance factories, where he had executive authority over 10,000 people. He returned to Cooper Brothers in 1946, full of enthusiasm to expand the then 173-person firm, partly through the application of military-type disciplines.

Among his first steps was a radical overhaul of the organisational framework. Out were the old generalist partners; in were separate departments dealing with audit, tax, executorship work, liquidation and receivership, secretarial work and investigations. Benson had seen manuals and procedures in operation in the munitions factories, and quickly realised that there was very little such control over what the audit staff scattered across London actually did. So he started to write an audit manual, setting out precisely the procedures for all audit work carried out by the firm. For 20 years this manual was simply an in-house document, regularly updated and amended. It was finally published in 1966 as Cooper's *Manual of Auditing*. The *Manual* was published under the name of Benson's partner, Vivian Cooper, so as to get the identification with the firm but without breaching the anti-advertising guidelines.

In the meantime Cooper Brothers was growing rapidly. Margaret Downes, who eventually became a partner in the Dublin firm of Coopers & Lybrand, remembered that

> 'Henry Benson was quite a powerful figure when I was with Price Waterhouse. Before I went to London I had never heard of Coopers. The well-known names were Price Waterhouse, Peats and Deloittes. In the 1950s Coopers was a name that was coming right up hard on the inside—he was a very, very tough guy but very dedicated—a very nice guy incidentally—but very determined to achieve his ambitions. He drove that firm; he was absolutely the driver of Coopers & Lybrand.'[52]

In 1957 Cooper Brothers had established with the US firm of Lybrand, Ross Brothers and Montgomery an international practice working from 1973 under the common label of Coopers & Lybrand. In 1961 Benson was appointed by the Northern Ireland Government to investigate the viability of its 300-mile railway system. (He was an inveterate acceptor of official assignments—his autobiography *Accounting for Life* (1989) has a full six-page appendix listing his appointments to a bewildering variety of committees and public bodies. Institute past-president Cornelius Smith gave this book a cool review in *Accountancy Ireland*, calling it 'a Churchillian chronicle' and suspecting that 'some Irish readers may be put off by the tone'.[53]) Benson's report, published in the summer recess of 1963, caused a predictable storm, not least because he proposed cutting Derry's links with County Tyrone and the south-west of the province at the expense of 400, mainly Catholic, jobs.

During his time in the North he evidently cast an acquisitive eye on the Irish profession, for the Craig Gardner partners' meeting minutes record an approach in 1963 from Benson. It was rejected, partly because of the business already flowing from other UK firms and partly from a wish to retain independence. Unfortunately, records do not survive, but it is likely that Sir Henry (as he became in 1964) approached other firms in the South at this time, such as Stokes Brothers & Pim, presumably receiving the same rebuff. He probably did not approach one large Irish firm, Kennedy Crowley, which had formed a partnership with Arthur Young of New York in 1963.[54] In the event, the first Irish amalgamation for Coopers & Lybrand was in 1965 with the Belfast firm of Rawlinson, Allen & White. Three years later in October 1968 came the formation of the Dublin branch with the notifications that three Dublin firms—Kevans & Son, Kean & Co., Peterson, Morrison—with Cooper Brothers in London, had formed an Irish firm to be called Cooper Brothers, later Coopers & Lybrand.

Cooper's Manual of Auditing

Sir Henry was a tough master. His biography in the British *Dictionary of National Biography* ascribes this to his time in the Guards, where their 'rigid, unswerving discipline, attention to detail and determination that anything undertaken should be as good as human endeavour could make it, made an impression on Benson which remained with him throughout his life'.[55] One aspect of this was Cooper's *Manual of Auditing,* use of which as Margaret Downes recalls, was 'absolutely *de rigueur* once we joined with Coopers.'

The *Manual* proposed a completely different rationale for audit than had been customary. Instead of the traditional concern with error, fraud and misrepresentation, which translated into exhaustive checking of specific transactions, the *Manual* announced that 'the system of internal control in force in the client's office forms the foundation on which the audit must be based'.[56] To that end, fully a quarter of the 620-page book is devoted to model internal control questionnaires, the forerunner of many audit questionnaires used today.

In this context, the auditor's principal task was to examine the system to ascertain whether it was appropriate and effective. This was a rational solution to the audit problem that very large companies, with hundreds of thousands of transactions every year, were presenting the profession. On the other hand it could be argued, as for instance a reviewer in the accountancy journal *Abacus* did, that 'it is possible to become over-absorbed with the practices, procedures and internal control systems'.[57] They are not after all 'ends in themselves'. Following his wartime experience in Royal Ordnance factories (with their enormous influx of newly trained workers), Benson chose to standardise by controlling the work processes, rather taking the route more congenial to the professional ethos of standardising skills.

Specifically, Cooper's *Manual* argued that an audit should be structured as follows:

- An examination of the system of book-keeping, accounting and internal control . . .

• Comparison of the balance sheet and profit and loss account or other statements with the underlying records . . .

• Verification of the title, existence and value of the assets appearing in the balance sheet.

• Verification of the amount of the liabilities appearing in the balance sheet.

• Verification that the results shown by the profit and loss account are fairly stated.

• Where the audit is that of a statutory body, verification that the statutory requirements have been complied with.[58]

Fraud is not mentioned in the book, and it is clearly stated that 'the primary responsibility for safeguarding the company's assets and preventing errors and defalcations rests with the directors'.[59] The legwork of 'ticking and scratching' that formed so large a part of the articled clerks' time is reduced: 'the detailed checking undertaken by the auditor should be kept to a minimum'. If tests show the system is sound, 'no useful purpose is served by increasing the detailed checking'.[60] The so-called 'book-keeping audit', the traditional method of simultaneously writing up the books and doing the audit, was frowned on:

> 'where a firm assists in writing up the financial books of a client and is also responsible for the audit, the writing up of the books does not in any way constitute an audit . . . the staff engaged on writing up the books should not be employed on the audit'.[61]

The *Manual,* which is evidently aimed at the audit manager or senior, rather than the partner,[62] is extremely prescriptive. It dictates the exact content and physical structure of the audit file ('each permanent and current audit file should have thin manila index sheets' separating major subheadings),[63] which of 15 different audit ticks and marks to use for each type of check,[64] and the number of items to check for purchase, wages, etc., e.g. 'verification of cheque payments 30 to 50 items, verification of sales 10 to 30 sales'.[65] Considerable attention was paid to the system of 'points' or problems and matters arising, elsewhere called 'Notes and Queries'. Points could be 'interim', 'final' or 'future'; generally, they would require to be cleared by the partner in charge of the audit.[66]

The number of items to verify is not selected by any kind of statistical sampling, though there is an attempt to relate the depth of audit checking to the quality of internal controls. The *Manual* required the auditor initially to assess the quality of the client's internal controls. Five grades were described, ranging from A, large companies with well-defined internal controls and active internal auditors, to E, small companies with little or no internal controls and cash movement and book-keeping in the hands of a single person. The intensity and depth of the audit was dictated by the grade. Most Irish companies at the time would have been graded D or E.

When the *Manual* was introduced to Ireland with the establishment of Cooper Brothers in Dublin, as Margaret Downes remembered, 'it was quite demanding and new to some of us. We were moving in that direction, but this stopped us in our tracks.' More gently, similar improvements in professional practice were being introduced though connections with London firms such as Craig Gardner with Price Waterhouse and Stokes Brothers & Pim with Peat Marwick Mitchell. The demands of American regulations with respect to Irish subsidiaries were another influence. Certainly Coopers were significantly ahead of the game, with their *Manual* being quickly used as the basis of training of new entrants to the profession. By the 1980s, however, all major firms had their own manuals, but by then Cooper's *Manual* had deeply influenced the profession.[67] For Ireland, as Margaret Downes confirmed:

> 'it was significant [in the development of our practice]—the difference between the late 1950s and the mid to late 1960s was quite enormous in professional practice—a lot moved forward.'

A new image of accountancy

By 1968 the tide had changed, and a new image of accountancy was emerging. Addressing the second residential conference of the Irish Institute in 1962 the Scottish accountant William Murray had told his audience that many people regarded 'the chartered accountant in industry and practice as unimaginative, non-creative, and hidebound by traditional accounting practice and legal constraints',[68] but the growing demand for management information was a chance to break out of that stereotype. And now it was happening. With the steady movement of accountants in business from backroom to boardroom, a new idea of accountancy began to impinge on the public consciousness.

In this spirit, the new edition of the Irish Independent *Guide to Careers,* published in 1968, started its article 'Accountant' with a resounding declaration that the accountant 'is a key figure in every branch of commercial and industrial enterprise'. 'The highest efficiency', we are told, 'at all levels of industrial and commercial activity is more necessary than ever before.

The accountant has the training, the background and the experience essential for sound judgement on plans to achieve this requirement.'[69] The article notes how the 'prestige and importance' of the profession has grown remarkably since the 1930s: 'the number practising in this country has grown from some 400 to more than 2,500.' At another level, high-profile mergers and acquisition activity by sharp operators such as accountant Jim Slater, the best-known UK stock market player and company operator in the late 1960s and 1970s, also demonstrated to the public that there was more to accountancy than prudence and dry conservatism.[70]

There were, the *Guide* explained, several ways to become an accountant. It dealt first with the Institute, noting the necessity for articles and the possibility of both graduate and non-graduate entry. A major change in the conditions was also noted in that 'today nearly all Articles are entered without premiums and there is often a small progressive salary'.

Although the Institute, with some 2,000 members and students, was comfortably the largest professional body, there were other routes to professional qualification, such as[71]:

- the Association of Certified and Corporate Accountants, a body incorporated in Britain with 300 members in its Irish branch (still going);
- the Association of International Accountants, also incorporated in Britain with 46 members in the Republic (still going);
- the Institute of Cost and Works Accountants, incorporated in Britain with 170 members in Ireland (now renamed CIMA);
- the Irish Society of Certified Public Accountants, incorporated in Ireland in 1943, currently with approximately 160 members and 90 students (now called CPA Ireland);
- the Society of Commercial Accountants, incorporated in the UK with branches in Belfast and Dublin; the Dublin branch had 114 members (eventually became part of the Institute of Company Accountants, which merged with the Association of International Accountants in 2003);
- the Institute of Company Accountants, incorporated in Britain with 45 Fellows, 102 Associates and 71 students in Ireland (merged with the Association of International Accountants in 2003);
- the Society of Incorporated Cost Accountants, founded in Ireland in 1963, with 20 members.[72]

The main advantage of most of these was that pre-qualification experience was gained in companies and commercial environments rather than in practice.

In the late 1960s a grand scheme was evolved by the English Institute to combine the most active of the accountancy organisations into a single body made up of three regional institutes in England & Wales, Scotland and Ireland.[73] This would have thrown six bodies together—the three Institutes of Chartered Accountants (Ireland, Scotland, and England & Wales), the Association of Certified and Corporate Accountants, the Institute of Cost and Works Accountants, and the Institute of Municipal Treasurers and Accountants. The combined membership in Britain and Ireland of these bodies was 90,000 with some 80,000 students, of which the Irish members amounted to 2,700. This highly ambitious idea proposed that the full 'Chartered Accountant' qualification be divided into streams (business, practice, public sector), with appropriately reserved functions. There was also proposed a lesser qualification of 'Licentiate Accountant' for those not able or willing to undertake the increasingly demanding full qualification. Members of the Irish Institute voted overwhelmingly in favour of such a scheme at a Special General Meeting in April 1968 (78 votes to 18), and twice more in postal votes of all members. In the crucial vote in June 1970, most of the bodies concerned (the Irish and Scottish Institutes as well as the ACCA and the others) voted by at least 74 per cent in favour of the great merger. The members of the English Institute, however, had cold feet and voted only 55 per cent in favour, well short of the required two-thirds majority. So the steam went out of this foresighted proposal. At the AGM of May 1971, the Irish Institute's President, D. H. Templeton of Ashworth Row and then Price Waterhouse of Belfast, was obliged to announce that the proposed scheme had been rejected.

Practice and theory

By this time the question of accounting standards was coming to the fore. These would eventually force the world-wide profession to examine its basic principles and practises.

One of the most successful accountants of the day was the first President of the Institute to be born after the creation of the Irish Free State in 1922, Sir Desmond Lorimer. He was born in Belfast and became a partner of Hugh Smylie, where he had served his articles, in 1952, having briefly set up his own plate. While with Smylie he set up a computer agency (in 1966) that eventually employed 200 people.[74] He was involved in other businesses, notably as financial director of Viyella. When Smylie & Co. joined Deloitte in 1976 he retired from the profession, cherishing his independence. This gave him more time for his public service, notably as chairman of the politically highly sensitive Northern Ireland Housing Executive, for which he was later knighted.

In his Presidential speech to the Annual Dinner of the Institute in October 1968, Lorimer (who had begun his career in 1944 in a professional atmosphere he described as 'fairly stagnant') identified 'the great challenge of our time'—radical change from scientific, technological and social innovations.[75] He ended his speech however with a tough-minded outburst: 'Government policy', he said,

> 'has always been a bit beyond me, particularly its use of theorists, when we live today in a practical age. We in Ireland however, both North and South, are fortunate that, unlike Whitehall, we are not bogged down with "Intellectual Whiz Kids" or to use another name "Theoretical Idealists" who influence Government policy and in my opinion can be a threat to the economy of the country. Theorists have a very important part to play but I feel it is better that that part should be played in areas removed from those where policy is decided.'

Unfortunately, as Keynes famously pointed out, the real difference in policy-making is not between theory and practice. As he put it:

> 'The ideas of economists and political philosophers, both when they are right and when they are wrong, are more powerful than is commonly understood. Indeed the world is ruled by little else. Practical men, who believe themselves to be quite exempt from any intellectual influence, are usually the slaves of some defunct economist.'[76]

The real contest, said Keynes, is between theory examined and theory unexamined—taken for granted, so long believed as to be unchallengeable.

As practical men and women, accountants have tended not to be absorbed by academic debates on principles. Thus it happened in Britain in the 1950s that the unassailable conventions of conservatism and prudence exposed clients to property-based takeovers. In Ireland, as Howard Robinson pointed out, firms worked with whatever accounts were presented by the client; they did not, as far as he could deduce, attempt to impose some theoretical best practice. The debate over inflation accounting in the 1970s was to expose the problems with this practical approach.

Chapter Seven
Ireland Coming of Age: the 1970s

Always remember that there are only two figures that can be relied on in a balance sheet: the issued share capital and the cash at bank. Everything else is more or less made up.

William Thompson, Senior Partner of City of London firm
Ball Baker Deed in the 1970s[1]

For Ireland, north and south, the 1970s was an abrasive, demanding, stressful, coming-of-age era, with considerably more going on than punk, bell-bottoms and bad hair. This applied in many domains, not least in the accountancy profession. Economically the decade was dominated by increasing global inter-dependency, manifest in three major ways: in what was then called the EEC, in the roller-coaster of oil prices and in the willingness of successful companies to expand overseas. This was also the decade in which 'inflation' ceased to be a technical term used by economists and became a daily practical reality for all business dealings: in the Republic consumer prices increased four-fold in the 10 years to 1983.

Politically, the decade was dominated by the Troubles in the North. These ignited in 1969 and by the end of 1979 had claimed 1,600 lives and millions of pounds worth of destruction. In the small centre of Belfast regular bomb scares became a feature of office life. A lesser-known consequence of the Troubles was the burning of pubs, which as accountant Hugh O'Hare remembered, were overwhelmingly Catholic-owned (including the pub owned by former President Mary McAleese's family). In all, 183 pubs and off-licences were destroyed in the Troubles, a regular loss of audit and accountancy work to Hugh O'Hare's growing practice, which by the mid-1970s employed eight chartered accountants. (We have seen Hugh O'Hare in the 1950s being refused articles by a leading Belfast firm because he was a Catholic.) Luckily several of his clients invested their compensation in the property business, which gave his practice a new lease of life.[2]

For Hugh O'Hare, undoubtedly the worst of it occurred on 21 July

1972 (so-called 'Bloody Friday'), when the IRA exploded a series of bombs in 23 sites across the city. The cascade started at 2.10 in the afternoon in Smithfield Bus Station, and ended at 3.30 pm. Nine people were killed and 130 injured. Among the casualties was Hugh's wife, 37-year-old Margaret O'Hare (a Catholic, whose brother was an SDLP councillor), who was killed by a car bomb as she pulled up to a shop in the mixed Cavehill Road area, where three of her children were inside. Her 11-year-old daughter, also in the car, was seriously injured. A young Protestant boy, who tried to warn people about the bomb, was killed at the same time, as was a 65-year-old Catholic. The children in the shop were not hurt. There had been no warning.

It was not only the relentless pummeling of the IRA bombing campaign that devastated the Northern Irish economy in the 1970s, though that was enough of a cause, particularly since they especially targeted British-owned businesses, to inhibit further such investment. In the 1960s a major contributor to employment growth had been the synthetic fibre industry—an industry dependent on plentiful supplies of oil, with the result that Northern Ireland became more dependent on oil than any other region of the UK. So when the oil shortages of the 1970s arose, the region was trebly hit in transport costs, in electricity and in industrial power. As a result, 'during the six years 1973–9', wrote the historian Jonathan Bardon, 'Northern Ireland's manufacturing output suffered a dramatic decline of five per cent annually. In that period jobs in the region's manufacturing sector were being lost at the rate of three per cent per annum. Much of this was due to the reluctance of outsiders to invest in such a violent and unsettled area'.[3]

A feature of the governance of Northern Ireland was the use of chartered accountants in official roles. Darwin Templeton chaired the Northern Ireland Development Advisory Committee in the 1970s, and when he retired he was succeeded by Sir Eric McDowell, who had qualified with Wilson, Hennessy & Crawford. He remained in place when the body was renamed the Industrial Development Board. Sir Desmond Lorimer, who had trained with Hill, Vellacott & Bailey, became, as we have seen, first chairman of the Northern Ireland Housing Executive in 1971. These three also served as Presidents of the Institute. Tony Hopkins, who had qualified in London, became the first FCA to become a Permanent Secretary in the Northern Ireland Civil Service—he later returned to private practice with what became Deloitte in Belfast.[4] This mobilisation of accountants in official roles echoed the practice which had begun in the UK during the

First World War, but was much less conspicuous in the South, as we saw in Chapter Three.

The violence spilled over into the Republic on several occasions in the early 1970s, most notably with the simultaneous bombings of Dublin and Monaghan in May 1974. Ruthless fund-raising excursions by the IRA became a feared part of the environment. Businesses such as Jefferson Smurfit, which traded both north and south, were told that they needed 'protection'. A number of high-profile kidnappings increased nervousness. So when the new Smurfit factory in Dublin's Walkinstown suffered a series of fires in 1971, in the jittery atmosphere of the time it was quickly assumed that the IRA was to blame. The Gardaí could find no evidence, however, and later it was discovered that ill-designed fork-lift trucks were more likely to have been the cause. Nevertheless, the fear remained and the board of Smurfit's ordered security precautions for its senior staff.[5]

The Republic's relationship with its old colonial master was significantly shifted by membership of the Common Market (as it was then called), for which the citizens voted in May 1972 by a decisive five to one. (The North joined as part of the UK in January without the excitement of a referendum.) An important factor was the redefinition of the Industrial Development Authority in 1970 as a stand-alone agency to stimulate foreign direct investment. Its successes in that area radically changed the industrial face of the Republic. In the process the incoming companies demanded a whole new standard of service from its accountants, such as in meeting the audit standards demanded by US head offices, and notably in tax-planning services.

Coming of age

In the Republic, the 1970s were full of shifts away from the old modes to the norms of modern European states. Coming-of-age events were common, as Ireland adjusted its neo-colonial legislation to modern conditions. For instance:

- *In respect of women:* in July 1972 the minimum age of marriage was raised from 12 for girls (and 14 for boys) to 16. In July 1973, the Civil Service lifted the ban on employing married women. In March 1976 the European Economic Community rejected the Irish Government's request for derogation on equal pay for men and women. In November 1976 the ban on women serving as jurors was lifted. In 1979 the first woman cabinet minister in modern times, Máire

Geoghegan-Quinn, took office as the Minister for the Gaeltacht.[6]

• *In respect of the Catholic Church:* in 1970 the hierarchy lifted the ban on Catholic students attending Trinity College, Dublin, originally imposed in the 19th century; two constitutional referenda were held, one to reduce the voting age to 18 and the other to remove the special position of the Catholic Church. Both were approved by substantial majorities. In April 1974, the Archdiocese of Dublin finally gave up the idea of building a cathedral in Merrion Square and handed it over to the public. The Pope's visit in September 1979 was an intense popular success, though his pleas to the IRA had little effect.

• *In respect of the economy:* in February 1976 the increasing number of telephone lines forced the Department of Posts & Telegraphs to split its national telephone directory into two volumes. The following month the export board, Córas Tráchtála, announced that for the first time at least half of Irish exports were of manufactured goods, and that non-UK exports represented over half of export value.

• *In respect of Europe:* very soon after joining in 1973, the Republic of Ireland became the first of the nine EEC members to apply for aid from the regional fund (July 1975). In March 1979 Ireland joined the European Monetary System, and Britain did not, so the link with sterling, dating from 1826, was broken.

• *Internationally:* by the early 1970s the US seemed to be unable to meet its insatiable demand for oil, a new circumstance with profound geo-political consequences. Ireland's dependence on imported fuel was dramatically illustrated by a series of oil spills in Bantry Bay, County Cork, in April 1972, October 1974 and January 1979. This dependence led to the Republic's inflation being the highest in Europe in 1976. In August 1970, Ireland abandoned its paranoid fear of communism: the Soviet news agency TASS opened an office in Dublin, and in November 1970 opposition to China's membership of the UN was abandoned.

The accountancy profession

The prestige of the profession was high at this time and this was reflected in the salaries accountants could command, especially from the large companies. The Irish Management Institute's *Executive Salary Survey 1970* recorded that in companies with over 1,000 employees, the median salary for a head of the accounting function was £4,790, compared to £3,694 for production and £4,140 for marketing. The average industrial wage at this time was £1,294, well below the starting salary of £2,000 to £2,500 that a newly qualified chartered accountant could expect.[7] Accountancy was well rewarded by comparison to, for instance, a principal officer in the Civil Service (£3,475 pa), a Colonel in the Irish Army (£3,220 pa), a Chief Superintendent of An Garda Síochána (£3,040 pa), a branch manager of a bank (£3,040 basic, i.e. without commission for selling insurance, which could possibly add a further £1,000).[8] Surviving data for a Dublin firm, Craig Gardner, suggests that the profession was developing rapidly. Between 1961 and 1971 fees charged rose from £177,000 to £593,000, which even taking inflation into account was comfortably more than doubling. By 1971 the then 14 partners had an average profit share of £12,700 (by no means was all of this take-home, of course). The rampant inflation of the decade pushed fees up tenfold, but because the number of partners had doubled to 30 by 1981, the average share in real terms went down.

A side-effect of the economic growth since the late 1950s was a remarkable expansion in the accountant's natural habitat, the office. Between 1961 and 1981 the Republic's census recorded a near doubling of the number of clerical workers, from 77,926 to 140,199. An increasing number of those were women, a trend helped by a quick response to the easing in 1973 of the official ban on married women working in the Civil Service, in state bodies and by convention in large private companies.[9] The 1981 Census, reporting the marital status of workers for the first time, found that now 24 per cent of female clerks and 29 per cent of female typists were married

Table 1: *The ever-growing office*

	1961	1971	1981
Clerical workers	77,926	103,199	140,199
Of which, women	59%	65%	72%
Accountants	2,378	3,418	11,127
Of which, women	2.9%	2.4%	10.6%

Source: RoI Census of Population: *Occupations* Table 2 1961, 1971, 1981

Most of the 3,418 self-described 'accountants' in the country in 1971 were chartered, with some 2,000 members and students in the Republic, but there were 200 Cost and Works (later to be CIMA) members, 500 Association of Certified and Corporate Accountants (ACCA)[10] members and 200 members of the Institute of Certified Public Accountants. The 1981 Census reported a great increase in 'accountants', to over 11,000 (see *Table 2*). Only half of this increase can be attributed to growth in the various accountancy bodies. The Institute's membership working in Ireland (north and south) rose from 1,975 to 3,586 in the same period, and membership of the other bodies (ICWA, ICPA and the recently renamed ACCA) had doubled to just over 2,000.[11] Even the 40 per cent growth in general clerical staff, and the general development of the economy and of the tax system, scarcely account for the enormous increase in numbers of self-described 'accountants'.

Table 2: *ICAI members and Census return of accountants*

Census date	ICAI members in Ireland	'Accountants' in RoI Census	ICAI %
1951	658	1,446	45%
1961	1,367	2,378	57%
1971	1,975	3,418	58%
1981	3,586	11,127	32%
1991	5,821	9,783	59%
2002	10,055*	14,822	69%
2011	14,312*	27,116	53%

* Membership data is all-island except these two, which are RoI.

Source: ICAI *Membership Lists* and Occupation Tables of the Census. *The Census return for 1981 is clearly anomalous. On a straight-line basis one would have guessed the figure for all accountants should be 6,600; the ICAI figure is a much more in-trend 54 per cent of that.*

In 1978, 90 years after the granting of the Charter, the profession was still predominantly male. On the Council of the Institute sat 25 men and one woman (Margaret Downes, who became in 1982 the only woman President so far). There were no women on the committee of the Leinster Society (the Dublin Society as was).[12] Male dominance was equally reflected in the pages of the Institute's journal *Accountancy Ireland*, with 88 per cent of those pictured being male. However, things were gradually changing. At the beginning of the decade there had been just 82 women reported as accountants in the census, or 2.4 per cent of 'accountants', by 1981 this had crept up to 1,188, or 10.6 per cent.

In 1975, the Institute demonstrated a new self-confidence by accepting the invitation of the Union of European Accountants (UEC) to host its 1978 conference in Dublin. Margaret Downes was appointed chair of the organising committee, which chose as its theme 'Looking forward to 1998'. The keynote address was delivered, on the tenth anniversary of the crushing of the Czechoslovak 'Prague Spring', by Professor Ota Sik, formerly Deputy Prime Minister to Alexander Dubček. His suggestion that the new wave of the future was likely to be a combination of capitalism and communism evidently baffled most of the 1,400 guests from 24 countries. (The monolithic Soviet bloc of the 1970s, then led by the grim-faced *apparatchik* Leonid Brezhnev and symbolised for many by the Berlin Wall, was not attractive.) More familiar technical ground was covered by businessman/banker Don Carroll (on value-added accounting) and the French President of the UEC (who discussed the relative importance of the balance sheet and the profit and loss account).[13]

The great bank strike of 1970

Symbolic in many ways of the old era was Ireland's antiquated banking system. Like so much of the country it changed radically between the late 1960s and the 1970s. Writing in 1971, Michael Fogarty of the Economic and Social Research Institute wrote that 'Irish banking has changed more since 1965 than in the whole of the previous century'. The individual banks had been quite small (the Royal Bank, for instance, one of the components of what was to become AIB, had just 500 employees, as had the Hibernian Bank, which became part of the Bank of Ireland Group.) Employees were recruited from school (no graduates), and worked away from their home towns, living in digs, often with quite poor facilities (in the days before launderettes, how and where to wash and dry shirts was always a problem). A recruiting surge in the 1920s meant that for years promotion had been very slow, with a man taking perhaps 20 years to get from back office to the customer counter and, if he was lucky, achieving promotion to branch manager only five or six years before retirement.[14]

Over time, the value of bank staff's incomes had been eroded, from three-and-a-half to four times the average industrial wage in the 1930s (with income tax paid by the bank) to only twice the average industrial wage in 1971 (and income tax paid by the earner).[15] With reducing incomes, local prestige had waned. In the old days it had always been the bank manager who became treasurer of the local clubs—now it was more likely to be an accountant. Women were obliged to retire on marriage (a rule insisted on by the union). Banks did not recruit staff from other banks; partly because they literally spoke different languages, using different banking terms. The work was highly routinised, and the management structure was extremely flat, with as many as 100 people reporting to the general manager.[16] Moving from these old ways was always going to present tremendous personnel and operational challenges.

Even if the boards of the banks had not been, as one former senior manager put it, like a bunch of well-intentioned bishops, 'decent but remote, detached, and impervious to advice from below',[17] this was a recipe for industrial problems. The catalysts for change were the establishment of the Bank of Ireland Group as a single unit with the takeover of the National Bank in 1966, and in September 1966 the simultaneous welding of three constituent banks into Allied Irish Banks. The new groups had a dynamic view of the range of services banks should supply, putting considerable sales pressure on an inadequately prepared staff. It was not, incidentally, until Minister for Finance Richie Ryan obliged the banks in 1975 to provide mortgage funds that they entered the housing market (in violation of the old adage 'borrow long, lend short'). Previous to this the main source of housing finance was the building societies, which financed loans out of deposits and were struggling to bring in enough money.

This was the background to a series of three prolonged strikes—May–July 1966, May–November 1970 and June–September 1976—which meant that the banks were out of action for a full 12 months in the decade. These bank closures, as Professor Antoin Murphy of TCD wrote: 'deprived the public of direct use of, on average, well over 80 per cent of the money supply'.[18] Conventional wisdom might have expected the economy to implode, like a body suddenly deprived of all its blood. In fact, life went on. At the beginning of each of the strikes there was a fall in retail sales, but thereafter a learning process taught buyers and sellers to work around the lack of cash, so that in eight out of the 12 months of the strikes, retail sales were more or less as expected. By what the publisher Michael Gill of Gill & Macmillan called 'ingenious patience', business trundled on as before, incidentally providing an insight into this stage of the Irish economy.

The strikes had various effects on the accountancy profession. Traditionally, one of the first tasks of the audit team was to reconcile the cash book with the bank balance. Ideally the balance shown by the bank would be the same as the balance in the cashbook; in practice, because of leads and lags (cheques signed but not cashed, cheques received but not put into the bank, standing orders, direct debits, bank charges, etc.), the task was not trivial. Once complete, however, the 'bank rec' was a powerful proof of the accuracy of the most important of the company's books. For six months in 1970, however, this basic prop of the old-fashioned audit was unavailable.

If the strike presented problems to accountants in practice, it was arguably worse for accountants in business, who had to find the cash to pay workers (not until the 1979 Payment of Wages Act was payment by cheque normalised) and to pay for stock and raw materials. Luckily, cash businesses such as supermarkets, cinemas, local shops and pubs were all happy to exchange cash for cheques made out by people they knew. A few companies were able to finance purchases with the proceeds from export sales, and set up overseas bank accounts accordingly. Trevor Morrow of Metcalf Lilburn in Limerick recalls how he was persuaded to use his regular visit to London to carry £140,000 in mixed currencies to be deposited in Coutts on behalf of a travel agent. John Blake Dillon of Craig Gardner remembers working on the Waterford Glass audit of that year and being incarcerated in a stifling security room (it was particularly hot that summer), counting the tens of thousands of pounds worth of miscellaneous cash picked up from supermarkets and stores around the country.

Three American banks and some smaller merchant banks were able to process current account transactions, especially for larger companies. But these banks had no branch networks and only limited ability to process any substantial new volume of business. At this time the Irish pound and sterling were still at par, so there was a marked increased usage of sterling notes and coins. Dividends, credit transfers and share certificates were locked for the duration, as were deeds left for safe-keeping. Pensioners and others dependent on interest and receipts from government stock had to wait. Stock exchange transactions fell steeply. When the normal supplies of cheques ran out, stationers provided blank cheque forms, and there was a sizable traffic in nondescript pieces of paper dignified with a 3d stamp in an attempt to give them legal status.

Ireland was still a small, relatively intimate society where sufficient trust operated to enable commerce to flourish without banks, in a way that would be difficult today. 'The negotiability of personal cheques', Antoin Murphy writes, 'depended on the degree of information and personal contact that the acceptor had about the issuer of the cheque.'[19] Since this was generally high, inconvenience was minimised, though there was a clear reluctance to accept third-party cheques. Irish society was still like a vast Victorian novel, in which all the characters are connected, and often related. When the banks reopened and the mess was unravelled, it did not appear that this trust was substantially misplaced. Considering the opportunities, it was remarkable that a mere 750 fraud cases were investigated by the Gardaí (though admittedly this was 10 times the usual number).

The weary strike finally came to an end in November, and the bank officials returned to a hideous cleaning-up job. Although there had been no strike pay, the officials were not financially worse off, since most of them had found work in Britain, and made up any shortfall with the overtime needed to clear up the backlog of transactions. Nor had the banks themselves suffered particularly, having had no wages to pay and having been able to use the money in their vaults on the international money markets. Looking back over the strike, industrial relations specialist Michael Fogarty deplored the waste caused by poor negotiation skills on both sides. He recorded the 'widespread strain, cost, inconvenience and uncertainty to users of bank services' for the sake of an agreement that he characterised as 'a ridiculous mouse'—an agreement that could have been, and was in other occupations, achieved with nothing like the national cost.[20]

Decimalisation and VAT

Just as the banks were finally sorting out the backlog, on 15 February 1971 the currency was decimalised, changing from the pounds, shillings and pence system of high antiquity to a pounds and pence system. The 240 old pennies to a pound changed to 100 (new) pence to the pound. Inevitably, there were teething problems and grumbles about opportunistic price rises. The Institute had established a Decimal Currency Committee to advise members on problems with the transition as early as 1969, with Edmond Grace as chairman.[21] In practice, no doubt due to careful preparation, the changeover was surprisingly smooth. In offices across the country accountants had to set up a 'decimal changeover account' to sweep up the bits and pieces that did not quite transfer neatly. Six weeks after the changeover, the Department of Industry and Commerce reported that it had received 382 complaints of overcharging, 'nearly all' of which it believed arose from genuine misunderstandings or confusion about the new system, such as the stallholder who simply changed the price of apples from 6d to six new pence, a 240 per cent increase.[22] A year after the change the Consumer Association was less positive, believing that the 10 per cent increase in the cost of living over the year had largely been caused by traders taking advantage of the opportunities offered by the changeover.[23]

The Consumer Association feared that similar opportunities for traders to exploit confusion would arise with the imposition in the Republic of VAT in November 1972, replacing existing turnover and wholesale taxes (this EEC-mandated tax was introduced into Northern Ireland in April 1973), and the forthcoming change from Imperial to metric measurements. VAT was obviously a concern to accountants, and in November 1971 the Institute asked the Minister for a delay to allow companies to catch up with the changes. For months there was a storm of angry controversy as economists, consumer spokesmen and traders issued dire warnings and government spokesmen tried to pour oil. In the event (and with a few last-minute changes, such as the zero-rating of food, medicines and eventually books) the new tax came in smoothly. Receipts in the first six months were £55 million, 20 per cent more than the receipts had been in the corresponding period from the predecessor taxes, turnover tax and wholesale tax.[24] What was barely commented on was that VAT, like PAYE before it, represented a substantial shift of tax-gathering effort from the Revenue Commissioners to individuals and companies. These reforms simply would not have been possible without the accountancy profession. Taxes on income (mostly PAYE) and taxes on expenditure (mostly VAT) are two of the highest sources of government receipts and the Government is dependent on the work of accountants and accounts clerks for compliance. In 1983 Francis O'Brien of UCD quoted a British study that suggested that tax gathering for PAYE and VAT cost on average 0.92 per cent of turnover, and was regressive in nature, in that compliance costs for smaller companies could be almost twice as much.[25] No doubt this extra activity contributed to the continuing increase in the number of members of the ICAI in Ireland and indeed to the number of accountants in all.

Foreign direct investment

The new policy of economic openness initiated by the Republic's Industrial Development (Encouragement of External Investment) Act of July 1958 and the First Programme for Economic Expansion (November 1958), the establishment of the Industrial Development Authority (IDA) as a state-sponsored body in April 1970, and membership of the EEC from 1972, stimulated an influx of foreign capital that completely recreated the Irish economy in the years following. By 1985, when the impetus was beginning to weaken, foreign companies of one sort or another employed as many as one-third of the manufacturing workers. The key industries were chemicals (notably pharmaceuticals), healthcare and metals (including electronics); the one sector sparsely represented was the traditional food and drink business.

Table 3: *Progress and impact of FDI 1960–1985*[26]

Year	FDI employment	% of manufacturing workforce
1960	3,043	1.8
1965	12,856	6.4
1970	29,349	13.1
1975	46,539	20.6
1980	67,485	27.3
1985	69,430	33.0

As well as the IDA's activities, there was in the 1970s a flurry of locally based corporate activity that promised to shake things up and provide new opportunities for the profession. There was, for instance, the growth of the old box company Jefferson Smurfit, which by a series of takeovers, mostly notably of the ramshackle Hely Group (which had comprised not just print but prams, TVs, toys, musical instruments, bicycles and dog requisites), had pushed itself up to number four in *The Irish Times*' corporate listings. By 1971, Michael Smurfit's company had 40 trading businesses employing 3,300 people. Similarly, Tony O'Reilly's Fitzwilton conglomerate reached the peak of its success in 1974 with interests in a bewilderingly wide diversity of areas (textiles, fertilisers, newspapers, building materials, retailing, etc.) and a turnover of £40 million and 4,000 employees. The initial success of Fitzwilton (which was fading, even by 1974) attracted other operators until shell companies abounded, most of which failed. There was the Michael Smurfit-backed TMG, and there were Moore Holdings, Brooks Watson and Harcourt Holdings, all of which flashed briefly across the financial sky before vanishing. Very often the only thing the members of these conglomerates had in common was reporting to the central accounts department and a belief in the magic ingredient 'managment'.

Lifestyle or business

The impact of this striking growth was immediately felt in the professional arena, particularly by the large accountancy firms. As in other parts of national life, the 1970s were a coming-of-age for the accountancy profession. We have seen that as late as the 1960s the typical Irish firm of accountants was small, with only a few generalist partners. Even the largest, Craig

Gardner, was small enough to enable all the partners to assemble every morning around a big table in the board-room to open the post. One of these was Bruce Lyster, who became a partner in 1965, having been identified, as we have seen, as potential partner material before he had qualified (one consideration was what turned out to be the old-fashioned thought that as a Protestant he would be acceptable to clients such as the Representative Church Body and the Freemasons.) As he remembers, professional life 'was a lifestyle arrangement' not a business.[27] The casual attitude often taken to the billing of clients was indicative. Until Lyster computerised Craig Gardner's collection and analysis of fees in the late 1960s (writing his programs in machine code, as had to be), the exact contribution of each partner was veiled in the decent obscurity of a hand-written ledger. The new system produced a monthly print-out detailing fees earned, work-in-progress, fees unbilled and so on, by partner and even by audit clerk. What you measure is what you get. A newly business-like atmosphere evolved not only in Craig Gardner but also in Kennedy Crowley, under Alex Spain's leadership, and in other firms. The influence of the ever-rising inflation rates, forcing close attention to cash flow, was, as Margaret Downes of Cooper Brothers remembered, an additional motivation.

By the end of the 1970s, the small firms that still characterised the business at the beginning of the decade had clumped together, like blobs of mercury in a Petri dish, into a series of much larger firms.[28] The precipitating factor was very often the interest of large British firms, and many of these amalgamations began in the North. Thus, Cooper Brothers' first Irish connection, in 1965, was with the Belfast firm of Rawlinson Allen & White; only some years later did they create the Dublin firm. In 1969, Deloitte Haskins & Sells combined with two Belfast firms (Wilson Hennessy & Crawford and Robert Walsh), moving to Dublin in 1973 to combine with Briscoe Smith and Gardner Donnelly. Price Waterhouse drew in the Belfast practice of Martin Shaw, Leslie & Shaw in January 1976, a few months before the merger with Republic of Ireland practice Craig Gardner was announced. Other firms started first in Dublin: these included Peats (with Stokes Kennedy Crowley), and Klynveld, Main, Goerdeler (with Reynolds McCarron). Coopers Brothers' Dublin office was formed in October 1968 by amalgamation with several small firms, notably Peterson Morrison, Kevans and Kean, and in that same year Arthur Andersen brought in Frank Barrett from South America to head up its new office in Dublin.[29] The limitations of the still-current Partnership Act of 1890, restricting the number of partners to 20, resulted in some complex arrangements. Haughey Boland for instance also practised as Kenny McHugh and some of the partners as Howarth, Haughey Boland and others as Laventhol & Howarth, all from the same office in Amiens Street.[30]

Not every firm was happy with its own progress. We have seen that for a long time Craig Gardner and Stokes Brothers & Pim were the leading firms in Dublin. In a surprise move in late 1972, Stokes Brothers & Pim amalgamated with the fast up-and-coming firm of Kennedy Crowley to create by far the largest firm in the Republic. The combined firm of Stokes Kennedy Crowley had 20 partners and employed 400 people. Craig Gardner at this time had 12 partners.[31] The Craig Gardner partners were much put out that Stokes Brothers & Pim should have merged with the brash newcomer rather than themselves.

Just before this surprise, Bruce Lyster had circulated a memo casting a cold eye on the firm's recent progress, concluding that 'we are not growing anything like as rapidly as our main competitors' and 'little major new work of any consequence has been gained in recent years', with the exception of jobs passed on by their London partner, Price Waterhouse. While the details were specific to Craig Gardner, his general analysis could no doubt have been echoed in the other larger firms. In his view audit remained the strategic key to success, and he identified five potential sources of new clients. These were merchant banks, North American banks (newly arrived in Dublin to handle the IDA projects from the United States), state agencies, solicitors and clearing banks. None of these sources had recently proved particularly fruitful for Craig Gardner. No work of any consequence had come from an American bank or a state agency; A. & L. Goodbody was the only solicitor to provide business, and that tended to be estate duty cases. Although two out of the three Irish merchant banks were Craig Gardner clients, Lyster believed that the traditionally remote, stand-off style of the partners meant that these banks 'see more of some other firms assisting their clients with loans than they see of us'.

There was therefore, as he put it, a 'marketing problem'—a term that his predecessors would no doubt have thought quite inappropriate for a professional firm. (The senior partner at the time was Gerard O'Brien, who had been with the firm since 1927. A busy man, who was also part-time Professor of Accounting in UCD, he was well known for briskly commenting after meetings: 'now we can get on with some work'.) However, it was clear that the old casual ways were not working; Craig Gardner was going to have to invest in both practice development and administration, even at the expense of removing otherwise effective earners from the front line. The very least that should be done was to complete the national coverage, not least because 80 per cent of IDA projects were based out of Dublin. This led to amalgamation with the venerable Cork firm of Atkins Chirnside (in 1973) and with two Limerick firms, Coffey Gubbins (in 1975) and Metcalf Lilburn (in 1976).

Like other firms at this time, Craig Gardner was faced with an important strategic dilemma. How was the balance between bread-and-butter auditing and the newly emerged specialist services (tax planning, management advisory services, etc.) to be managed? Traditionally the generalist (audit) partner had been the key contact between the firm and the client, and he brought in specialist tax and other services as he perceived the need.

Lyster identified certain problems in continuing this model. There was, he noted, going to be increasing pressure on the independence of the audit function, not least, or so he thought likely, from the accounting standards which were just beginning to be issued. As Irish representative on the London-based Accounting Standards Steering Committee, he foresaw that they were likely to erect a wall of technicalities between increasingly demanding clients and the firm. Much better, he suggested, to create multiple streams, each capable of selling services to the client.

This was a watershed time in the development of the profession. 'Chartered accountants', wrote a perceptive journalist in 1978, 'are being pulled in two different directions by forces that grow stronger every year . . . the simple fact is that auditing and basic tax are forming a smaller and smaller part of the average accountant's workload.' He estimated that the annual audit and the associated tax compliance work, which had been 80 per cent of the workload 'now just makes it to 50 per cent'.[32] The new direction was clear from the rapid growth in importance of specialist departments in City of London firms.[33]

The new approach was stressed by Stephen Epstein, senior partner of Stokes Kennedy Crowley's US partner Peats, at the SKC conference in 1978. He described how his firm pitched for business and actively looked for ideas to sell to potential customers, approaches that had a distinct touch of novelty in Ireland. He declared: 'I am a businessman . . . we must go out and market our products'. As *The Irish Times*' journalist quoted above wrote: 'ten years ago . . . such naked commercialism would not have sat well with the detached, professional image.'

On the other hand, in a paper to the 1978 Union of European Accountants conference in Dublin, Bryan Rankin of Thomson McLintock of Edinburgh noted a strong body of opinion that believed 'the auditor cannot be independent if he is involved with the provision of other services . . . it may be that the inevitable outcome will be the creation of two or three types of practice, perhaps dealing with audit, taxation and other management and advisory services.'[34] No doubt an audit-only business, if such could have survived, would have borne a greater resemblance to the old idea of professional practice as a lifestyle rather than a profit-maximising business. Perhaps such did exist, but they certainly were not to occupy the high ground of the profession in the future.

A major watershed for the Institute was the production in 1970 by the Education and Training Committee of its *Derryhale Report*.[35] Until then, as Ben Lynch, the newly appointed Director of Education put it, provision 'was very haphazard'.[36] Classes were available in Rathmines, many trainees took correspondence courses, and individuals offered grinds. This report, drafted by Lynch, was a development of ideas initially expressed in the *Whelan Report* on the objectives of the Institute. The *Derryhale Report* urged the development of an all-graduate profession (in 1969, 47 per cent of trainees were graduates). The key commitment, however, was that the Institute recognised that the current 'fragmented pattern of tuition', relying on the market to supply what was needed, was no longer adequate. The failure rate for each of the five exams prescribed was awkwardly high, and there was a consciousness that, as the report put it, 'if the Institute is to attract students of adequate calibre it will need to ensure that proper educational facilities are available'. A nine-month, full-time course was being piloted in Belfast, and this was only the start. A significant new commitment to training had been made.

The introduction of financial accounting standards

Before 1970, neither the Irish nor the British professions had been much bothered with detailed accounting or auditing standards. Specific ethical rules (for instance against advertising and touting) there certainly were, and once in a while a member of the Institute would be reprimanded by the Ethics Committee for infringing the rules. Richard Hewat, managing director of Heitons, who qualified with Stokes Brothers & Pim, remembers being asked to sit as a business member on the Institute's Ethics Committee. 'They said the post was virtually honorary, as the committee doesn't sit very often.' Cooper's *Manual of Auditing,* published in 1966,[37] mentions standards only in the context of the auditors of a subsidiary of a US firm having to follow those laid down by the American Institute of Certified Public Accountants. The *Manual* does refer occasionally to the gentle 'Recommendations' issued by the English Institute, a series which began in 1942 with a recommendation on the accounting for wartime Tax Reserve Certificates. Typical of these was N18 'Presentation of balance sheet and profit and loss account', issued in October 1958. This disarms potential criticism from the start by stating that 'businesses are so varied in their nature that there must be flexibility in the manner of presenting accounts', and then goes on: 'the function of the balance sheet is to present a true and fair view of the state of affairs of the company as on a particular date . . . a balance sheet is therefore mainly an historical document which does not purport to show the realisable value of assets such as goodwill, land, buildings, plant and machinery; nor does it normally purport to show the realisable value of assets such as stock in trade. Thus a balance sheet is not a statement of the net worth of the undertaking, and this is normally so even where there has been a revaluation of assets and the balance sheet amounts are based on the revaluation instead of cost.'[38] With such an array of what the balance sheet was *not*, it was difficult to see what it *was.* These recommendations were particularly nondirective in respect of profit and loss accounts, noting that 'there are differing opinions as to what should be included in the amount shown as the profit and loss of the year . . . [and] each of these opinions has arguments in its favour.' Behind all was the almost Platonic ideal of a 'true and fair view' which was supposed to emerge when men of integrity and technical skill addressed a set of accounts.

The Irish Institute had begun tentatively to issue its own recommendations (generally on the implications of new legislation to members from 1967), the first of which was a statement on the balance sheet treatment of contingent liabilities under the Redundancy Act. Another was on the interpretation of the Solicitors Accounts Regulations.

It took two dramatic British cases for public pressure on the profession to lead to the establishment of the first of the accounting standards boards in 1970. These crystallised a grumbling feeling among investments specialists and journals such as *The Economist* that all was not quite as it seemed in published accounts. This feeling was underlined in 1964 when the washing machine company Rolls Razor collapsed spectacularly just after publishing 'clean' accounts. But it was the takeover battles of the mid to late 1960s that really exposed a problem, as widely different profit statements often emerged from the same data. Thus, Management A, under attack, might be excused for promoting an optimistic view of, for instance, stock and work-in-progress valuations; while the incoming Management B could reasonably take a more pessimistic view, particularly since there was then a lower benchmark against which their own performance would be judged.[39]

The first of these cases, as dramatically memorable as the 1930s *Royal Mail* case, was when the General Electric Company took over its rival Amalgamated Electrical Industries in 1967. This was a noisy, messy takeover with overtones of anti-Semitism in the City of London as the GEC boss Arnold Weinstock was accused of asset-stripping a good old British industry. Three months before the end of the financial year the AEI directors, who were opposing the takeover, announced a profit forecast of £10 million for the financial year. Following the takeover the published accounts revealed a £4.5 million loss. As one discussion put it: 'while £5m of the total £14.5m difference could be attributed to matters of fact, £9.5m was due to judgements regarding accounting principles and bases.'[40] Confusing the issue, there was a suspicion that GEC wished to present AEI's results in the worst possible light so as to discredit the old management and justify factory closures. Nonetheless, the take-home message for the newspaper-reading public was that one set of accountants had approved a profit forecast of £10 million and another, using the same information, thought that a loss of £4.5 million was right.

Then came the Pergamon affair. In the course of a large investigation into Robert Maxwell's affairs it emerged that the £2 million profit declared by the company's auditors, Chalmers Impey, was reduced on re-examination by Price Waterhouse to a loss. The inspectors were 'not satisfied that any of these [audited] accounts showed a true and fair view' of the affairs of Pergamon 'at the material time or of the profits reported for the relevant period'.[41] Once again the valuation of stocks and work in progress were crucial elements.

It had of course long been recognised that judgement entered into the production of accounts. What was dismaying for the public to learn was just how much impact that judgement had, and how non-standardised the whole practice was. Each auditing firm, it seemed, had its own precedents and judgements as to what was true and fair. The investing public was not happy to realise that if they wished to compare two sets of accounts, they had first to consider and evaluate the impact of different accounting policies.

In January 1970, the Institute of Chartered Accountants in England and Wales announced the formation of the Accounting Standards Steering Committee (ASSC); this became the Accounting Standards Committee (ASC) in 1976, and the Accounting Standards Board (ASB) in 1990. The Irish and Scottish Institutes were invited to participate and became members of this body in the same year, followed by the Association of Certified Accountants (now the ACCA) and the Institute of Cost and Management Accountants (now CIMA) in 1971. The first Irish representative on the ASSC was W. Bruce Lyster of Craig Gardner, and he was joined in the following year by Frank Barrett of Arthur Andersen. The process was that after internal discussion the committee would issue an Exposure Draft; in controversial cases more than one turned out to be necessary. Thus the first exposure draft was issued in July 1970, and the associated accounting standard issued by the new committee was the Statement of Standard Accounting Practice on *Accounting for the results of associated companies* This was SSAP1—for a listing of the first 20 published standards, see the Appendix at page 165. (This was an attempt to tackle the abuses uncovered in the Pergamon report.) It was less clear how these new standards were to be enforced—for years the toughest sanction was the 'expectation' of the professional bodies that the standards would be followed, or if they were not this fact would be noted in the accounts. At one point the possibility was raised that the then-combined London and Dublin Stock Exchanges would refuse to list companies not following the standards, but they declined to accept that responsibility.

Some years before this, the American Accounting Association, which is primarily an academic group, had issued a dramatic statement called *Statement of Basic Accounting Theory* which boldly declared that 'accounting is the process of identifying, measuring and communicating economic information to permit informed judgements and decisions by users of the information'.[42] Professor Robert Sterling, a distinguished US commentator on accounting matters, described this new approach as 'revolutionary when its contents are compared to contemporary practice and education' and 'the stuff that revolutions are made of'. What excited him was the idea that accounts were no longer to be seen as primarily communications between the company and its shareholders. Companies were part of society and had therefore to be accountable to that society. Financial reporting was the way in which a company gave information to society. It was as if accounting reports were a kind of information tax, levied for the privilege of limited liability.

On this side of the Atlantic, a similar view surfaced in the Accounting Standards Steering Committee's *The Corporate Report* (1976), which began with the words, 'our basic approach has been that corporate reports should seek to satisfy, as far as possible, the information needs of users: they should be useful'. The historian of the British/Irish standards process, Professor Brian Rutherford, comments: 'Unstartling as this proposition appears today, it was actually quite a radical development in the mid-1970s for a professional accountancy body to countenance the notion that its principal product should be generally useful.'[43] *The Corporate Report* was an attempt to put flesh on the public interest aspect of professional activity—the idea that there was something beyond client interest that should be considered. It also addressed the accusation that setting of standards or rules for this or that specific element was a mere set of tactics lacking principles or an overarching strategy, a state of affairs militarily described as 'the noise before defeat'.[44]

The second standard produced, SSAP2 *Disclosure of accounting policies,* did attempt to address the fundamentals, but was too timid. It specified the four 'fundamental accounting concepts' which should underlie the preparation of financial statements, namely the traditional ideas of going concern, accruals, consistency and prudence. Unfortunately, as Taylor and Turley comment, 'this set of concepts in fact represents a mixture of principle, convention and assumption, and in practice the ASC [did] not find it easy to follow these rules when setting standards. The conflict between the prudence and accruals concepts has often arisen in the context of new standards but contrary to SSAP2 the ASC has not always allowed prudence to prevail, for example the valuation of long-term contract work in progress (SSAP9) and the capitalisation of development expenditure (SSAP13).'[45]

A good deal of the 'radicalism' ascribed to *The Corporate Report* (and this is not normally a complimentary term in the profession) lay in its acceptance of the fashionable contemporary view that there was more to business than profit, and that accounts should reflect social aspects of business organisations. To that end, it proposed to add to the balance sheet, profit and loss account and cash flow analysis, formal values-added statements, employment reports, accounts of dealings in foreign currency and with government agencies, and statements of future prospects. One of the Irish representatives on the ASSC, Frank Barrett of Arthur Andersen, described *The Corporate Report* as 'one of the best things we did'. Others were more critical, and there was not much regret when the new Conservative Government elected in May 1979 put its ideas on the back burner, though it continued to be referred to by thinking accountants.

At the same time there were other factors pushing the accountancy profession into familiarity with formal standards. Many of the larger British and Irish firms had increasingly close associations with US companies which had long been used to the detailed prescriptions from the Securities and Exchange Commission. As a result, the practice in the larger firms, such as Deloitte, Touche, Coopers and, importantly, the London office of the US firm Arthur Andersen, was markedly different to the more traditional styles of the many smaller firms, even those that had Stock Exchange-quoted clients. The larger firms and therefore the Institute were conscious that there were wide differences in practice.

These variations made the individual firms vulnerable if, as was increasingly possible, the client sued. In 1972, David Rowe of Kennedy Crowley raised the issue in *Accountancy Ireland,* noting that, as yet, contested law suits against Irish auditors were rare, since accountants much preferred to avoid publicity and 'will compromise or settle out of court, even if they have a strong case'.[46] However, the rise in the number of cases in the US, and to a lesser extent in Britain, had been discussed during the Institute's Annual Conference in 1970, and David Rowe declared that there was a 'feeling of uncertainty and perhaps insecurity as to what direction the law might take', especially since claims could easily be 'enormously out of proportion to the culpability of a negligent auditor'.

Behind the need to write down standards was a waning of automatic professional authority. Many professional groups, notably politicians, the clergy and the medical profession, felt the same.[47] A suit or a soutane was no longer enough to stimulate respect. For the medical profession, the old days when 'doctor's orders' was a command were long gone, as the eager take-up of alternative medicine proved. David Rowe identified without enthusiasm 'some move away from the generally accepted standards of the profession as being an adequate measuring rod for the procedures used by the auditor'. Clients and accounts users were now less likely simply to accept professional expertise—the accounting equivalent of 'doctor's orders'—at face value. As increasing numbers of qualified accountants joined client firms, there was a shift in balance of technical power between auditors and client firms.[48] Auditors were typically faced with client finance managers as skilled and knowledgeable as they were (they had after all trained in the same firms and passed the same exams) and who necessarily had incomparably more detailed knowledge of the affairs and aspirations of the client company. Not only did they know where the bodies were buried but they also had a specific loyalty and sensitivity to the aims and objectives of senior management.

The development of standards was also an attempt to strengthen the arm of the external auditor against self-serving management. The existence of a knowledgeable and acquiescent professional team can give the so-called dominant senior managers considerable power to present accounts as they want them.[49] This factor became even more important with the wider use of financial management techniques after the Stock Exchange big bang in the 1980s. Professor Ed Cahill of UCC has pointed out how the combination of a dominant senior manager and aggressive accounting policies were key factors in three of the most spectacular Irish corporate reversals of fortune in the 1990s—Goodman, Kentz and GPA.[50]

Accounting for inflation

The issue of inflation accounting tested the standards process severely. Price inflation had greatly accelerated across the developed world, but particularly in Ireland and Britain, from the late 1960s onwards. As economist Kieran Kennedy wrote, 'the consumer price index rose at an annual average rate of 8.3 per cent between 1968 and 1972, about double the average rate previously experienced since the Second World War.'[51] It got worse as the decade progressed. Inflation rapidly became the economic background to every decision, a factor in every calculation. When every financial forecast had parallel columns headed 'Cash' and 'Inflation-adjusted', it became clear that a basic assumption of accounting, that a pound yesterday is the same as a pound today, was being undermined. Confusingly, the impact was not uniform, even across a single set of accounts. The resale price of stocks and goods went up, for instance, while the value of cash and debts went down. In 1982 Howard Robinson recorded, from his own experience, how 'accounts purported to show profits in concerns which were finding the continuation of business increasingly difficult, if not impossible, owing to their inability to replace stock at increasing costs . . . it became increasingly difficult for an accountant to persuade a client who was a realist that he was making a profit when he was not able to draw out of his business anything on which to live, and to add insult to injury was being taxed on such "profits" calculated in the old-fashioned way without regard to the effects of changes in the purchasing power of money.'[52]

The newspaper columns of course reflected this interest. Thus, in the first five years of the 1960s the word 'inflation' was used only once every few days (fewer than 500 times in five years) in *The Irish Times*, but it came up as many as 4,680 times in the first years of the 1970s. Over the whole decade of the 1970s the word was used on average four times a day. Pressure on wages began to be felt; as Professor Joe Lee put it: 'growing trade union aggressiveness was reflected not only in intensified strike activity but in national pay agreements which took scant account of economic reality and further fuelled inflation. The 1970 agreement allowed the average male worker an 18 per cent increase over an eighteen month period, the 1972 agreement a 21 per cent increase over eighteen months.'[53]

Industrial unrest was only the start, however. Over the previous 25 years the developed world had become increasingly dependent on the great international trade in oil. Cheap, readily available oil encouraged unmoderated usage in factories, power plants, homes and cars. The average daily consumption in the developed world went from 19 million barrels a day in 1960 to 44 million in 1972.[54] Heretofore the great US oilfields of Texas had been able to meet US demand; but now, more than 10 years before this was expected, expert opinion began to believe that those fields had reached and passed their peak. The US became dependent on the world oil market, of which the key suppliers were the Islamic countries of the Middle East. These of course deeply resented the US's continuing support for Israel, and were now in a position to exert pressure. In 1973, various OPEC countries, led by Saudi Arabia (the world's largest oil exporter), announced drastic restrictions in world oil supplies with a view to forcing a change in US policy. Very quickly the price of oil quadrupled.

Because of Ireland's dependence on imported oil (and Northern Ireland even more than the Republic), this immediately struck at Ireland's balance of payments, and inflation rose remorselessly, hitting highs of 21 per cent in 1975 and 20 per cent (after another strike with the oil weapon) in 1981. In a bare 10 years, from 1973 to 1983, the consumer price index in the Republic quadrupled. We have seen the effects of similar rises on the North's industrial development.

Thinking accountants had long been conscious that the key difference between the economists' definition of income and their own had been the economists' insistence that a theoretically sound concept of profit (defined as an increase in real wealth) had to include fluctuations in values of assets and the purchasing power of money.[55] In practice, of course, these are notoriously difficult to assess, so the profession had chosen to ignore theory and stick with the comfortable precision of historic costs and the illusion of stable monetary values. But as asset prices rose with inflation, recorded values moved increasingly out of kilter with reality.

In the light of the double-digit inflation of the late 1960s and 1970s, it was felt in the profession that something had to be done. During Frank Barrett's five years on the ASSC, numerous standards dealing with such matters as deferred taxation, depreciation and extraordinary items were argued and produced. However, from his first meeting in mid-1972, at which Provisional Standard 7 'Accounting for changes in the purchasing power of money' was discussed, to the end when Exposure Draft 18 'Current cost accounting' was on the agenda, the problem of asset valuation in inflationary times was never far from the table. 'There was scarcely a single day's meeting', wrote Barrett, 'into which this problem did not thrust its ugly head.'[56]

The Accounts Standards Steering Committee made a stab at the problem in 1973 with an Exposure Draft, also called 'Accounting for changes in the purchasing power of money'. This was unenthusiastically reviewed in *Accountancy Ireland* by future President of the Institute Purvis Bruce (Atkinson & Boyd, Belfast) but others, notably Don Carroll, a member of the Institute's Council, were enthusiastic. As chairman of cigarette manufacturer P. J. Carroll and Governor of the Bank of Ireland, Carroll was in a position to act. Under his influence the annual accounts firstly of Carroll's, and subsequently the bank, included inflation workings. No doubt this contributed to the Carroll's accounts winning the first Published Accounts Award of the Leinster Society in 1978. But the profession as a whole was not convinced, and in January 1974 the British Government took a hand and appointed Sir Francis Sandilands to explore the issue. His analysis showed that there were broadly two ways in which accounts could be inflation-proofed: either by adjusting historic costs using an index-based multiplier, or by making adjustments to asset valuations based on replacement cost. Sandilands went for the latter, called 'current cost accounting'. His proposals were incorporated in the now-renamed Accounting Standards Committee's subsequently notorious Exposure Draft 18 in 1976.

ED18 aroused a storm. A total of 746 responses to the Draft were received by the Committee, three times the number of the next most responded to (and that was an inflation-related proposal, too). Four times as many practising firms as usual responded. Only 5 per cent supported the Draft.[57] In half-page articles in *The Irish Times,* first the well-known industrialist Noel Griffin FCA, managing director of Waterford Glass, and then Howard Kilroy, FCA, financial controller and later chief operations officer of Jefferson Smurfit, poured scorn on the proposals.[58] They thoroughly agreed with the common complaints received by the ASC: that ED18 was too complex, too subjective and too costly. So elaborate indeed was the system, Griffin mischievously argued, that 'the number of professional accountants in the country would increase enormously'.

Howard Kilroy in particular deplored the proposed departure from, as he put it, 'the one great standard—FACT'. Sliding over the crucial point that inflation renders historic cost an illusion, he disingenuously declared that 'historic cost accounting is objective, and open to very little manipulation'. Since one objective of the standards process was to strengthen the hand of the auditor against in-house professionals, of whom Griffin and Kilroy were prominent examples, perhaps their opposition should not have come as a surprise. Some weeks later, Alex Spain, who was the immediate past-President of the Institute, was given a whole page in *The Irish Times* to refute these attacks, arguing that the fears of complexity and cost were exaggerated. 'It is', he wrote, 'strangely reminiscent of the worries before the introduction of decimalisation and we are all aware that when that great day came that it was an accounting non-event.'[59]

However, the weight of accountancy opinion was against him. Conscious no doubt of the general lack of enthusiasm both among their majority of members in business and also those in practice who foresaw considerable difficulties in auditing current cost accounting accounts (and the disproportionate burden on SMEs), in June 1977 the Institute of Cost and Works Accountants in Ireland joined the Institute of Certified Public Accountants and the Institute of Chartered Accountants in Ireland in rejecting ED18 in whole or in part.[60] In July, ED18 was withdrawn after a special general meeting of the English Institute voted against it. Theory once again lost out to practice. Inflation was to continue to be a plague for some years, and a new Exposure Draft was produced covering current cost accounting in 1979, followed by a Statement of Standard Accounting Practice (SSAP16) in March 1980. Two months later UK inflation peaked at 22 per cent year-on-year; but then, as a result of a restrictive monetary control policy, it dropped for virtually 32 successive months, reaching under 5 per cent in 1983.[61] A similar pattern occurred in Ireland somewhat later in the 1980s. With this, the urgency of inflation-conscious accounting faded and the issue slipped off the table.

Future course

By the end of the 1970s, the ASC had issued 20 standards and exposure drafts, though two of these had been withdrawn after considerable controversy. There were also a number of EEC accounting directives. In November 1979 Howard Kilroy of Jefferson Smurfit took the opportunity of an invitation from the Leinster Society to return to the attack. 'At the end of the day', he declared, 'there has been no improvement at all emanating out of the multitude of guidelines issued.' The profession was moving away, he believed, from the ideal of pragmatic simplicity towards a legalistic reliance on small print. 'The sense of disenchantment among management for the accountancy profession and the auditor is growing.'[62] Actually, as we shall see, over the next decades the profession was able to expand its services and become even more important to management.

One striking event in 1979 was to have substantial consequences for Irish business. In March 1979 the Republic decided to join the European Monetary System, in the forlorn hope that the monetary discipline implicit in tracking hard currency countries such as Germany would help control inflation. Very soon sterling moved so far away that Ireland would have had to devalue to maintain the link. Ireland stuck within the EMS band, thus breaking a 150-year connection. Now at least half of Irish trade with the North and the rest of the UK required foreign exchange transactions, a new challenge both for in-house accountants and auditors. Dealing with foreign exchange presented tax planning opportunities too.

As the decade wore on trade union militancy in the United Kingdom escalated (as it did also in Ireland and continental countries such as Italy), climaxing in the famous 'winter of discontent' of 1979. During this crisis local authority workers' strikes left rat-infested piles of rubbish in city centres; so many unburied bodies were held in storage depots in Liverpool that public health officials began to speak of burial at sea; and a leader of striking ambulance drivers notoriously declared: 'if it means people's lives will be lost, that is how it must be'.[63] For Ireland (north and south) 1979 was the worst ever year for industrial action, starting with a strike of oil-tanker drivers in Northern Ireland causing a state of emergency to be declared. A thoroughly frightened British electorate elected Mrs Thatcher and the Conservatives to power, and very different social, industrial and financial policies were emerging as the new background to the development of the profession.

Appendix: The First 20 Statements of Standard Accounting Practice [64]

For each standard I have noted the date of the first relevant Exposure Draft (in some controversial cases, e.g. inflation, extraordinary items, and deferred taxation there were three or four); the issued date and any variants; and the number of comments received in response to the ED, and, as an index of participation, how many of those came from practising firms (as opposed to accountancy bodies).

SSAP1 *Accounting for associated companies* (ED Jul 1970, issued Jan 1971, amended Aug 1974, revised Apr 1984) comments 152, of which practising firms 22.

SSAP2 *Disclosure of accounting policies* (ED Feb 1971, issued Nov 1971) comments 69, of which practising firms 13.

SSAP3 *Earnings per share* (ED Feb 1971, issued Feb 1972, revised Aug 1974) comments 66, of which practising firms 18.

SSAP4 *The accounting treatment of government grants* (ED Mar 1973, issued Apr 1974) comments 76, of which practising firms 14.

SSAP6 *Extraordinary items and prior year adjustments* (ED Sep 1971, Jul 1972, issued Apr 1974) comments 83, of which practising firms 17.

SSAP7 *Accounting for changes in the purchasing power of money* (ED Feb 1973, issued May 1974, withdrawn 1977) comments 113, of which practising firms 13.

SSAP8 *The treatment of taxation under the imputation system in the accounts of companies* (ED Jun 1973, issued Aug 1975) comments 67, of which practising firms 18.

SSAP9 *Stocks and work in progress* (ED May 1972, issued May 1975) comments 153, of which practising firms 21.

SSAP10 *Statements of source and application of funds* (ED May 1974, issued July 1975) comments 98, of which practising firms 22.

SSAP11 *Accounting for deferred taxation* (ED May 1973, issued Aug 1975 withdrawn 1977) comments 67, of which practising firms 18.

SSAP12 *Accounting for depreciation* (ED Feb 1975, issued Dec 1977, revised

Nov 1981) comments 101, of which practising firms 21.

SSAP13 *Accounting for research and development* (ED Feb 1975, issued Dec 1977) comments 66, of which practising firms 15.

SSAP14 *Group Accounts* (ED Aug 1977, issued Sep 1978) comments 85, of which practising firms 18.

SSAP15 *Accounting for deferred taxation* (ED May 1973, issued Oct 1978, revised May 1985) comments 115, of which practising firms 26.

SSAP16 *Current Cost accounting* (ED May 1979, issued Mar 1980, mandatory status suspended June 1985) comments 746, of which practising firms 83.

SSAP17 *Accounting for post-balance sheet events* (ED Mar 1978, issued Aug 1980) comments 91, of which practising firms 23.

SSAP 18 *Accounting for contingencies* (ED Mar 1978, issued Aug 1980) comments 81, of which practising firms 21.

SSAP19 *Accounting for investment properties* (ED Sep 1980, issued Nov 1981) comments 107, of which practising firms 21.

SSAP20 *Foreign currency translation* (ED Oct 1977, issued Apr 1983) comments 107, of which practising firms 20.

Chapter Eight
'The old concept is dead': The 1980s

The emphasis on profits and on earnings per share has certainly contributed towards the 'creative accounting' that some companies developed during the 1980s—for example the improper use of pre-acquisition provisions and extraordinary items, off-balance sheet finance, capitalisation of expense items, changes in asset lives for depreciation purposes, reductions in pension fund contributions and reserve accounting.
The Financial Reporting Commission of the Institute of Chartered Accountants in Ireland *Report* (1992)

The 1980s opened with a televised broadcast to the nation by a chartered accountant who had reached the highest executive office in the Republic. In a solemn, impressive address on 9 January 1980, Taoiseach Charles Haughey outlined the country's bleak economic plight: 'the picture I have to paint', he said, 'is not, unfortunately, a very cheerful one . . . as a community we are living away beyond our means . . . taking us all together we have been living at a rate which is simply not justified by the amount of goods and services we are producing.' Despite widespread public approval of this analysis, over the next few months he proceeded to do exactly the opposite of what he had said he would do—in an attempt to buy growth he increased public spending and borrowing. Haughey's government greatly increased the number of public servants, and settled pay claims 'with such abandon', as his great rival Garret FitzGerald put it, 'that average rates in the public service rose by almost 30 per cent in 1980'.[1]

Unbeknownst to all but a very select few was the fact that Haughey's own finances and spending were in exactly the state he had described for the country as a whole. He was living far beyond his official means and was dependent for his magnificent lifestyle on handouts from rich supporters. A few days before, the AIB had forgiven him £400,000 of his £1 million debt, allegedly after he had told the bank 'I can be a very troublesome adversary'.[2] In the comfort of his fine Gandon mansion at Kinsealy after the broadcast, he perhaps reflected that 'like many other great moralists and preachers, he had been eloquent on a point in which his own conduct would ill bear examination'.[3]

There was not in truth much room for economic or political manoeuvre. Inflation was running at over 18 per cent and unemployment was 115,000 by the end of 1980, on its way up to 17 per cent by 1986.[4] This was, as Paul Tansey wrote in *The Irish Times,* the year that 'for the first time since Ireland's takeoff in the 1960s the steam began to run out of the economy'.[5] The tax system was dangerously dependent on a narrow base of earners. Deflation in Britain hit Irish exports and at home consumer spending was down on the previous year. In an attempt to stimulate growth, the Fianna Fáil governments of Jack Lynch and Charles Haughey had, as Garret FitzGerald argued, 'increased the volume of current public spending by almost half, more than doubled in real terms the annual level of borrowing and almost trebled the national debt'.[6]

In the North, the political situation grew increasingly poisonous as violence and intransigent propagandising from both sides escalated. Bomb scares and bag searches remained part of everyday life. About 300 IRA prisoners had been on 'dirty protest' for years, and in May 1981 this was to escalate into a full-blown hunger strike. In the end, 10 people starved to death and 61 were killed in associated disturbances. It was estimated that the extra security costs to the Republic from the Northern violence could have been as much as £200 million a year.

Northern Ireland's fragile economic base, and its position on the periphery of a state which itself had the poorest growth record in Europe, looked unhopeful. As Timothy Quin of the Northern Ireland practice of Touche Ross described, during this time 'the main concern of businessmen and professionals in Northern Ireland was to keep their heads low and carry on business as usual'. And in some minds doubts arose about whether the Institute could survive in its existing form: 'chartered accountants who had strong Unionist inclinations began to question their own participation in an all-Ireland Institute. Many southern members, concerned about the security situation, showed reluctance to attend conferences and other meetings in the North.'[7] However, the much-valued connection had withstood a tougher challenge with the establishment of the Irish Free State in 1922, and it held.

The continuing violence and the international publicity during the hunger strikes frightened off potential investors into Northern Ireland. Between 1979 and 1981 no fewer than 110 substantial manufacturing plants closed their doors. The last of these, the Grundig plant in Dunmurry, squarely blamed 'disturbances of a political nature'. In 1982 the flagship DeLorean sports car factory (which the IDA in the Republic had turned down) finally collapsed, with a dead loss of the £80 million that had been pumped in. This was the prelude to a decade that was to get much worse before, towards the end, some light was visible at the end of the tunnel. The aircraft manufacturer Shorts announced a profit in 1983, the first since 1975. The Northern Ireland economy remained vulnerable, nevertheless, and heavily dependent on subventions from Westminster.[8]

Three professional developments

For the accountancy profession, however, things were not so bleak. A new multi-disciplinary configuration or business model promised to expand opportunities. In April 1979 the soon-to-be President of the Institute Noel MacMahon summed up the enormous changes that had occurred in the previous decade.[9] He identified three aspects in particular: 'the search for improved standards of accounting and auditing; the growth in the complexity of taxation legislation; and the advent of low-cost computers.'

The gathering storm of complaints of ambiguous and variable accounting and audit work had led to the development by the profession of an increasing body of formal standards. These generally had, as MacMahon put it, 'important effects in raising the standard of financial reporting'. However, there was far from unanimity about the new standards. Cornelius Smith (President of the Institute 1973–4) identified a *philosophical* contest between 'accountants and their powerful clients', and users who demanded 'uniformity over as wide an area as possible'.[10] He warned that this 'chronic malaise' would cause stress, though without expanding on this classic 'political theory' dilemma, between the powerful who want as much freedom as possible and the users who, for protection, need rules. Part of the problem, he claimed, came from 'ungentlemanly pressure groups', though he does not specify these more closely.

Perhaps he was thinking of the US, where it was certainly the case that standard setters were subject to fierce pressure on particular issues, from both corporations and accountancy firms. The American accounting scholar Professor Zeff attests to 'a series of attempts by bodies representing [accounts] preparers to diminish the FASB's ability to issue rigorous standards, among which was an attempt to revise upward the required voting majority on the Board to slow down the Board's ability to issue standards.[11] Smith's particular fear was the loss of the self-regulatory power; ultimately he thought the public would 'make up our minds for us', and that the profession would lose its prized self-regulation.[12] The contest over standards certainly exposed a dichotomy in the heart of the profession, between the accountant as scrupulous and learned professional and the accountant as pro-client business advisor.

When a new standard made some form of current cost accounting mandatory for large companies in 1980, compliance was weak. Although Irish inflation peaked in 1982 at 21 per cent, both journalists and the Irish business community generally 'were wedded for the time being to historic cost accounts', as research by Edmond Grace (then of the Manchester Business School, whom we have last seen as chair of the Institute's decimalisation committee) showed. Journalists were apparently 'too busy' to get their heads around the new concept, so continued to headline historic cost figures. Despite the formal standard, many companies did not produce inflation-related figures, a proportion that Grace believed 'appeared to be affected by whether or not they appeared profitable'. Looking closely at a sample of 33 companies listed on the Irish Stock Exchange, he found that if the accounts were adjusted for inflation, fully two-thirds did not cover the issued dividends.[13]

Table 1: *Difference between historic cost outcomes and current cost outcomes from selected year-end reports*

	Historic cost		Current Cost	
	Profit (£m)	Dividend cover	Profit (£m)	Dividend cover
Bank of Ireland	52.7	4.0	12.8	nil
Jefferson Smurfit	17.4	1.9	8.6	0.7
Jones Group	2.2	3.6	1.9	3.2
Clondalkin Group	2.8	4.3	2.2	3.0
Brooks Watson	0.4	nil	(0.6)	nil
Arnotts	3.4	2.7	2.6	1.4

Note: In most cases companies foregrounded the historic cost data and published the inflation-adjusted figures as a supplement to the annual report. In each of these cases the profit and dividend cover outcome is worse in current cost terms than in historic cost terms.
Source: The Irish Times 18 May 1981[14]

The standard setters' attempt to impose an unwonted rigour was widely resisted, though opponents often showed little attempt to address the real problem, which was that inflation made nonsense of adding values from different years as if they were the same. Thus, Mark Hely-Hutchinson, Managing Director of Guinness (which was very soon to suffer from its own version of the dominant senior manager problem), told the Association of Certified Accountants in July 1980 that accountancy bodies should keep to a minimum of rules, 'as heavy regimentation would blunt skills of judgement and interpretation'. Inflation accounting, he declared, was suitable only for large firms.[15] A couple of years later, now CEO designate of the Bank of Ireland, Hely-Hutchinson returned to the fray. The problem with standards, he declared, is 'the multiplicity and frequency of changes, and the problem of using them' in practical business planning. For good measure he threw in complaints about the fees: 'it is galling to have to spend a six-figure sum each year simply to be told that one's own accountants are doing a good job'.[16]

Also in 1982, Vincent Cruise, Managing Director of Hickey Ltd of Cork, argued to a seminar of the Munster Society of the ICAI: 'people like myself in the world of business find it extremely difficult to explain to ourselves, let alone our fellow directors, the relevance/need for so many of these standards.'[17] He singled out the standards relating to depreciation and accounting for inflation as particularly objectionable. In a revealing phrase, he described them as 'totally irrelevant to the needs of business'. The only effect, he sarcastically suggested, was to extend financial statements from eight to 20 pages 'with consequential effects on audit fees.' Just thus, in a flat-earth society, might the advocates of great circle navigation be derided.

In *Accountancy Ireland*, Alex Spain, Frank Barrett and Noel MacMahon defended the accounting standards, arguing that public accounting had a wider mandate than simply meeting 'the needs of business', in Vincent Cruise's words. Information about businesses was a public good, though for historic reasons the cost of maintaining that good was charged to the individual company rather than the State. Noel MacMahon bluntly stated that 'the significant failure' of the profession in the 1970s was the 'agonisingly slow pace with which we and our colleagues in other countries have coped with the accounting and reporting issues created by withering inflation which has over-shadowed our lives.' The failure to grapple adequately with the intellectual issues involved was no doubt a function of the severely practical nature of the professional formation. With hindsight, of course, we can see that when inflation came down rapidly in the mid-1980s, the still unsolved problem sank into insignificance.

There were other aspirations. Margaret Downes (President of the Institute 1983–4) reverted to the ASSC's 1975 *The Corporate Report*'s proposal that a company's wider obligations to employees, shareholders and society should generally be included as part of the annual accounts. She argued that accountants 'must take a leadership role in the development of more meaningful annual reports and the development of annual social performance reports'.[18] This explicit rejection of Milton Friedman's idea that businesses have no responsibility other than to make profits was quietly ignored in the neoliberal wave that came in with Mrs Thatcher's election in 1979 and Ronald Reagan's in 1980.

The second change MacMahon identified was the 'extraordinary growth in the complexity and range' of taxation services provided by accountants. Coming into office in 1973 the new Fine Gael-led Government had tax reform high on its agenda, and a rapid sequence of innovations followed its election: capital gains tax, wealth tax, capital acquisitions tax, taxation of farm profits, corporation tax and a unified system of income tax. Crucially, as we shall see, each of these taxes was riddled with well-meaning concessions, exemptions and reduced rates. At the same time sophisticated overseas investors were highly alert to local and international taxation consequences of decisions. A combination of increasing ability to address these problems, and the outreach provided by international associate firms (which the solicitors did not have), gave the large accountancy firms a significant edge over legal rivals, to the point where in the 1990s there was common speculation about the largest accountancy firms tucking a solicitors' practice or two under their wings.

Where it had in the past been a low-level consideration, tax now became a key decision area, even for smaller businesses. Writing in 1979, MacMahon stressed the importance of this change by noting that now 'it would be an exception to find any businessman making a significant investment decision without giving detailed consideration to the tax consequences of such a decision'. Tax departments in the larger firms boomed, boosted by recruits from the Revenue Commissioners. Specialist sub-departments dealing with capital, income and corporate taxation emerged.

The third innovation of the 1970s, which Noel MacMahon described as 'probably the single most important factor of change', was the introduction of computers, an exponential step up in office automation from the cumbersome accounting machines of older days. In the beginning computers were expensive and required air-conditioned rooms and highly trained operators, often working around the clock to complete complex program suites. These were followed by mini-computers, of which the Burroughs B80 was a typical example. A B80 provided a multi-part system, including a desk with a built-in dot matrix printer spewing out sprocket-driven fan-fold paper reports, and storage capacity provided by double-sided 8-inch 'super minidisks', with a capacity of 1MB. A proprietary operating system and application software came as part of the package. The cost was between £13,000 and £20,000, depending on the configuration.[19] Gradually, the old ledgers began to be replaced by print-outs.

Initially such machines were used, nervously, for repetitious accounts and clerical tasks, such as payroll and sales; the next stage was to add functions such as stock control, and the introduction of some mathematics (such as Camp's stock replacement formula); finally, the new machines graduated to providing integrated management information systems. The benefits to the profession could be spectacular. Operating a small accountancy practice in Lurgan, Henry Murray estimated that the bulk of his work—incomplete records for farmers, publicans and hauliers—could be completed in half or less time by use of his newly installed mini-computer.[20]

Captivated by the power of the new machines, people began to speculate about the possibility of the 'paperless office' and its advantages. The best-known of these prophets was Christopher Evans, whose book *Mighty Micro* also foresaw the imminent decline of all professions, from accountancy to teaching, on the grounds that all the knowledge would now be available to everybody. This book was respectfully reviewed in *Accountancy Ireland* as part of a regular feature that certainly covered practice-relevant books, but by no means kept strictly to the narrow path.[21] In 1980, for instance, the anonymous editor (in reality the long-serving staff member of the Institute, Ben Lynch) had mischievously included a full page review of Bryan Breed's *White Collar Bird,* a sympathetic description of the experiences of middle-class men serving prison sentences—'solicitors, accountants, clerks, businessmen', as the blurb had it. Later in the decade there were notices for the best-selling management book *In Search of Excellence,* and also for *Creative Accounting: How to Make Your Profits What You Want Them To Be*, which the reviewer thought would come as a shock to the uninitiated but no surprise to the professional.[22]

For the profession, the development of computer usage provided a substantial impetus to the development of management consultancy by accountancy firms. Previously, firms had been chary of claiming expertise outside of the accounts department, but because the new technology was used company-wide, firms providing IT advice were necessarily involved with the needs and possibilities of other areas. Management consultancy services quickly overtook secretarial as a contributor to profits and in some firms, such as Arthur Andersen, became a major activity. Eventually, the development of consultancy and tax services led to the elevation of non-chartered accountants to partnership.

Accountants making a mark

Charles Haughey was not the only prominent accountant in national life. Also in politics was the Kildare chartered accountant Charlie McCreevy, later to become Minister for Finance and European Commissioner. Almost as well-known were Vincent Finn, Director General of RTÉ from 1985, and Gerry Dempsey of Aer Lingus. In banking there was Don Carroll of P. J. Carroll and the Bank of Ireland, a vigorous supporter of inflation-related accounts, Niall Crowley, chairman of Allied Irish Banks and Sean Fitzpatrick, MD of the still tiny Anglo-Irish Bank. Among the prominent businessmen were Noel Griffin of Waterford Glass (whose early death in a boating accident in 1981 was much lamented), Lochlann Quinn of Glen Dimplex, Brian Slowey, MD of Guinness, Jack Casey, MD of New Ireland Assurance and Paul Conlon, CEO of CIÉ. About 7 per cent of the 1,000 names listed in the 1984 edition of *Who's Who in Ireland* were from the profession, including non-chartered accountants such as for instance Frank Feely ACCA of Dublin Corporation, Kieron Fearon CIMA and MD of Coyle Hamilton, and Bertie Ahern, who 'worked as an accountant in the Mater Hospital'.[23]

Inside the chartered profession, one of the most respected accountants was Frank Barrett of Arthur Andersen (President of the ICAI 1982–3). Barrett was from a staunchly Republican background. His father was a successful leader in Clare during the War of Independence, and later died prematurely from the effects of a hunger strike in an English gaol. After qualification in Dublin, Barrett worked in Venezuela, coming to Dublin in 1968 to set up the Arthur Andersen office. This became the most highly regarded practice in Ireland. His famous mantra 'think straight, talk straight' reflected his personality, which, as a colleague said at his funeral, combined 'a strong self-belief and vision, a deep knowledge of international audit best practice and an honourable fearlessness'.[24] He retired in 1987.

With 6,200 members by the centenary of the Charter in 1988, it was inevitable that there would be men and women in the profession who did interesting things in their 'life after 5.30', as the headline in *Accountancy Ireland* put it, evidently before the long-hours culture kicked in.[25] Golf and membership of golf clubs of course loomed large, but there were also, for instance, surfers (Brian Britton ex-SKC was past-president of the European Surfing Association); people involved in charities (Des O'Donohue of Deloitte was for many years Treasurer of the St Vincent de Paul Society, Alex Spain was Deputy-Chairman of the National Maternity Hospital and Tom O'Higgins was on the board and later chairman of Concern); an Olympian (rower David Gray of Price Waterhouse Belfast took part in the Moscow Olympics in 1980); and people in civic life (Desmond Miller of Stokes Kennedy Crowley followed Gabriel Brock as President of the Dublin Chamber of Commerce).[26] In response to the tough financial times, the Leinster Society of Chartered Accountants had set up and ran a free and confidential financial advice service called the Financial Information Service Centre, which had 11 centres around Dublin and centres in Cork, Limerick, Naas and Waterford. Press officer Niamh Brennan, then lecturing in accounting in UCD, explained: 'anyone who has any sort of financial query can come along and we will deal with it . . . most people come to us with tax problems—this seems to be the most incomprehensible part of Irish finance.'[27] Less publicly, accountants commonly filled the treasurer role in sporting and other clubs up and down the country.

Considering there were fewer than 3,000 members of the Institute when most of these started their careers, this is a striking record of business and social prominence. Looking for reasons why, we might adduce the demanding training (pass rates in the final examination rarely reached more than 50 per cent) and a sense, appealing to the ambitious, that the profession offered much broader scope, in business and practice, at home and abroad, than for instance engineering or law.

After Charles Haughey, perhaps the accountant best known as such to the general public of the 1980s was the unfortunate C. Russell Murphy. Before his death he was recognised as a patron of the arts and the theatre (taking blocks of seats on opening nights for distribution to friends). Sole partner in Henry M. Murphy & Co. (his father's firm), he qualified in 1947 and became one of the leading specialists in taxation and company law.[28] He built up a strong business in liquidations, being appointed as such to several publicly quoted companies including Matt Talbot's old employer, the timber merchants T. & C. Martin. Some later well-known public figures were articled to him, including Margaret Downes and Paddy Masterson, who was to become President of University College Dublin and the European University Institute in Florence.

Murphy also had a personal client list, including many of the best-known names in show business, who employed him to look after their financial interests. When, after a long illness, he died at the age of 59, he was widely respected; his funeral was attended by, among many others, the Tánaiste and the Chief Justice of the day. In an obituary notice, broadcaster Brian Farrell identified him as a *beau ideal* of a certain type of accountant. He described Murphy as an accountant 'in a mould that might seem long since fractured by the pressures of contemporary business life. He maintained the ideal of a personal relationship with clients that spilled beyond any narrow bounds and became a seamless robe of concern and protection . . . prudence, discretion, judgement, foresight and knowledge—Russell had the professional virtues in abundance.'[29]

Unfortunately, very soon after this was published, rumours began to spread that all was not well. Murphy's original choice for executor, a member of staff, stood aside and the High Court appointed Laurence Crowley of Stokes Kennedy Crowley to take over the execution of the estate. It soon emerged that by a combination of mistaken investments (one particular property deal going sour) and extravagance, he had lost in the region of £1.5 million of his clients' money. What made this a *cause célèbre* was the fame of these clients. They included Gay Byrne, Ireland's premier broadcaster, who was devastated by the loss of his life's savings, Douglas Gageby, editor of *The Irish Times,* and the playwright Hugh Leonard. The latter could not resist waspishly commenting: 'I understand that I have lost more than any of the others affected, but my losses are proportionately lighter.'[30] Leonard was considerably less philosophical in his column in the *Sunday Independent* about his losses and about accountants generally. Embarrassingly, it was just then, as Henry Saville of Stokes Kennedy Crowley's Belfast office and the Institute's Council remembered, that Hugh Leonard had been invited to be the after-dinner speaker at the annual conference in Newcastle, County Down.[31] Gay Byrne attempted to sue some of Murphy's employees, arguing that they were *de facto* partners, as well as the Institute of Chartered Accountants in Ireland, but the cases were struck out in 1986 and that was the end of the matter.

The professional services model

In the 1980s the third business model of the profession, as a provider of professional financial services, became established. In this, the Irish firms were tracking the market-driven path trodden by their international partners in the US. By 1990 what was then the Big Six firms in the US (see *Table 2*) had firmly restructured their businesses. In 1975, between 60 and 75 per cent of their business had been audit; by 1990 none of the Big Six had as much as 60 per cent of its fees from audit, and Arthur Andersen had less than 50 per cent. Ten years later PricewaterhouseCoopers had barely 33 per cent from audit, and Touche Ross had only 31 per cent.[32]

Table 2: *The emergence of the Big Four*

<table>
<tr><th>Big Eight</th><th>Big Six 1989</th><th>Big Five 1998</th><th>Big Four 2002</th></tr>
<tr><td>Arthur Andersen</td><td rowspan="4">Ernst & Whinney merge with Arthur Young to form Ernst & Young</td><td rowspan="4">Coopers & Lybrand merge with Price Waterhouse to create Pricewaterhouse-Coopers</td><td rowspan="4">Arthur Andersen surrenders its licences to practice</td></tr>
<tr><td>Arthur Young</td></tr>
<tr><td>Coopers & Lybrand</td></tr>
<tr><td>Ernst & Whinney</td></tr>
<tr><td>Deloitte, Haskins & Sells</td><td rowspan="4">Deloitte, Haskins & Sells merge with Touche Ross to create Deloitte & Touche</td><td></td><td></td></tr>
<tr><td>KPMG</td><td></td><td></td></tr>
<tr><td>Price Waterhouse</td><td></td><td></td></tr>
<tr><td>Touche Ross</td><td></td><td></td></tr>
</table>

In Ireland, as Noel MacMahon testified, there opened up two fruitful new areas in particular: tax planning and consultancy. On the tax side the increasing complexity of the tax system after the 1975 reforms opened up avenues, and the demands of the international incoming companies opened more. On the consultancy side, a combination of the growing interest in numerate, information-led management and the simultaneous explosion in computer use were perfect opportunities for accountancy firms.

The profession's previous business models, first with accountants as specialists in insolvency, and secondly as generalist auditors, were steadily superseded. David Chapman of Chapman Flood, founded in 1981, one of the new middle-sized firms doing well, put it bluntly: 'the old concept of the auditor is dead'.[33] Not that the changes were uncontested. Many hankered after the fast-disappearing professional lifestyle. In discussing the change, John Callaghan, managing partner of Stokes Kennedy Crowley, which had developed over the decade to become the largest firm on the island with over 700 staff, recalled how 'an eminent accountant' some years ago gave warning to an Institute conference that 'we were in danger of being changed from a profession to a business'.[34] Many years later Cecil Donovan of Touche Ross (President of the Institute 1987–8) reflected that the new commercialism threatened 'a lowering of standards and ethics. It can also breach the essential of independence.'[35] A sceptical Timothy Quin of Atkinson & Boyd (later Touche Ross), Belfast, believed that 'corporate pressures in the audit market and the use of the audit as a loss leader in the marketing of a wider range of professional services [was leading] to more and more shortcuts in audit procedures.'[36] As a result he proposed that 'the arguments grow stronger for purification of the audit process and for its separation from the provision of other professional services'.

John Callaghan, however, accepted with relish the market-driven inevitability: 'whether we like it or not', he wrote, 'the modern practising accountancy firms are in business—the business of providing a range of professional services . . . it is only if practising accountants recognise that they are in business and act like businessmen' that they will succeed. And he identified the key to this success as 'quality of client service'.[37]

To provide these new services there was an organisational restructuring, most clearly seen in the larger firms.[38] In the ideal form of the old style, a group of generalist partners were involved in a loose coalition, each relating exclusively to his own clients for all their needs, and drawing on a common pool of clerks (qualified and unqualified seniors, and trainees) and other staff as required. The partner might be expected to give preference to the two clerks articled to himself. The first intermediate management level, audit managers, only appeared in the 1960s. The senior partner was normally just that, the oldest, and acted as chair and convenor of meetings and, if necessary, representative of the firm, but had little directive power. He typically retained all or most of his client load.

Because of the much larger numbers involved (by 1986, 12 Irish firms had 100 or more staff), the ideal form of the new configuration necessarily involved a much more elaborate management hierarchy. This now stretched from the 40 or more equity partners and salaried partners through service directors, managers, assistant managers, qualified and nearly qualified seniors to new clerks. The numerous partners were specialised, with one group doing audit, another tax, a third consultancy and so on. Each group was headed by a managing partner who was also a member of the managing partners' committee, chaired by an elected managing partner. He (invariably *he*) would be much more directive in managing the growth of the practice and be involved with little direct client work, except at a representative level.

In common with the country as a whole, money was increasingly visible (Ireland's first 'Rich List' was published in *Irish Business* magazine, January 1989). The old obscurity as to which partner was contributing how much was gone as computer-based billing and costings were introduced. Now the many more, younger, partners were under pressure to deliver fees. As a result, as Patricia Barker reported the results of a survey in the early 1990s: 'Irish accountants are working very long hours. 45 per cent of the men and 33 per cent of the women work in excess of 50 hours a week and there is a high incidence of work-related social activity and of nights spent away from home.'[39] In the US firms, where those hours would have seemed self-indulgently low, the CEOs of Big Eight firms such as Deloitte Haskins & Sells and Touche Ross began to challenge the traditional idea that partnership was, as Cecil Donovan put it 'a bonding for life, and a privilege which was greatly valued'.[40] In the 1960s the then CEO of Price Waterhouse in the US ran into a storm when he tried to remove a rogue partner; 20 years later multiple partner layoffs were not unheard of.[41] These giant firms wanted to be seen not as a professional firm dealing with business, but, as the Deloitte Haskins & Sells CEO put it, 'a business that happened to market professional services', and as such underperforming partners were as secure as underperforming salesmen in consumer goods companies.[42] In Ireland, as KPMG managing partner Terence O'Rourke believed, things were less abrupt: in his experience partners failing to achieve targets were moved sideways, and then usually (highly competitive individuals as they invariably were) felt the situation sufficiently to move to a less stressful environment.[43]

The new paradigm entailed a shift from the stiff, old production-oriented approach to a more flexible, customer-oriented style. In earlier times, it was taken as a mark of the professional ethic that regardless of what the client thought, 'the professional man or woman, like the craftsman, tends to put the job first, and will not be satisfied with second best'.[44] The new business-oriented stance was less insular, more looking towards the client for approbation. 'Alumni clubs' of people who had qualified in the firm and gone into industry were established as marketing tools—at first politely called 'practice development'. These clubs became important sources of contact between professional firms and businesses—what the well-known managing partner of US Arthur Andersen, Leonard Spacek, called his 'fifth column: when they got into business, they remembered their alma mater'. To that end he did his best to ensure that even those who had no prospect of a partnership remembered their experience with Arthur Andersen positively.[45]

From Europe there was a sense of unease about the impact of cross-selling on auditor independence. In 1984, the 'Eighth Directive', on auditors and auditing, talked vaguely of insisting on the 'independence' of the auditor, though without defining what this might entail.

Part of the new environment was the spread in Ireland of the practice, prevalent in the US since the 1970s, of asking several competitive firms to present their ideas and fees for the audit—a practice an earlier generation would have regarded as distasteful as advertising. As it happens, the ban against competitive bidding was only reluctantly lifted by the US professional association, the AICPA, in 1973 under federal government pressure against anti-competitive arrangements. This governmental action made a drastic change to the American profession, giving rise to cut-throat competition on audit fees and subsequent dependence on non-audit services.[46] An Irish example of such proposals survives from the successful 1988 bid for a state-sponsored body from one of the 'Big Eight' and shows the new 'service' culture in full flower.[47] The 'Proposal to Serve', as it is headed, offers: 'a highly efficient audit' incorporating 'value for money' and 'regular contact with the audit team'. Obviously there was no question of moving outside compliance standards, but the audit committee could hardly mistake the implications of a 'highly commercially oriented advice arising from our business approach to the audit' and 'an imaginative and constructive approach to accounting and auditing issues'. This bid document certainly does not celebrate the virtue of 'professional scepticism'. In the firm's newsletter the success of the bid was reported with the comment 'we will be aggressively looking for opportunities to provide [non-audit] services'.[48]

Although audit was still by a long way the biggest part of most firms' workload, by 1987 John Callaghan of Stokes Kennedy Crowley believed that the 'market for audit services is not growing and it is unlikely to do so at any appreciable rate in the foreseeable future'.[49] Of course, the newly diversifying firms were not going to stop doing audits. The function was too big and too embedded for that. Thus, Craig Gardner's total fee income for 1988 was £17.3 million, of which fully half came from audit—and of course an equivalent number of voting equity partners, who were unlikely to vote for any separation of powers. (The rancorous Andersen split on those lines was still in the future.) Craig Gardner's biggest fees at the time were from Waterford Glass (billed at £360,000) and Independent Newspapers (£161,000). By far the largest audit fee paid in Ireland at this time was the £961,000 that Jefferson Smurfit paid to two firms, Kinnear and Ernst & Whinney. Stokes Kennedy Crowley charged Cement Roadstone £465,000 for their audit, and Irish Distillers £181,000.[50]

Accountancy firms needed to look for growth from a range of other services. John Callaghan instanced an ambitious menu of possibilities: 'information systems, tax planning, corporate financial advice, pensions and compensation packages, strategic planning, management structures, marketing, distribution and production processing, management training and executive recruitment.'[51] No doubt he also had in mind the possibilities that the 1979 split with Sterling and the 1986 'Big Bang' deregulation of the UK financial sector might deliver, as well as the hoped-for consequences of the 1987 IFSC enabling Act. Not that anything was going to be handed over on a plate. Callaghan saw stiff competition to the profession generally, but especially perhaps to the Big Firms emerging from the banking sector, from solicitors' firms and others.

Amalgamation

Following the *Derryhale Report* of 1970, the Institute had begun to take increasingly seriously its responsibilities for education of trainees, which had previously been generally left to firms, technical colleges and postal tuition courses. Although the Institute, with 4,000 members in 1980, was comfortably the largest accountancy body in Ireland (north and south), this was not the whole story. The Association of Certified Accountants (which eventually became the Association of Chartered Certified Accountants (ACCA)) had 1,000 members in Ireland, the Institute of Cost and Management Accountants had 700 members and the Institute of Certified Public Accountants in Ireland had 350 members. There was also a new qualification of accounting technician with its own professional body attached to the Institute of Chartered Accountants in Ireland. Each of these bodies had its own administrative centre, separate training programmes, educational facilities and examination schedules.

In 1981, a radical plan emerged to amalgamate all these and create a cost-efficient unified body with 6,000 members and 7,000 students. Apart from the savings in costs and administrative effort, a unified body would have great advantages in political lobbying and would even perhaps have been able to achieve such goals as the establishment of a statutory register. Perhaps also there was a recognition that as the number of Institute members in practice became a minority, the character of that body was likely to change. There were, of course, problems with the proposal: what would the new amalgamated body be called? How would the amalgamated members be designated? What 'practice rights' would be available, given that the certified and cost accountants had little or no audit experience? What problems would arise from the fact that the ACCA and CIMA bodies were branches of UK parents while the Institute and the CPAs were locally based? What transition arrangements would be in place for already qualified members and for students? As we have seen, this was certainly not the first time such ideas of amalgamation and registration were mooted, and once again voting members dashed the elected officials' hopes. In February 1982, Institute President Noel Stewart (Belfast-based partner in Coopers & Lybrand) sadly admitted that yet again it had become clear that, as he put it, 'the chances of developing a detailed scheme that would attract the necessary support from the membership of the four bodies' was unacceptably low and discussion had been broken off.[52]

At the beginning of the decade Craig Gardner sent a summary of the top firms in the Irish market to its international partner Price Waterhouse. The two largest firms were Craig Gardner and Stokes Kennedy Crowley, with just under 600 staff. Of these, some 60 per cent were in audit and 15 per cent in tax. The balance were in secretarial services, consultancy and insolvency. Quite soon after this report, amalgamations among firms recommenced. In 1981 Cooper Magennis and three smaller firms combined to associate themselves with Touche Ross. This meant that what were then 'Big Eight' US accountancy practices were represented in Ireland. Some, such as Coopers & Lybrand, Arthur Andersen, Arthur Young, Ernst & Whinney and Deloitte, Haskins & Sells practised under their international names, while for the moment Stokes Kennedy Crowley (Peat Marwick), Craig Gardner (Price Waterhouse) and Cooper Magennis (Touche Ross) kept their Irish names.

The surging growth of the profession in Ireland can be seen when the figures in *Table 3* below are compared with comments from Howard Robinson's *History of Accountants in Ireland*.[53] He records that in 1962 there were 116 firms in Dublin; 'only 23 firms had more than two partners: Craig Gardner had ten Dublin partners; and another firm had seven partners; a third firm had six partners; there were five firms with five partners; three with four partners and 12 with three partners.' In 1962, the 23 multi-partner firms had 86 partners in total, one fewer than the top two firms had between them in 1986.

Table 3: *Top accountancy firms mid-1986 (ranked by numbers of staff)*

	Partners	Staff
Stokes Kennedy Crowley	44	711
Craig Gardner	43	633
Coopers & Lybrand	34	414
KMG Reynolds McCarron	28	272
Touche Ross	29	272
Oliver Freaney	34	247
Ernst & Whinney	19	213
Haughey Boland	13	202
Arthur Andersen	10	190
Arthur Young	9	140
Kinnear	19	116
Deloitte, Haskins & Sells	8	100

Source: *The Irish Times* 20 December 1986. The average ratio of partners to staff is 1:12.

The next significant amalgamation news came a few years later when, in 1986, Haughey Boland announced it was merging with Deloitte Haskins & Sells. This pushed the combined firm to Number 4 in the rankings. A year or two later KMG Reynolds McCarron and Stokes Kennedy Crowley followed the international combination of Peat Marwick and KMG to create the Irish office of KPMG, though for the moment continuing to practice under the Stokes Kennedy flag. Of course, not all merger plans went smoothly: in 1984 a mega-merger between Price Waterhouse and Deloitte, Haskins & Sells fell through, and in 1989 the merger of Arthur Young and O'Hare Barry collapsed when the Arthur Young team wanted to follow the international merger that had created Ernst & Young, and managing partner Aidan Barry decided he was not interested in being part of such a large operation. The combined firm would have had 53 partners and 620 staff.[54]

By the end of the decade the order at the top of the table was much the same (ranked by fees billed) but it was noted that several smaller firms, such as Simpson Xavier and Chapman Flood, were pushing ahead.

Table 4: *Accountancy firms' income in 1989*[55]

Firm	*Fees 1989 (£m)*	*International Associate*
SKC	25	KPMG
Craig Gardner	18	Price Waterhouse
Coopers & Lybrand	14	Coopers & Lybrand
Ernst & Whinney	10.5	Ernst & Whinney
Deloitte Haskins & Sells	8	Deloitte Haskins & Sells
Arthur Andersen	7.5	Arthur Andersen
Touche Ross	6.5	Touche Ross
Arthur Young	5.5	Arthur Young
BDO Binder Hamlyn	3.8	BDO Binder Hamlyn
Grant Thornton	3	Grant Thornton
Oliver Freaney	2.8	Spicer & Oppenheim
Simpson Xavier	1.8	Horwath & Horwath
Pannell Kerr Forster	1.6	Pannell Kerr Forster
Farrell Grant Sparks	1.4	IMPACT
John Woods	1.1	Moores Rowland
Chapman Flood	0.93	Nevill Russell/Summit
Gilroy Gannon	0.9	Touche Ross
Hayden Brown	0.9	N/A
Bastow Charlton	0.8	N/A
O'Connor Leddy Holmes	0.98	Urbach Hacker Young
Kenny Mathews Hogan Clarke	0.73	N/A
Duignan	0.7	N/A

Source: *Finance* magazine August 1989

It had long been obvious that a small number of large firms were dominating the industry. For instance, of the 15 presidents of the Institute between 1967 and 1981, only three were not members of the large firms. (One of these three, in 1978–9, was Gerry Dempsey of Aer Lingus, the first president from industry.) It was, however, only when firms became less coy about their incomes that it was possible to see how marked the domination of the 'Big Eight' actually was. The total fee incomes for the top 22 firms, as listed in *Finance* magazine, was £116.4 million. Of this, the top eight firms garnered fully £95 million (82 per cent), and the top three just over £57 million (49 per cent).

The sophisticated package offered by the big firms was not, of course, suitable to all. Younger, smaller practices were adept in providing personalised, partner-level service, often at considerably lower fees to small and medium-sized concerns that did not require the full panoply.[56] And there were still numerous sole practitioners, many of whom were still engaged in the kind of 'book-keeping audit' that had long passed out of the hands of the Big Eight. The Institute had recognised this in the formation in 1977 of the Small Practitioners Standing Committee, chaired by future President Cecil Donovan.

Tax—the flammable issue

A few days after Haughey's television appearance in January 1980, as many as 700,000 people marched in protest against the tax system, 300,000 in Dublin and the rest in 36 towns and cities across the country.[57] It was (and remains) by a long way the most widely attended protest in the history of the Irish State. Responding to a Trades Union Congress appeal, workers brought everything but vital services to a halt: factories, shops, offices, schools, banks, restaurants and even pubs closed. Trains, buses and planes were grounded.

The protest was against the injustice of the tax system, which had certainly leant heavily on the captive PAYE workers in recent years. Income tax as a per cent of GNP had risen from 5.6 per cent in 1970 to 11.9 per cent in 1980. At the same time, inflation had eroded allowances and effectively narrowed bands so that, for instance, whereas a married man with three young children had paid 2.8 per cent of average industrial earnings in tax in 1970; by 1980 this had soared to 14.3 per cent.[58] The narrowing of the bands meant that over 40 per cent of taxpayers were faced with a marginal rate of 45 per cent or higher. Before 1975, fewer than 5 per cent of Irish taxpayers had paid tax at more than the standard rate. Other drains on personal spending were also up: social insurance contributions had doubled in the same time, and VAT had risen nearly 40 per cent—there were five VAT bands, running from zero to 35 per cent. Receipts from corporate profits tax, by comparison, had fallen from 2.7 per cent of GNP to 1.7 per cent. With good reason, PAYE workers were convinced that farmers and the self-employed paid considerably less than their fair share.

Despite the vociferous concerns about the inefficiency and injustice of the tax system, the monster protest march achieved nothing. Five years later, the income tax bands had been widened, a bit, but the top rate had gone from 60 to 65 per cent, and income tax represented an even higher proportion of the total revenue. The main governmental reaction to the march was to adopt a traditional method of putting an awkward problem on the long finger—they appointed a Commission. (The first Commission on Income Taxation had reported in 1962 and included recommendations on death duties, sales taxes, capital taxation and the organisation of the Revenue department.) The new Commission was headed by Miriam Hederman-O'Brien and included two economists, two trade unionists and two accountants—James Gallagher, head of taxation at Arthur Andersen, and Patrick O'Neill, described as a farmer and accountant.[59] The reports of this Commission began to be issued in July 1982, starting with *Direct Taxation*. The governments of the day kept to the tradition—they widely admired the result, and did nothing.[60]

Tax, both in terms of incidence and justice, remained a hot topic throughout the 1980s. (In that barometer of public concerns, *The Irish Times,* the simple word 'tax' was used nearly twice as often in the 1980s as in the 1960s: the phrase 'tax avoidance' was used over 10 times as often.)

As usual in tough economic times, the public wondered if the rich, aided by the accountancy profession, were 'getting away with it'. An article in *The Irish Times* expressed the point thus:

> 'the *raison d'être* of accountants is the taxman. Nobody would be half as interested in employing accountants if income tax, corporation tax, capital gains tax, capital acquisition tax and all the other nasties didn't exist . . . an accountant's ingenuity is stretched each year to find other new ways of avoiding tax for his client . . . the ordinary man in the street can benefit only marginally from an accountant's advice.'[61]

Opportunities for tax mitigation typically arose because the simple money-raising objective became confused by a well-meaning attempt to favour one activity or another. In his *History*, Revenue Commissioner Seán Réamonn told the archetypal story of the Entertainments Stamp Duty originally introduced in 1916 and finally abolished in 1961. Over time, various exemptions were introduced (for instance, for entertainments promoting Irish, or those with a substantial percentage of live performance). Soon it was learnt that in cinemas up and down the country managers were gaining tax relief by hiring elderly fiddlers to play to an empty house from, as it were, 2.30 to 8.00pm, and then showing films to a packed hall thereafter.[62] Examples like these reinforced the Revenue Commissioners' distaste for such exemptions, which always complicated their prime task, that is, to collect the required tax as quickly and cheaply as possible.

Despite this distaste, exemptions and incentives became a favourite political tool, especially in the new taxes introduced in the 1970s. As Joe O'Broin of Craig Gardner put it in his book, *Tax and Business Decisions* 'the operation of incentives has become highly complex with the introduction of new taxes in recent years. Every new tax—corporation tax, capital gains tax, gift and inheritance tax—contains its own form of incentives.'[63] *Tax and Business Decisions* details some of the everyday business actions that might have tax implications:

- Investment in building or machinery
- Dispersal of fixed assets
- Setting up an export project
- Investment in trading stocks
- Financing arrangements
- Mergers and take-overs
- Undertaking research
- Paying dividends
- Setting up a manufacturing project
- Group re-organisation.

Not only did the potential for tax mitigation affect so many decisions, but because rates varied so widely, the effects of failing to take tax into account could be significant. For instance, the capital allowances for retail establishments was nil, for market gardens and farm buildings 30 per cent, but for intensive farming 54 per cent. Industrial buildings (including hotels) attracted 100 per cent, as did machinery. The effective rate of corporation tax ran from nil for exports and Shannon-based companies to 45 per cent for trading companies, 54 per cent for service companies and 56 per cent for investment companies. The piecemeal evolution of the system of incentives stimulated complexity. For instance, certain operations, such as book publishing, design services and fish farming, qualified as 'manufacturing' for the purposes of export and were thus entitled to 100 per cent export sales relief, but were *not* so classified for the purposes of corporation tax. A series of cases established, on the other hand, that blending tea, bottling bulls' semen, pasteurising milk and ripening bananas were all 'manufacturing' within the meaning of the Finance Act and so could avail of favourable corporation tax rates. (Not that things came easily; it took Stokes Kennedy Crowley five years to prepare and win the 'banana case'—*Inspector of Taxes v. Fyffes Banana Processing Ltd*—with the final judgment being made in the Supreme Court.[64])

The complexity of the system and the demand from clients for tax work meant that tax departments became increasingly prominent in accountancy firms. In Joe O'Broin's own firm, Craig Gardner, for instance, the tax department grew from a mere 16 people in 1970 (6 per cent of all employees) to 85 in 1980 (15 per cent of all) and 150 in 1990 (26 per cent). This latter figure included 14 partners, or as many as the whole firm had in 1970. By 1990 the tax department contributed 34 per cent of the firm's surplus.

It was the policy of the law to consider only the 'letter' of a scheme and not to look behind this front. In the early 1980s, two English cases, *Ramsay v. Inland Revenue* (1981) and *Furniss v. Dawson* (1984), seemed to allow the Inland Revenue to look behind the letter of a set of transactions to the underlying motivation. In 1989, in a case called *McGrath v. MacDermott (Inspector of Taxes)*, the Revenue Commissioners brought to the Irish High Court a complex series of transactions engineered solely (and admittedly) to achieve artificial losses for the purpose of avoiding capital gains tax.[65] Justice Mella Carroll refused to follow the English cases, declaring that it was not for the courts to inquire into the motivation behind transactions, as long as they were each and cumulatively legal. Ms Justice Carroll pushed the problem firmly back into the lap of the Government, saying, as *The Irish Times* reported: 'tax laws were for the legislature to enact, and if the lawmakers failed to plug a hole in advance or even to enact a general anti-avoidance law then the courts could not be expected to intervene'. The Supreme Court endorsed her decision.[66]

The elaborate efforts to reduce the contribution to the exchequer of rich men and women such as the McGraths, especially in the dire economic circumstances of the mid-1980s, gave rise to ambiguous feelings. On the one hand, it was infuriating for the ordinary PAYE worker to have to pay so much tax. On the other, there was a general view that if any tax mitigation was available it should be grabbed with both hands, combined with a rueful admiration of 'cute hoors'. So if the well-known actor Joe Lynch of the TV soap *Glenroe* was able to channel his earnings through the Isle of Man, like other entertainers and sportsmen, good luck to him.[67] The 'cutest hoor' of them all, Charles Haughey, aided by his former colleagues from Haughey Boland, Des Traynor and others, was widely admired in this light.[68] In 1984 Taoiseach Garret FitzGerald took the moral high ground, as usual, arguing that 'extraordinarily insensitive' tax avoidance by wealthy people was causing unease and instability in the country. FitzGerald referred particularly to a procedure called 'bond washing', which exploited the fact that bond prices rose just before an interest payment was made. If the investor sold just before the payment, he created a tax-free capital gain. This was perfectly legal in Ireland, though prohibited in Britain. FitzGerald went so far as to describe such schemes as 'one of the major political problems we face'.[69]

ICAI President Margaret Downes took an unusual step for the Institute at that time in responding directly and publicly. The problem as she saw it was that the Government continually adds tax incentives and allowances to a tax structure already 'riddled with anomalies'. It was hardly for Government to complain if people quite legally responded to these incentives and took advantage of what was on offer. 'In my view', she said, 'the government is insensitive and causing uncertainty for sincere and thrifty people who are trying to invest their money.' She put her finger on the practical difficulties of FitzGerald's position by highlighting the legal but morally grey area between ordinary tax avoidance ('a couple both earning £9,000 could save £1,200 by marrying between now and April 5th' wrote *The Irish Times* on St Valentine's Day in 1983) and highly artificial schemes that teetered towards evasion. Exactly at what point, she asked to be told, does legal tax avoidance become unacceptable?[70] Years before, Institute President David Telford had asked that tax compliance be addressed 'in the spirit of the income tax laws', but the taxpayer who could afford professional advice was looking for something more precise—in effect, the payment of as little tax as possible inside the law.

The cheerful amorality of tens of thousands of depositors in evading DIRT during the 1980s, actively aided by the banking system, suggests that FitzGerald's view was not widely held. The results of the 1988 tax amnesty, in which 170,000 people owned up and delivered over £500 million to the exchequer, rather confirmed this. The scale of this windfall, one-sixth of the 1988 income tax receipts, was reminiscent of the back-duty cases of the 1920s. Anecdotal evidence suggested that the vast majority of payers were not actually hardened tax dodgers, but self-employed and small business people who had fallen behind and were glad of the chance to tidy things up.

Women in accounting

A rather late consequence of the forceful feminism of the 1970s (exemplified by the 1971 stunt of importing still-illegal contraceptives from Belfast by train) was the slowly growing number of women becoming members of the profession. There had of course been precursors, starting with Eileen Woodworth, whose father had been a signatory of the Charter petition. She qualified in 1925. She was followed by others, in ones and twos, for the next 50 years. It was not until 1977 that as many as 1 per cent of members were women.

Until the 1980s few women chose accountancy. In fact, the profession just beat engineering and the Army at the bottom of the per-cent-of-women table. The 1981 Census reported that 62 per cent of teachers were female, 25 per cent of medical practitioners, 20 per cent of the legal profession and 1.4 per cent of accountants. Part of the reason for the poor showing may have been the old idea that women were 'naturally' not good at maths, and so girls' schools put less effort into teaching the subject. Slowly thereafter things changed. In 1984, Niamh Brennan (who had qualified with Stokes Kennedy Crowley) noted that there were then 221 female members of the Institute, of whom two-thirds were working in professional offices. There were 24 women 'in practice' (i.e. running their own business or at partnership level), most of whom were sole practitioners. Of the eight in partnerships only two were in large offices, of whom the best-known was Margaret Downes of Coopers & Lybrand.[71]

Two years later, in 1986, Marie O'Connor became Craig Gardner's first female partner. On the way up, she, like most of her female colleagues, had been subjected to low-level prejudice and occasional discrimination. When she started in the early 1970s, most women's career paths were simple: they would work for a while, get married and spend the rest of their lives looking after house and children. They would also drop out of the public world; exceptions applied, but generally even unmarried women could not get a mortgage without a male guarantor, nor could they purchase goods on hire-purchase without a male guarantor, nor could they serve on a jury. If married, they could not receive gynaecological surgery or collect the Children's Allowance without their husband's written permission.[72] Only 7 per cent of women worked outside the home, though this was to change in 1973 when the ban on married women working in the Civil Service and other state arenas (which by convention extended also to large companies) was raised as a result of pressure from the EEC.

When Marie O'Connor applied for a place in the accounting class in Rathmines Technical College, she was to be the only women in the class. Her interviewer commented sarcastically: 'if you're looking for a husband, you'd have a better selection in UCD'.[73] She joined Craig Gardner in 1974 and encountered there few overt prejudices, but audit managers sometimes felt obliged to check in advance if a woman clerk would be acceptable. One client frankly replied, 'Oh yes, send down lots of little girls, but not as a senior!'

Patricia Barker, who qualified with Stokes Brothers & Pim in 1973, recalled how the appearance of a woman auditor could cause a bit of a stir. There was the time she went to the B&I, the semi-State shipping company, to check that the wages were being handed out properly. '"Will yiz shurrup and listen!', bawled the clerk to the queue, "this girl wants to make sure you are all there, physically".' The ribald implications of this took a minute to sink in, and then the men erupted with laughter and a rich variety of suggestions. On another occasion she turned up to do a physical stock-check at Irish Distillers in Midleton in 'a pale lilac number with a flared miniskirt'—no wonder the startled clerk (vividly aware of the fungus-covered state of the old warehouse with its wall-to-wall cobwebs) called to his boss, 'th' otter's here and it's a woman and she wants to taste the whiskey!'[74]

The women who entered the profession at this time certainly did not 'drift' into it, unlike perhaps some of their male colleagues who might have taken up accountancy for want of other ideas. They were clearly identifiable as pioneers and subject to all sorts of ancient prejudices. For instance there were lingering feelings that women were not technically able, or that they lacked qualities such as ambition, assertiveness and leadership, though there was no evidence of the former from the exam statistics (in May 1994 *Accountancy Ireland* reported that nine out of the top 11 places in Professional Two that year were women), or the latter from women's achievements in other fields. More problematic was the question of children. Even in firms with equal numbers of men and women starting as trainees, at every stage of promotion, as time demands grew, fewer and fewer women were present. In Patricia Barker's research three-quarters of women accountants questioned clearly attributed this to motherhood. 'There is evidence, however,' she wrote, 'that these professional mothers do not want to give up their profession completely and are anxious to find ways and means of combining career with motherhood.'[75] In a profession that was rapidly escalating the degree of commitment it demanded of senior people, this was a tough ask. Ironically, had the cultural configuration permitted, it would have been much easier for such women in the gentlemanly 1950s.

The centenary year

The British Prime Minister James Callaghan once said that every 30 years or so there came to be a change of the tide of public opinion, against which politicians struggled in vain. Such a change produced the elections of Margaret Thatcher in 1979 and Ronald Reagan in 1980. The hallmarks of their economic policies were tight control of money supply, low taxation, reduced government spending and light touch regulation. This tide hit Ireland some few years later, in 1987, when Ray MacSharry became Minister for Finance and immediately initiated such a wave of public expenditure cuts he was dubbed 'Mack the Knife'. At the same time, section 30 of the Finance Act 1987 initiated the formation of the International Financial Services Centre (IFSC) in Dublin.

By the Institute's centenary year of 1988 the world had changed very considerably from when just 31 accountants petitioned the Privy Council for a Charter. There were now 6,200 members. In those early days Belfast was one of the most prosperous places in Britain and Dublin barely more than an elegant backwater. Belfast had world-scale industries in shipbuilding, linen, rope-making and tobacco, not to mention the hosts of ancillary businesses. By contrast, the South was then predominantly agricultural, with a few industries, such as Guinness and Jacobs, that were very close to their agricultural sources. As we have seen, the strength of the accountancy profession in the North had been a marked feature of the membership of the Institute for its first 50 years.

Now, driven by foreign direct investment from the US, from Japan and from Europe, the Republic's economy was showing new strength, and with it the local accountancy profession. Two-thirds of members of the Institute now came from the Republic and less than one-fifth from Northern Ireland. Part of this of course was caused by the new importance of the European Union. In a commemorative book of essays published to celebrate the Centenary, Timothy Quin of Touche Ross in Belfast noted the historic shift: 'whereas Belfast remains a provincial city, Dublin has become a capital city and a financial centre of some importance.'[76]

Perhaps as a consequence the focus of the larger practices in Dublin and Belfast were different. In Belfast they saw themselves 'operating on a Belfast–London axis . . . at least two of the Big Eight firms have Belfast offices that are wholly integrated within their UK partnership. Others are independent Northern Ireland partnerships linking in with their Great Britain counterparts.' Of Dublin practices, only Stokes Kennedy Crowley operated on an all-Ireland basis. Quin hoped, however, that since 'world-wide economic and commercial pressures [were] making political boundaries less important for accounting firms, EEC influence and closer correlation of the Irish and UK economies may well make the Dublin–Belfast axis a more meaningful mode of operation in the future.'[77]

In the course of the centennial year, the Institute elected its second president from industry, Eugene Greene, Managing Director of Goodalls, a food manufacturing company based in Dublin. In the customary interview with the Editor of *Accountancy Ireland*, the new President looked forward particularly to the changes the single market of the EEC planned for 1992 would produce. As a businessman, rather than a practising accountant, Eugene Greene was quite critical of the way the efforts of the Institute had been always been biased towards practice. 'We do not give the same service to our members on industry.' He went on to speculate whether it would be sensible to set up a separate division within the Institute catering for those in industry, financial services and commerce. Towards the end of the interview this Donegal man expressed particular pleasure in the fact that the Institute continued to be an all-Ireland institution and 'had maintained a strong sense of community between members in Northern Ireland and in the Republic throughout a period of turbulent change on this island'.[78]

In respect of the professional firm, Timothy Quin looked forward with some apprehension to various changes. These seemed likely to continue due to the growth of multi-disciplinary businesses, with giant accountancy firms following the logic of the provision of professional services and taking first lawyers, then computer engineers and marketing specialists under their wing. (Following its international partners, PwC in Ireland established Landwell Solicitors in 1999, though the firm was acquired by Beauchamp Solicitors in 2012.) To meet the needs of the EEC's Eighth Directive, the audit side of the practice would, he speculated, be hived off into a semi-autonomous unit. This expansion would demand much more capital. Legislation permitting, this would most likely be supplied by incorporation and flotation, or the selling of equity to banks, insurance companies and other financial institutions.[79] As Alan Gibson (President 1987–8) put it, in this view of the future, chartered accountants would 'face the challenge of remaining a learned and objective profession whilst responding to the ever-changing market place'.[80]

Chapter Nine
The Rise and Rise of Accountancy: the 1990s

[We start by] assuming that the existing state of affairs will continue indefinitely, except in so far as we have specific reasons to expect a change. This does not mean that we really believe that the existing state of affairs will continue indefinitely. We know from experience that this is most unlikely. The actual results of an investment over the long term very seldom agree with the initial expectation.

John Maynard Keynes, The General Theory of Employment, Interest and Money (1936)

In November 1989 the cruel Wall that had split Berlin for nearly 30 years was torn down. With it came the end of the hostile world-contest that had been the background to everyone's lives since 1917. The mighty struggle between capitalism and communism had been fought both directly and by proxy all over the world, and now capitalism—individualism, property and the market—had won. This was so profound a change that the American historian Francis Fukuyama famously called it 'the end of history'. Another historian, Eric Hobsbawm, noted that 'there can be no serious doubt that in the late 1980s and early 1990s an era in world history came to an end and a new one began'.[1] For him, what he called the 'Short Twentieth Century' ran between two iconic events: the outbreak of the First World War in 1914 and the collapse of the Berlin Wall in 1989.

Inevitable as the result might now seem, especially from this side of Europe, it should be remembered that, at the international conference of accountants hosted by the Institute in Dublin a mere 10 years before, a professor of economics from Czechoslovakia had proposed that the ideal for the future was a combination of the two systems. Modestly accepting the plaudits for the change were two leaders of the Western world, Ronald Reagan and Margaret Thatcher, for whom 'the market' was a magic space where economic miracles occurred. Although they left the political stage in 1989 and 1990 respectively, their successors, George Bush and John Major, hardly represented policy change.

Irish people had looked on the Cold War as fascinated spectators, but spectators in a game that had not much affected them. Fleeting attempts were made by establishment figures in the 1960s to persuade the public that Ireland was in some way in the front line in the fight against communism. It was claimed that sinister infiltration of the trade union movement was likely (there were, we were told, *at least* 100 members of the Communist Party in the country), or failing that, since the country lacked radar defences, a sudden air attack from Russian paratroopers swooping down from 20,000 feet and taking over the country during the night.[2] But even the possibility of 'misguided missiles'—one alone could incinerate the whole of inner Dublin from the Four Courts to the North Circular Road—failed to alarm anyone very much.[3] The one exception to the general insouciance was the Cuban Missile Crisis of late 1962, which certainly succeeded in filling the confessionals for the week or so of its duration.

The Celtic Tiger

In the Republic, 1987 had witnessed a major economic turning point, ushering in what Peter Sutherland has called a 'sparkling period' for the Irish economy, which lasted until 2002.[4] Taoiseach Charles Haughey and his Minister for Finance Ray MacSharry, having promised during the election to increase public expenditure, suddenly reversed course on being elected and began a stringent course of fiscal rectitude. Patrick Honahan has suggested that the goad was a real fear of 'a financial melt-down, with foreign and domestic financial market refusal to rollover debt'.[5] MacSharry's path was made considerably easier by the self-denying 'Tallaght Strategy' in which, in the general interest, Fine Gael leader Alan Dukes agreed not to oppose appropriate tax hikes and expenditure cuts. Steadily, and harshly, the excesses of the late 1970s and early 1980s were corrected, in a way that the Fine Gael/Labour coalitions of 1982–7 had been unable to agree on.

In the January following the election, *The Economist* published an uncomfortable survey of the Republic, reminding us of those excesses. It noted the country's 'extravagance, frustration, debt' caused by 'a passionate desire to enjoy the same lifestyle as its former masters'. 'Ireland', it wrote, 'is easily the poorest country in rich north-west Europe. Its gross domestic product is a mere 64 per cent of the European Community average.'[6] *The Economist* pointed out that economic growth had averaged only 0.2 per cent over the previous five years, including negative growth in three of those years; unemployment was 18 per cent of the labour force and national debt was 125 per cent of GNP. Ireland, it seemed, was a basket case, a banana republic, only tolerated at the big table of the EEC because it was so small.

Extraordinarily, once the public finances were restored to order a new combination of factors came together which created the phenomenon latterly called 'the Celtic Tiger'. The most important factors in Ireland's success in the 1990s were the advancing European project and the globalisation of world trade. From the beginning, voters in the Republic had been enthusiastic Europeans, combining a lively awareness of benefits from the Common Agricultural Policy and regional funds with an enthusiasm for getting out from under the influence of the old colonial master. The initial referendum vote, in 1973, was passed by 83 per cent; the next landmark, the Single European Act of 1986 was passed by 70 per cent; and the Maastricht Treaty in 1992 which ultimately led to the creation of the Euro, was passed by 69 per cent. Quite quickly, Ireland became skilled at extracting money from various European funds. As economist Antoin Murphy commented, however, 'there was still some way to go to learn the other side of the European story, namely the need to accept stronger fiscal discipline'.[7]

It was another piece of good luck, skillfully ridden, that Ireland shifted towards Europe just at the time when major US corporations, especially in information technology and 'big pharma', realised that, particularly with the Single European Market on the horizon, 'the establishment of a European base from which they could market their goods became a priority'.[8] As a result of the IDA's efforts over two decades there were already companies from the US and many other countries in Ireland, and they were able to report positively on the experience. By the late 1980s and early 1990s Ireland was well positioned to serve as America's entry point into Europe with a new raft of products.

A second factor was the very low corporate tax rate. Paradoxically, Ireland was able to offer this because of its weak manufacturing sector. Countries such as France or Germany with well-established manufacturing industries simply could not afford to undermine their existing tax receipt structure with such rates. Later on, Ireland consolidated its reputation as a low tax regime by reducing personal tax rates. Once companies were established in Ireland, whether as manufacturers or in the newly created International Financial Services Centre (IFSC), transfer pricing, as the tax skills of local and corporate accountants took into account international tax differentials, enabled maximum benefit to be gained. The scale and importance of transfer pricing is difficult to estimate.[9]

Ireland of course had other advantages besides tax rates. It was English-speaking, and clearly committed to Europe, as Britain was not. Its young people were well-educated, flexible and easy to work with. Crucially, wages were low by European standards—as late as 1999 the OECD found that Ireland's wage cost per hour averaged at DM24.27, which made it 17th out of 29 OECD countries, with Germany being top at DM46.96 per hour, France at DM33.04 and the UK at DM31.09.[10] Industrial relations were orderly, with almost 100 per cent adherence to agreements under the Social Partnership arrangements which had started in 1987, trading low wage increases for lighter taxation. Ireland had a lighter bureaucratic touch, and its size made possible quick access to key decision-makers in government or finance. And finally, not to be ignored, was the 'diaspora dividend'—the fact that 40 million Americans claimed some affinity with Ireland, a point underlined by successive visits from US presidents.

Such was the success of the new policies, combined with developments in Europe and the growing enthusiasm of US companies for access to Europe, that as early as 1994 the phenomenon was nicknamed 'the Celtic Tiger' by a Morgan Stanley researcher,[11] and by 1997 *The Economist* was eating its words in a lead editorial entitled 'Ireland's shining light'. 'Today', the journal now wrote, Ireland 'is about as prosperous as the European average and getting richer all the time.'[12]

The accountancy profession

The 1991 Census revealed that there were 9,800 accountants in the country, of whom nearly a quarter were women.[13] The proportion of women members of the Institute, at 12 per cent, was considerably lower than the Census figure, though the much higher proportion of women students suggested that this was about to change. Even if we assume that half of all accountants were in business, the number in practice, relative to the population and the economy, is large compared to the 11,800 *wirtschaftsprüfer* (public auditors) in Germany or a similar number of *commissaires aux comptes* in France. For historical reasons Ireland had followed the US and the UK in making accountancy, and not for instance engineering, the language of business. For a generation or more, accountancy had been seen as the ideal launching pad for a career in general management. Quietly, in business after business, the accountant became a key figure. The Institute's membership list for 1995 shows how the profession had in fact become central to so many Irish businesses: a sample shows members as senior managers in companies as varied as Adair Printing, Aer Rianta, AIB, Avonmore, Bank of Ireland, Bord Bia, Cadbury Ireland, Campbell Catering, CIÉ, Clondalkin Group, DCC, FBD Holdings, Fyffes, Golden Vale, Heitons, Independent Newspapers, Irish Film Institute, Kingspan, NTMA, Odlums, Silvermines, Temple Bar Properties, Toyota Ireland and Waterford Stanley, to take just a few pages.

One typical such accountant in business was Leo O'Donnell, the 69th President of the Institute of Chartered Accountants in Ireland. He was born in Derry in 1937, before his family moved back to their home county of Sligo in the 1940s. Here he was educated at Summerhill College, where as a new boy at the age of 13 he was immediately faced with the life-changing decision of studying either Greek or commerce. He chose commerce, the first step to a career in accountancy. After school he was articled with Kean & Co., one of the founding firms of what has now become PwC. Qualifying in 1960, he worked for a couple of years in Price Waterhouse in London and then in Dublin before plumping for industry in 1963. He joined the paint company Harringtons and Goodlass Wall in Cork (now part of the Dutch AkzoNobel group) and then moved in the early 1970s to W. & R. Jacob as Finance Director, then Personnel Director and finally Managing Director for 20 years. During that time he saw the company merged with Bolands to form Irish Biscuits and move the factory to Tallaght, County Dublin. He continued (at least until the death of the initiator Frankie Byrne) the famous Jacob's Awards for radio and television. These had been started in 1962 in the time of his predecessor as Managing Director, Gordon Lambert, also a chartered accountant.

In the customary Presidential interview in *Accountancy Ireland,* O'Donnell stressed the value of the chartered accountancy qualification in business: 'the habit of disciplined thinking, the sense of objectivity and the emphasis on integrity instilled into the training of a chartered accountant [are] invaluable assets. Different career paths, of course, require different temperaments, but the young chartered accountant is uniquely equipped to pursue a wide variety of post qualifications careers.'[14]

Accountants in practice tended to be less high profile, apart from the well-known liquidators such as Laurence Crowley and Tom Grace, the ex-rugby international.

The best-known accountant in public life was still Charles Haughey (Taoiseach until 1992). In 1991 Haughey became the first recipient of the Institute's new Distinguished Member Award at a special dinner at which over 600 members and guests attended.[15] The presentation of this award suggests that if such a highly connected set of men and women had no knowledge of his financial circumstances, the secrets were well-kept. Another well-known political accountant, Charlie McCreevey, was still a backbencher: his opportunity was to come with Haughey's successor, Albert Reynolds. A new political name from the profession, Joan Burton, gained her first seat on Dublin Council in 1991.

Most of the accountants identified by the Census were members of the Institute of Chartered Accountants in Ireland, which now had 6,800 members (up from 4,000 in 1980); of the other main bodies, the Chartered Association of Certified Accountants (later ACCA) had 1,350 members and the Chartered Institute of Management Accountants (CIMA) had 800. Another body, the Institute of Certified Public Accountants in Ireland (ICPAI), also claimed 800 members.[16] These three, with the Institute, made up the Consultative Committee of Accountancy Bodies–Ireland (CCAB–I) which had been established in 1988 to coordinate their activities, particularly in respect of the standards-creating process going on in London, but with a mandate also to liaise with the government departments in respect of forthcoming legislation that might affect the profession as a whole. There were also 42,000 book-keepers (mostly women). This was a new Ireland—for the first time ever, as the Census showed, there were more accountants in the country than priests and nuns.

The thousand or more young people entering the profession in 1990 had a wide set of possible destinations. The first choice was: practice or industry? And in both the second choice was: big, medium or small? Newly qualified accountants could join one of the 'Big Seven' (progressively to be whittled down, mostly by amalgamations, to what is now the 'Big Four'), that is (in alphabetical order): the hugely respected Arthur Andersen; Coopers & Lybrand; Craig Gardner; Deloitte Haskins & Sells; Ernst & Young; Stokes Kennedy Crowley; and Touche Ross. These, in common with the market as a whole, had grown rapidly in recent years. In 1987, the fee income of the top seven firms was £85 million—in 1990 it was £142 million, a striking rise in conditions of low inflation—a simple indication that the new range of services in addition to simple audit was extremely acceptable to the business market. The market was still substantially skewed. As much as 78 per cent of the fees earned by the top 24 accountancy firms went to the Big Seven. The logic of amalgamation (at least for the partners) is exposed by the fact that this 78 per cent of fees was earned by a disproportionate 66 per cent of partners (see *Table 1*). The fee income per chargeable staff was just 15 per cent better in the Big Seven firms.

Table 1: *Accountancy firms in 1990 with more than £1 million in fees*

Firms	*Fees (£m)*	*Partners*	*Chargeable Staff*
SKC (the only firm reporting all-island figures)	30	47	706
Craig Gardner	22	45	527
Ernst & Young	18	44	410
Coopers & Lybrand	16	37	365
Arthur Andersen	10	12	179
Deloitte Haskins & Sells	9.5	16	308
Touche Ross	7	25	190
Grant Thornton	3.7	14	72
Oliver Freaney	3.1	10	85
IFAC[17]	3		130
Simpson Xavier	2.5	10	78
BDO Binder Hamlyn	2.2	7	54
Pannell Kerr Foster	2.2	5	54
Bastow Charleton	1.8	10	38
V. F. Nathan	1.6	5	52
Farrell Grant Sparks	1.6	3	41
Cooney Carey	1.6	7	42
O'Hare Barry	1.5	7	42
Chapman Flood	1.2	3	26
O'Connor Leddy Holmes	1.2	7	30
John Woods	1.2	9	26
McGrath & Co.	1.1	5	36
Hayden Brown	1	7	19
Gilroy Gannon	1	6	40
Top 24 firms totals	144	341	4250
Top seven totals	112.5	226	2685
Top seven as % of top 24	78.13%	66.28%	63.18%

Source: Finance July & August 1990

The amalgamations of previous decades had swept up once well-known second-tier names such as Reynolds McCarron, now part of KPMG, and Haughey Boland, now part of Deloitte Haskins & Sells. So the second tier of those firms with an income of £1 million or more consisted mostly of new names, with only Oliver Freaney (whose founder came to prominence in the late 1940 and early 1950s as a GAA star) standing. Some of these, such as Grant Thornton and Pannell Kerr Forster, were the Irish representatives of international groupings; others, such as Simpson Xavier and Farrell Grant Sparks, were of new local growth. Below this level again there were numerous firms with only one or two partners—in fact, 550 of the 950 firms in Ireland were sole practitioners, no doubt performing exactly the task their professional ancestors performed in the early days of the profession—i.e. using book-keeping and accountancy skills and other technical knowledge to translate the messes of everyday life into a format that the rest of the world could handle.

Within a year or two after qualification, half or more of new accountants had left practice and taken jobs in industry, the public sector or the non-profit sector. A growing number moved into academia. There they gave what was rapidly becoming an all-graduate profession their all-important first taste of accounting. In the past the introduction to accounting involved being told to add up enormous columns of figures: now it was on the benches of a lecture hall. Among the new wave of accountancy teachers, following from Des Hally, were Frank O'Brien and Pearse Colbert in UCD, Ed Cahill in TCD and Keith Warnock in UCG (now NUIG). The opportunities in industry were widening all the time, and were a long way from the 1930s, when the most likely opportunity had been to double as company secretary and accountant.

The growth of management education had established numeracy as the basic language of business, and this no doubt contributed to the rapid growth in prominence of the profession. The pages of *Accountancy Ireland* showed a wide range of possibilities: on one page in November 1989, for instance, jobs were offered in corporate finance, in venture capital, in international audit, in project management, in strategic planning and as a straightforward financial controller. With a computer (of sorts) on every desk there was the growing field of management accounting and costing, modelling with spreadsheets, budget control with sophisticated software, and the planning and costing of new ventures and investments. In organisations such as Jefferson Smurfit, 'knowing the numbers' (not just the financial numbers) had become the key executive virtue, and it was the accountant who was the supreme numbers person.

One new field in which accountancy skills could be put to use (in business and in practice firms) was corporate treasury. David Thompson, a London-based member of the Irish Institute, described his job thus: 'a treasurer can save his company a lot of money. He may also make money, depending on the position of the business, but normally one is a borrower, so it is a question of finding the most economical ways of borrowing. These can be of great variety, and extend from for example using one's tax position to benefit from leasing, to issuing bonds and using the swap market or to covering one's problems with options. It is also vitally important to control the cash flow.'[18] The range of tricky technical products (foreign exchange hedging, financial futures, derivatives, interest rate swaps, options complete with caps, floors and collars, etc.) available to treasury managers expanded daily.

For nearly a decade increasing numbers of newly qualified Irish accountants had been responding to the lure of the big world outside Ireland. Lured by lavish full-page ads for jobs in Australia, Europe, the Caribbean and North America, it was now common for newly qualified accountants to head overseas, if only for a few years. Employees of the larger firms were often encouraged and facilitated by their firm's international connections. Others were conscious of the fact that in the mild recession of the early 1990s there seemed to be too many newly qualified accountants entering the job market. (As newly elected President Niall O'Carroll of SKC put it in 1992, 'the boom times are over for the time being'.[19]) In 1993 the four main accountancy bodies between them were training thousands of students, and the Institute alone was admitting some 500 new members every year.[20] Noting that of the 1,700 increase in membership since 1985, as many as 700 of these new members were now overseas (including nearly 200 in Australia), Institute Director Roger Hussey commented, 'one may theorise why this is—is it weak demand for accountants at home, heavy demand elsewhere, the opportunities offered by the high reputation of the qualification, the availability of better experience abroad or perhaps just some traditional wanderlust?' There was no question that 'a growing number of Institute members are now pursuing their profession either in Great Britain or overseas'.[21] The City of London (thriving under the freedoms created in the 'Big Bang' of 1986) was recruiting heavily—ads offered jobs to newly qualified ACAs at £28,000 or even more. This was a professional catch-up, for the stimulating opportunity to work overseas—perhaps for no more than a few years' 'work experience'.

A survey by the Leinster Society of Chartered Accountants in 1992 (which had recently elected Niamh Brennan as its first female chair) revealed that the average chartered accountant in the Republic five years after qualification was earning £29,000, plus a car. This was a little more than the average TD, who then earned £27,800. Other research a few years later found that there were many more men than women at the higher levels of £50,000 or more. Interestingly, it was found that 'there was a significant difference between the average wage of men with stay-at-home partners (£62,500) and those in dual career relationships (£41,034).' The authors reflected that 'in dual career relationships where issues of time, energy resources and salary have to be finely balanced, both partners make decisions on the optimal level of remuneration required by the family unit rather than an individual and organise their working lives accordingly.'[22]

The range of chartered accountants' incomes reported by the Leinster Society's respondents was wide, from the £205,000 of a banking executive to the £13,000 of a newly qualified accountant in practice. To put this into perspective, Albert Reynolds, who became Taoiseach in 1992, had a salary of £72,300. Managing directors in business and financial services topped that at £103,000. In general, qualified accountants working in financial services were paid better than those in industry, who were in turn paid more than those in auditing practice. Unfortunately, no data was collected on the incomes of partners in practice, since, as it was tactfully explained, they were paid a profit share, not a salary.[23]

Developments in audit

Even in the largest firms with a wide range of other services, audit, the predominant task since the 1900s, remained so, representing 40 per cent or more of fees. It also remained the basic training track for chartered accountants. Unfortunately, as a leading historian of accounting put it, audit was 'clearly the most controversial aspect of the accountant's work'.[24] By this he meant that it was under pressure from clients who looked upon audit fees with the same enthusiasm as tax, and at the same time (as economic activity expanded) presented every year more and more transactions to audit. No wonder audit was the source of intermittent disputes. In 1990 alone, KPMG was under attack from Aer Lingus (audit fee £503,000) for failing to spot accounting discrepancies in its subsidiary Aer Lingus Holidays; Ernst & Young was awaiting their day in court with AIB, and Price Waterhouse was smarting from a recent row with Waterford Crystal.[25]

The negative comments following a few examples of earnings management and well-publicised audit failures stimulated the growth of formal accounting and auditing standards. Over 20 years these grew from a series of vague 'best practice' suggestions, to a dense thicket of national and international standards; the profession attempted to support its members with rules laying down detailed standard treatments. The growing number of European and international standards merely added to the issues, particularly when they did not agree. In his discussion of the aircraft leasing company GPA, for instance, Professor Ed Cahill of University College Cork pointed out that in the crucial matter of when profits could be taken from operating leases, the US standards were different to those of Ireland and the UK. This meant that under UK and Irish standards GPA could declare profits in 1988–92 that were nearly 50 per cent higher than would have been allowed under US standards.[26] This GPA example underlines how significant (and therefore worth forcibly lobbying) the decisions of standards-setting bodies could be. Given the popularity of sale and leaseback arrangements, the treatment of leases became one of the most contested standard-setting areas.

As external conditions changed, audit techniques evolved. In the early days companies were generally sufficiently small for it to be practical to check a very large proportion of transactions. Taking over from amateur 'shareholder auditors', the professional auditor was perceived as reporting on the management's performance on behalf of shareholders. The textbooks continued until the early 1960s to give high priority to the detection of fraud. Professor Louden Ryan and his group asserted in the 1992 Financial Reporting Commission *Report* that 'most users [of accounts] believe that auditors have a duty to detect material fraud' and this difference was in fact part of the 'expectations gap' between what clients and the public think auditors do and what the profession believes possible.[27] In practice, the profession has traditionally provided little or no training in the detection of fraud, and has relied heavily on the dictum about the auditor being a watchdog not a bloodhound.[28] On the other hand, it was difficult to deny that the presence of a material fraud would prevent the accounts from showing a 'true and fair view'.

The progression and sophistication of auditing technique over the years was as follows[29]:

- *Book-keeping audit*, in which the auditor does the accounts as well as some checking. This has been historically by far the most common form. For small businesses it provided the auditor with a greater in-depth understanding of the business than any other method. However, because auditors are in effect auditing their own accounts, purists barely regard it as an audit at all.
- *Transaction audit*, in which the auditor is given at least a trial balance, if not a set of accounts, and performs more or less extensive voucher checks, bank reconciliations and (as late additions) physical stock checks and debtor circulations.

By the 1970s all-transaction audits came to be seen as less and less practical or necessary. Firms were more professionally managed and could now present their own accounts. And of course, even in mid-sized companies there were just too many transactions. At the same time, the overt objective of auditing shifted to the validation of financial statements proposed by the management of the concern. So two new approaches were proposed:

- *Balance sheet audit,* where the audit focus shifts from transactions to the verification of balance sheet items, especially stocks, accounts payable and receivable, and assets. The technique is based on the idea that the fundamental corporate objective is change (preferably increase) in shareholders' equity.
- *Systems audit* was highlighted in Ireland with the increased use of Cooper's *Manual of Auditing* after 1968.[30] Here the focus is on the internal control system and the dominant technique is the use of extensive questionnaires backed up with sample checks—a small 'judgement' rather than 'statistical' sample being usual; the theory being that if the control system works, all is well and the accounts will be true and fair.

Then, 'around 1980', writes the British historian of auditing, Derek Matthews, 'the audit changed again under pressure from clients who, in an increasingly competitive world, needed to reduce audit fees. In turn auditors had to cut their own costs by further reducing the testing of the clients' records and systems by only targeting the areas considered significant and with the greatest risk of error, and by an overall comparative analysis of the client's business and accountancy.'[31] The new approach was based on two concepts: audit risk and materiality, combined with analytic review.

- The *Audit risk model*, which was introduced into the US with Statement on Auditing Standards No. 47 in 1983, concentrates on trying to identify and evaluate risk in advance. The model requires a judgement of a combination of the following. First, riskiness of the environment (maximising for instance in an all-cash business); secondly, the quality of controls (called the control risk); and thirdly, the detection risk (i.e. how likely is it that existing audit techniques will discover any misstatement). This cumulative risk is then evaluated by materiality criteria. As one writer pictured the approach: 'an auditor undertaking the first audit of a newly floated company specialising in high-technology research and development [and driven by a charismatic entrepreneur] is engaged in a high-risk activity comparable to a Himalayan mountaineer. The re-appointed auditor of a private family company with a known and efficient accounting and control system and a helpful and concerned board of directors may be going for the audit equivalent of a Sunday stroll up Snowdon.'[32] Materiality was crucial: in neither case was an ill-controlled petty cash account to be treated as seriously as an unregulated director's loan system.

Most of these audit types were alive and well in the 1990s, especially the book-keeping audit and the systems audit. However, these could not go too far since, as a KPMG survey identified in 1995, less than half of Irish companies with a turnover of £20 million or more had fully functioning internal audit controls.[33] In this context the more sophisticated techniques certainly presented a difficulty.

A typical audit in the 1990s

A typical Big Six audit in Ireland in the 1990s required four or five staff on-site, with a senior (qualified) accountant accompanied by trainees of various years. Behind these, spending most of their time in the office, would have been a manager, perhaps an assistant manager and one or more partners. Despite increasing use of computers, audit still required considerable personal attention. In the late 1980s, Gerard Hanlon, a sociologist from TCD, conducted a series of interviews with staff engaged on audit.[34] A Big Six senior reported, 'when you start you do an awful lot of ticking and bashing, totting schedules and cross-totting balance sheets . . . I'd say the work is probably harder because you're under an awful lot of pressure. When you come in you'd do certain tests—it's called systems work. You make out a list and make sure they're dealing with their documents right, that they're filing them, that they're totting them correctly . . . you go through them and you tot them and see that somebody has signed it, that they've checked it and it's done right.'[35]

The environment could also be intimidating. The nice middle-class trainees (Gerard Hanlon found that 87 per cent of his interviewees, from partner to trainee, were from the professional employer class, compared to 62 per cent of ordinary industrial managers), fresh as they were from a world of libraries, lectures and exams, had rarely been inside an office of any sort and knew little of that environment's special jargon and rituals. There is the story of the unfortunate trainee who was told to pick a sample of debtors, but couldn't find anything but accounts receivable files, so lurked for half a day, too shy to ask anyone's help. Despite the increasing use of checklists and controls, in the process of the audit there was a reliance on the skill and knowledge of subordinates, a confidence that may not always have been well-based. Niamh Brennan recalled how a colleague in Stokes Kennedy Crowley, newly out of UCD, felt completely out of her depth when asked to check the board minutes of a plc for financial decisions. These were written as usual in the clipped and opaque language of a trained company secretary, behind which it was very easy for a novice to miss important points.

Like so much accountancy practice, audit work is almost always private between the client and the professional. A rare documented example of an audit professional operating in practice emerged in the Beef Tribunal *Report* of 1994. While working in the Cahir plant of the Goodman group on the audit for the year ending March 1986, John King of Stokes Kennedy Crowley spotted 'firstly one invoice which appeared odd and then on investigation a number of invoices' typed on ordinary paper on the same typewriter, purporting to be from various Northern Ireland hauliers. 'Odd' meant lacking telephone or VAT numbers, with vague addresses and all for unusually round sums. Eight names were identified in the end, and further research proved that none could be found in the Northern Ireland telephone book, nor in the company's records of haulage loads and destinations. There was no sign of their lorries, nor did their names appear in the year-end accounts, either as creditors or accruals. All the cheques (which amounted to £840,000) were cashed in Cahir. Then, working late one night at the Cahir branch the audit team spotted unusual activity around the accounts department, with a number of workers apparently being paid in cash, which, as John King put it, 'we thought was strange as we thought all payments were by cheque'.[36] John King reported both of these findings to his audit manager and the audit partner. The first thought was some kind of embezzlement, but the report about workers being paid in cash introduced a new legal dimension. Persistent pulling at this thread eventually led to the Tribunal and its *Report*.

The world of trainees in medium-sized or small firms was quite different from that of the largest, even down to the style of the office. Gerald Hanlon reported that in the Big Six firms security was tight and visitors corralled; in the smaller offices things were much more informal. Their work would be more akin to that done by their professional ancestors—small audits, incomplete records and 'shoebox jobs', in which a miscellaneous collection of vouchers, invoices and receipts would be bundled together, perhaps with a cash book, into a not-quite-complete set in a box. As trainees, their advantage was that they found out how a set of accounts was put together, something their friends in the Big Six might know only from their studies; but on the other hand they were never exposed to large-scale internal control systems, sophisticated corporate treasury, management reporting, and so on. When it came to seeking jobs after qualification, this difference became a problem. Interviewers knew the Big Six firms by reputation, and knew also that the potential recruit had had hands-on experience with large systems. Gerald Hanlon recorded how a man from an unnamed medium-sized firm was told that employers would only recruit from the larger firms: 'the only opportunity would be for me to join a [Big 6] firm . . . and hopefully progress from there.'[37]

With more glamorous options beckoning, in industry or other aspects of the profession, it was perhaps not surprising that Hanlon detected in the early 1990s among some audit staff a creeping sense that, as he put it: 'many accountants and clients view auditing as a waste of resources'. In the intense client relationships and an atmosphere prioritising 'service', it was perhaps hard to keep the wider societal requirement for sceptical auditing in mind. Hanlon was told by a Big Six senior: 'if you're in industry you'd feel that money was actually being made, and you're helping to make it. You're actually doing something that is real as opposed to just going in and annoying someone for two or three weeks and giving them a whopping bill at the end of it'. The idea of 'value-added audits' and the growing importance of the management letter were attempts to recreate a sense of the value of audit in the clients' minds. Consequently, 'there is now pressure on the senior [on the audit] to produce a good management letter for the client containing worthwhile suggestions for the future'.[38]

The expectations gap

In the 1990s the Irish profession became concerned with the so-called 'expectations gap', a term originally coined in the 1970s in the US and referring to 'the gap between the views of auditors and the views of users on what the process of audit adds to financial statements', as the Institute's Financial Reporting Commission put it in 1992. The Commission was set up, with the distinguished economist Professor Louden Ryan of Trinity College, Dublin, as chairman, to address what Institute President Tom O'Higgins described as 'the flood of unwarranted criticism of the profession'. In an interview with *Accountancy Ireland* Professor Ryan identified two key public concerns: first, the scope that existed for companies to manufacture profits rather than earn them, in other words 'creative accounting'; and secondly, 'company failure after the company had received a clean audit report', which he considered was especially frequent in Ireland. These were generally the result of problematic accounting decisions approved in the course of the audit. A vivid current example was Xtra-vision for which a change in depreciation policy resulted in radical changes in outcomes: the company's 'reported gross profit [for 1989 and 1990] represented a margin of 41.4 per cent and 41.6 per cent respectively. In the 1991 annual report the restated accounting policies resulted in the much lower gross profit margin of 11.2 per cent in 1990 and 19.5 per cent in 1991'.[39] The specific problem was that the straight-line depreciation originally adopted misrepresented the actual cash flow generated by a video for hire. Rental income, especially from the popular 'new releases', was high in the first six months and then tailed off rapidly until the video was sold after two or three years. Since depreciation was not matched to revenue, profits in the first year were overstated, an effect that was multiplied and, to a degree, hidden by the rapid expansion from 16 stores in July 1987 to 325 in June 1990.

In the 1992 book *Survey of Irish Published Accounts*, the UCD-based authors wrote of 'new and increasingly complex balance sheet arrangements, specifically designed to circumvent generally accepted accounting principles and to massage companies' gearing ratios, continue to be developed'.[40] The techniques were more popularly highlighted in another 1992 book called *Accounting for Growth,* which had as its central thesis the startling idea that 'much of the apparent growth in the 1980s was the result of accounting sleight of hand rather than genuine economic growth'. Described in an *Accountancy Ireland* review as 'a corporate version of a Scud missile', the book describes 12 accounting techniques which, though in themselves quite legitimate and in particular circumstances totally appropriate, could be used to manipulate financial results. The author, a researcher with a UK stockbroker, stressed that use of any one of these techniques could be legitimate. However, he claimed, they could be used to 'engineer' accounts, or at the very least to make a comparable price/earnings ratio difficult to calculate. His advice to investors was to assume the worst. The more of these techniques used, he proposed, the more the investor should take it that the accounts were being manipulated.[41] *Accounting for Growth* covered similar ground, though in more detail, as Ian Griffiths' *Creative Accounting*, published in 1986—and they became two of the books most borrowed from the Institute's library.

In their *Survey of Published Accounts*, Niamh Brennan, Aileen Pierce and Frank O'Brien from UCD identified the wide variations of accounting treatment possible inside the existing standards. They noted, for instance, that 93 audited accounts of their 138 sample companies opted to value stock at net realisable value, which if the traditional 'prudence' was being adhered to would mean it was lower than the cost of production. Net realisable value was variously defined as: 'selling prices less selling expenses' (17 cases); 'selling price less selling expenses and costs to completion' (37 cases); and 'selling cost less provision' (three cases). One-third of the companies valuing stock at net realisable value did not expand on what was meant.

Equally, the UCD team identified 17 sets of accounts in which some (unidentified) proportion of fixed assets was not subject to a depreciation charge. Of these, six accounts referred to high maintenance standards rendering depreciation unnecessary, four gave no reason at all, and others reported that the particular asset was already fully depreciated, or recently re-valued, or was stated at the lesser of cost and market value.[42] This work underlined a long-lasting professional dilemma, which might be stated thus: in the context of a one-to-one communication between a client company and its shareholders, such reporting could be appropriate, even optimal, but as soon as other users of financial statements are brought into the picture, the lack of comparability becomes painfully obvious.

The key proposal of the 1992 Financial Reporting Commission was that an Irish Financial Reporting Review Panel, on the model of the one operating in the UK, be established as quickly as possible by the four accountancy bodies in CCAB–I (i.e. ICAI, ACCA, CIMA and ICPAI). At this time 'standards continued to rely on the moral suasion of professional accountants to ensure their implementation'.[43] The purpose of the new panel was, as Roger Hussey optimistically put it, 'to have teeth, and also a reputation for biting'. It was to examine the financial statements of large quoted companies, semi-states, cooperatives and building societies, with a view to enforcing accounting standards. The Commission envisaged that the panel would ultimately have legislative backing and the sanction of applying to the courts for an order compelling an errant company to revise any statement that did not give a true and fair view of its affairs.[44]

In presenting his proposals, Professor Ryan and his Commission did not factor in how acutely aware leading accountants were of their clients' preferences for less regulation, a lesson recent accounting history might have taught him.[45] He urged that the Financial Reporting Panel be set up immediately by CCAB–I. He evidently believed that it would quickly enjoy the full support of the Irish Stock Exchange, as well as 'the accountancy profession, shareholders, trade unions, financial institutions [and] the tax authorities'.[46] Critically, despite the Institute's urging, the idea did not have the support of the Irish Government, in the person of Des O'Malley, Minister for Industry and Commerce (1989–92).[47] This lack of support was surprising in the light of O'Malley's speech a year before at the annual dinner of the Chartered Association of Certified Accountants (later the ACCA), in which he lambasted the profession, declaring: 'I cannot understand how a company which gets a clean audit certificate this month can come crashing down next month . . . I think the auditor could in general be a rather more vigilant watchdog than he has been up to now.'[48] The proposed Financial Reporting Panel never saw the light of day.

In the 1994 *Report* of the Beef Tribunal, it was discovered that clever tax evasion schemes had continued for years in some Goodman International plants, after the auditors had drawn them to the attention of management. On the other hand, as the *Report* put it, 'accountants were involved and they had put a lot of thought into it'.[49] So in 1995 the Finance Minister Ruairí Quinn proposed that auditors should have a statutory responsibility to report tax and other offences by clients (section 153 of the Finance Bill 1995). There was an immediate storm, with almost daily headlines for two months.[50] As never before, the profession was the subject of daily conversation in pubs and coffee shops. Accountants argued strongly and emotionally that they would be turned into 'spies', 'narks', 'stoolies' and 'informers' (as the letter writers put it). Equally forthrightly, the Institute's Chief Executive Roger Hussey declared that the row was about 'the right of a profession to set its own standards and more particularly the rights of the taxpayer to independent, professional and confidential advice'. Enactment of this section, it was argued, would have a negative effect on potential inward investors, diverting them offshore, or perhaps to Northern Ireland. It would reduce the privileged freedom of communication between accountant and client. Joe Gannon, Chairman of CCAB–I, declared that the 10,000 members of the combined bodies took strong offence at the proposed clause, attacking as it did the fundamental tenet of the profession, client confidentiality. The opposition to the clause was long and sustained, including a walk-out by the accountancy bodies from the Taxation Administration Liaison Committee, the liaison body with the Revenue Commissioners. Protests against this 'snoopers' charter' also came from other bodies to which it would have applied, such as the Law Society of Ireland, and in the end the offending section was replaced by a much less offensive section 172. The accountants had won their point, though formal recognition of the position of privilege was still to come.

The Tribunals of Inquiry into the beef processing industry, the Blood Transfusion Service and Dunnes Stores certainly raised questions. Of course, for the vast majority of accountants these events were quite remote from their normal working lives. Accountants ran thriving companies, conducted complex audits and solved problems without needing to consult standards or ethical textbooks. But the professional bodies were obliged to take the public feeling into account. As ICAI Chief Executive Sean Dorgan put it, it was no longer enough to declare that 'ethical standards were set and were enforced through peer pressure'.[51] Something more had to be done if the profession was to maintain its high standing. 'Chartered accountants,' he continued, 'no more than any other profession cannot be isolated from scrutiny, and such scrutiny is inevitable if public confidence is to be maintained.' But exactly how this was to be done was not obvious.

An increasingly technical environment

In line with the growing complexity of the commercial environment, professional accountants' lives were now weighted with professional technicalities. By 1990 the ASC had issued 24 SSAPs, of which three were subsequently withdrawn. They had also issued 46 Exposure Drafts and two non-mandatory Statements of Recommended Practice.[52] These were independent of auditing and ethical standards, which had their own exposure drafts and published standards. The blizzard of acronyms lent the discussions of these matters a deeply technical air. The 21 SSAPs extant in 1989 covered a range of accounting problems, from stocks to depreciation, goodwill and extraordinary items, though a conceptual framework for all these tactics, an agreed 'grand unified theory', eluded the standards setters, just as it eluded the astrophysicists.

The flow of exposure drafts, urgent-issue decisions and standards was not going to stop, and the volumes of rules grew steadily fatter. In 1993 the Institute's journal *Accountancy Ireland* began to publish a Technical Supplement in an attempt to help members keep up. The first issue, in December of that year, included:

- a report of the new Auditing Practices Board's standard on 'Auditors Reports in Financial Statements';
- a new Exposure Draft covering fraud;
- a new Exposure Draft covering the accounting for post year-end events and fraud;
- a detailed discussion of the conditions of the forthcoming tax amnesty;
- information on the newly widened scope of the business expansion scheme;
- how the Urgent Issues Task Force had rowed back on accounting proposals relating to the expenses of vacant leasehold property;
- how two cases in the High Court allowed the production of day-old chicks and the bottle-conditioning of stout to qualify for manufacturing relief;
- changes to the taxation of unit trusts announced by the Minister for Finance;
- details of continuing professional education courses in accounting software, arbitration, the Companies Register and completing Form P11D.

By 2011 the *Standards and Guidance* Compendium of the Auditing Practices Board ran to 2,180 pages. Two volumes of international standards from the International Accounting Standards Board ran to 1,328 pages (Part A *Conceptual Framework and Requirements*) and 1,947 pages (Part B *Accompanying Documents, Guidances, Examples, etc.*), respectively. The 2012 Wiley edition of the *US Generally Accepted Accounting Standards* weighs in at a relatively modest 1,320 pages.[53]

Businesses that wanted to float on both the New York and London Stock

Exchanges, for instance, had to have one set of accounts according to the US accounting rules and one according to the UK rules. Unfortunately, as Jerome Kennedy, managing partner of KPMG put it: 'There is a wide range of different treatments and applications even between the countries of the EU. Europe has a long way to go before we get one set of standards across EU countries.' Patricia Barker of DCU sensed 'a power struggle going on. Each state or area has its own rules but the world of business is becoming globalised and the accounting profession has not responded'.[54]

The new model thrives

By 1995 the fee income of the accountancy profession in Ireland was surging ahead, more than in step with the rapid growth of the economy—the top two firms, for instance, now had fee income of £67 million, 23 per cent up on 1990. These two (the old warhorses Stokes Kennedy Crowley and Craig Gardner) still represented one-third of the fee income of the top 25 firms, a similar position to the 1950s, when they had between them audited a third of the companies on the Irish Stock Exchange. This dominance by the larger firms was a worldwide phenomenon: a Lafferty report in 1992 estimated that the top 10 world accountancy networks (including the Big Six but also the likes of Grant Thornton and Pannell Kerr Forster) had 87 per cent of the fees generated by the top 27 networks. The Lafferty report accounted for this by what it described as the disproportionate expenditure on accountancy services in North America and Britain (the homelands of the Big Six). Firms in those countries received over half the world fee income. The report also made it clear how even after Independence in 1922 the profession in the Irish Free State followed the UK/US model, though perhaps the profoundly agricultural nature of the economy barely warranted it. This included a high legal audit requirement (compared to other European countries), a dominant role in tax and consultancy and (captured in the very earliest days of the profession) 'the insolvency franchise—something which is the domain of lawyers in the Nordic region'. The relative significance of the profession in Ireland was indicated by the fact that the fee income of the top 10 Irish firms was six times the equivalent group in Germany, as a per cent of GDP.[55]

The services mix for Irish firms was gradually shifting, with firms reducing their dependence on the contracting audit market, which suffered from fierce price competition. Now they provided a wide range of diversified services such as investigations, mergers and acquisitions, IFSC-related work and tax planning. Occasionally, a glimpse can be seen of the scale of this, as when *The Irish Times* reported the merger of Price Waterhouse and Coopers & Lybrand in September 1997. In 1996, Price Waterhouse earned £700,000 in audit fees from the Bank of Ireland and £3.6 million in non-audit services, and Coopers & Lybrand £1.1 million in audit fees from AIB and £400,000 in non-audit services.[56] Apart from high-profile insolvencies, which gathered headlines as they had done for generations, firms gained the public eye as a result of investigations and reports. These might be initiated by the firm itself to demonstrate sectoral savvy, for instance in the hotel industry, or by the Government and government agencies. The large firms, with their enormous resources, were used for an impressively wide range of government-related number-crunching and consultancy tasks. Thus, between 1990 and 1996 Price Waterhouse alone was commissioned to report on:

- the organisation of the Office of Public Works (OPW);
- Telecom Éireann;
- Dublin's Olympic bid;
- the organisation of the Defence Forces;
- the administration of the Department of Finance;
- An Post;
- errors in marking the Leaving Certificate art examination;
- the pay of the Bord na Móna CEO; and
- the relations between Michael Lowry and Dunnes Stores.

In the same period Coopers & Lybrand reported (among other purely financial matters) on: Harland & Wolff (by Coopers & Lybrand, Belfast); on proposals to simplify the tax system; on payments to the MD of First National Building Society; on the dental profession; on the film industry; on Tara Mines; on Killybegs fishing harbour; and on the book publishing industry. In 1990, Coopers & Lybrand had 48 per cent of its fee income from audit, 9 per cent from liquidation and the balance in various non-audit services.[57] Among these would have been the company secretarial service which had been part of the professional mix in firms and companies for a long time. Firms regularly supplied services such as attending formal board meetings to take and circulate minutes, keeping up the share register, preparation of returns to the Companies office, advising on company structures and formations and acting as secretary to trade organisations. In companies the first chartered accountants employed would often have been in the dual capacity as company secretary and accountant.

Table 2: *1999* Finance *Survey of firms with fees of £1 million or more*

	Fees £m	Partners	Chargeable Staff	Income per staff member £
PricewaterhouseCoopers	78	82	1,083	60,000
KPMG	66	45	792	64,188
Arthur Andersen	38	28	n/a	
Ernst & Young	34	36	461	57,432
Deloitte & Touche	33	34	396	63,707
BDO Simpson Xavier	18	28	226	57,222
Grant Thornton Group	10	21	205	44,248
Oliver Freaney	7	n/a	n/a	
Chapman Flood Mazars	6	10	77	58,824
Farrell Grant Sparks	5	11	61	60,795
IFAC Accountants	5	5	88	25,769
Bastow Charleton	4	7	82	41,115
Pannell Kerr Forster	3	n/a	n/a	
Russell Brennan Keane	3	6	74	33,511
V. F. Nathan	3	6	48	35,917
O'Connor Leddy Holmes	2	6	31	54,048
Orsmby & Rhodes	2	5	25	54,243
O'Hare & Associates	2	6	25	55,714
Hopkins O'Halloran Grant	2	3	40	35,673
Ryan Glennone & Co.	2	4	40	37,000
OSK	2	3	29	46,895
Brenson Lawlor	2	4	34	42,143
Hargden Moor	2	4	34	39,286
O'Donovan Caulfield Lavin	1	3	21	47,500
Caplin Meehan	1	4	18	44,542
Totals	331	361	3,890	56,386
Big Five % of totals	76%	62%	n/a	n/a

Source: Finance September 1999

The second half of the 1990s showed the profession continuing to improve its position. The market responded positively to the varied services mix. By 1999, total fees earned in public practice were more than double what they had been in the beginning of the decade and, because employment was only slightly up, income per staff member had gone from £31,300 in 1990 to £56,000 in 1999.[58] As *Table 2* shows, the number of partners in the top 23 firms had gone up by a mere 5 per cent, and the number of chargeable staff had actually dropped from 4,250 to 3,890. During the 1990s membership of the Institute rose remarkably, from 6,910 in 1990 to 11,647 in 2000.[59] The number of members working in Ireland rose by 77 per cent over the same period. By now well over half of members based in Ireland (60 per cent) worked in industry or business, where the constantly increasing use of numerical analysis gave the profession a strong and developing role.

The league table of the top 23 firms was still divided between the large (by the end of the decade, the 'Big Five', with the internationally initiated melding of Price Waterhouse and Coopers & Lybrand) and the medium-sized. An analysis of the top 2,500 companies, North and South, revealed that just over half were audited by one of the Big Five. Not surprisingly, 'the midsize practices had a higher percentage of the small to medium company audits, outside the top companies'.[60] Over the decade it can be seen that the mid-sized firms (i.e. those not in the Big Five but with more than £1 million in fees) had slightly increased their share of fees from 22 per cent to 25 per cent. Nonetheless, the Big Five still had 75 per cent of fee income and 62 per cent of partners. The mid-sized firms were led by such strong performers as: Simpson Xavier, led by the ebullient Anthuan Xavier (fees up from £2.5 million in 1990 to £18 million in 1999); Grant Thornton (up from £3.7 million to £10 million); and Chapman Flood (up from £1.2 million to £6 million). Between them, these firms had 50 partners in total, compared to PricewaterhouseCoopers' 82.

Another survey, published in *Accountancy Ireland,* confirmed that the year 1999 'had proved an excellent one for the accountancy profession'. Growth apparently came from all sides of the business 'from "bread and butter" audit work to corporate finance, consultancy and taxation advice, but many now see the non-audit areas as having higher margins and are benefitting from cross-selling in the HR, IT and consultancy divisions'.[61] Fee income per partner was well up, for example, reaching £1.46 million for KPMG.

Northern Ireland revives

The signing of the Good Friday Agreement in April 1998 gave new hope to the Northern Ireland economy, which as we have seen had been struggling in continued political turmoil. As Institute President Timothy Quin of Deloitte & Touche in Belfast put it, 'Northern Ireland is potentially facing a period of enormous opportunity for economic growth. Peace in Northern Ireland will bring prosperity and particularly an increase in cross-border relations with the Republic.'[62] More than 1,800 ICAI members were based in Northern Ireland. Distinguished among them was Bruce Robinson, Chief Executive of the Industrial Development Board. His plans looked forward to the creation of 23,000 jobs between 1998 and 2001, of which 18,000 were to be created by externally owned companies (including some from the Republic). 'The change in political climate', he said, 'and the international focus on Northern Ireland gives IDB a unique platform to make a powerful impact on target audiences and export markets.' He warned, however, that there was a legacy of the long period of Troubles. 'There is a misconception that it is difficult to do business with the Republic.' As in other parts of the economy, there was a task of realignment to be done: most of the larger firms in the North looked towards London rather than Dublin. KPMG was the only firm based in the South to report all-island fee income and to be controlled from Dublin. To overcome the barriers that undoubtedly existed, Robinson was keen to use the Institute's established status as an all-island body to build relations and confidence.

The Y2K phenomenon

From the mid-1990s the distant buzz of Y2K, the Millennium Bug, could be heard. In the years and months before the stroke of midnight on 1 January 2000, analysts and 'experts' speculated that, because older systems could not cope with four-digit dates (so 2000 was to them the same as 1900), disaster would strike the world's computers. As one put it: 'up to 50,000 mainframes will crash in succession causing a wave of economic, political and social chaos that will engulf the entire world.'[63] It was speculated that any device with a computer chip could fail, ranging from a nuclear power station and a Boeing 747 to a burglar alarm and a motorised wheelchair. With lip-smacking relish journalists and others multiplied the possibilities of disaster—in April 1999 a writer in *Accountancy Ireland* suggested that the auditor's favourite computer-aided sampling systems could well succumb to the Millennium Bug, and 'installing new systems and retraining staff could take several years'. More soberly, this was clearly a consultancy opportunity for IT specialists of all sorts, especially since the legal profession had made it clear that *if* things turned out badly and *if* companies had not taken proper precautions, shareholders, creditors and other stakeholders would have the right to sue. In a 1999 *Bulletin* the Auditing Practices Board recommended that auditors report on the state of Y2K preparedness of companies.

In the event, aside from a few scattered power failures in various countries, problems in data-transmission systems at some of Japan's nuclear plants (which did not affect their safety) and a temporary interruption in receipt of data from the US's network of intelligence satellites, the New Year arrived with nothing more than the expected hangovers. Was this because of all the preventive work, including the Y2K-compliant certificates demanded by many firms? Or perhaps the whole thing was a science fiction fantasy?

The paradox of the public image

There was throughout the 1990s, as we have seen, a very strong demand for accountants in business, and in practice clients appeared keen to avail of the new range of services. We have also seen how as business became increasingly numerate, accountants became increasingly prominent in management teams and boardrooms. Somehow these practical demonstrations of the value of accountants and accounting failed to find public expression. As David Simpson of Simpson Xavier (President 2000–1) put it, 'the issue of public confidence in the profession was never very far from the top of the [Institute's] agenda'.[64] Undeniably, the profession had a clear image as intelligent, active operators, whether providing tax advice, reporting into the running of government departments, or providing crucial expertise and advice in all sorts of industrial and business environments. In 1997 President MacAleese appointed an ex-President of the Institute, Noel Stewart of Coopers & Lybrand (NI), to the Council of State. But throughout the 1990s an increasing scrutiny was imposed on the financial reporting and audit functions. Dyspeptic headlines, such as 'REPUTATION OF AUDITORS TAKES A FURTHER BLOW' and 'EXTERNAL AUDITORS COME IN FOR HEAVY CRITICISM', were generated by the Public Accounts Committee's decision to set up a Review Group to examine 'the functions, independence and reliability of external auditors'.[65]

Much of this derived from the fact that because of their pivotal position, accountants were often uncomfortably exposed in high-stakes battlefields—in takeovers, in struggles for corporate survival, in companies hard-driven by ambitious managers. Accountants who found themselves either on the inside or the audit side of high-flying companies tended to be particularly vulnerable. In the 1990s, in the business crises of companies such as Goodman, Xtra-vision, GPA, P. J. Carroll, Waterford Wedgewood and Irish Shipping, as one academic observer put it, 'there was clear evidence of material accounting/financial reporting inaccuracies'.[66] In a number of these cases, as Professor Ed Cahill of UCC reported in his 1997 book *Corporate Financial Crisis in Ireland*, 'poor external financial reporting and disclosure were causal factors in the financial crisis'. The corporate crisis itself was often driven by dominant senior managers—for instance, Don Carroll of Carroll's, Larry Goodman of Goodman International, Donal Geaney of Élan, Richard Murphy of Xtra-vision and Tony Ryan of GPA. In the case of the engineering company Kentz, a combination of overtrading and poor internal financial controls drove the company to examinership in 1994. (Classic symptoms of trouble were the fact that audited accounts for 1991 and 1992 had not been submitted to the company's bankers by late 1993, and that there were extensive delays paying creditors and tax.) In September 1993, auditors KPMG had made clear (again) their unhappiness at weaknesses in the accounting and financial reporting structures of Kentz and declared that the group 'was operating at an unacceptable level of risk'.[67] It took another accountant, Anthuan Xavier of Simpson Xavier, to carry through a rescue package that, with the help of Malaysian investors, set Kentz back on its feet.

Unexpectedly, the questions being raised on accounting and audit were not caused by a decline in faith in the idea of audit as such—rather to the contrary.[68] 'Audit', often naïvely prescribed, was becoming an increasing part of public control of institutions: there were quality audits, safety audits, health audits, value-for-money audits, catering audits, clinical audits and even arts audits. Reflecting the new interest, the word 'audit' itself was used in the pages of *The Irish Times* three times as often in the 1990s as in the 1980s. The profession made little or no attempt to capture any of these new domains, though in theory their audit skills might have seemed suited.

To address the continuing problems of public image, the Institute initiated a marketing campaign in the late 1990s. The core of the campaign was to stress the quality of the Chartered Accountants 'brand'. A new logo was devised, intended to be 'authoritative, substantial and professional, but also modern and vibrant', as Chief Executive Sean Dorgan put it.[69] Members were encouraged to add this logo to existing stationery. 'A comprehensive marketing campaign' was initiated through press and radio, including local radio in conjunction with the National Ploughing Championships. In 1999, his replacement, the Institute's new Chief Executive Brian Walsh, presented the Institute as 'a significant business body playing a responsible role in the development of the Irish economy', a notably wider brief than the founding fathers would have considered. 'We have always had an involvement with, for example, government working parties and committees' Walsh declared, 'but a lot of what we do takes place behind closed doors. We need to be more assertive and to take more credit for the contribution we make.'[70]

At the very end of the decade Walsh addressed the still-niggling issue of the profession's public reputation: 'around 1993/4 the profession suffered an avalanche of criticism during the Beef Tribunal and subsequently in the Dáil . . . a few years later we had the Dunnes' payment and the McCracken report and all that arose from that. These events have had a negative impact on the perception of Chartered Accountants and that impact has been felt personally by many members.'[71] He asked, 'what has gone wrong with Chartered Accountants in the last twenty years?' Thinking no doubt of the vast majority of his members, he answered: 'Nothing.' Walsh was inclined to put the newly critical attitude to the profession in the context of a general loss of the automatic respect previously accorded to the professions. And the paradoxical contrast between the evident success of the profession in business and practice and the public view was not unique to accountancy. The opinion was commonly expressed, for instance, that the Irish health service was generally a shambles: 'though I must admit', the speaker usually added, 'that the time I was in hospital recently, I got great treatment and the nurses were lovely—and of course the cancer survival rates have soared.' The paradox was not to go away with the new millennium, either for the health service or the accountancy profession.

Chapter Ten
From Strength to Strength: the 2000s

Eight out of the top ten companies based in Ireland have a Chartered Accountant as CEO or CFO; Chartered Accountants are CEOs of 690 Irish companies, owners of 900 and board members of 2,800.[1]

By the start of the new millennium the Irish economy was looking good.[2] The comparison with the high-growth Asian states implicit in the phrase 'Celtic Tiger' seemed thoroughly justified. As economist Antoin Murphy put it: 'the rise of the Celtic Tiger began in earnest in 1994 and finished in triumph in 2000, when both GDP and GNP growth averaged 9.3 per cent. Ireland had successfully linked in with the remarkable technological revolution at Silicon Valley and created a European platform for US multinationals to export into Europe. Combined with sound macroeconomic policies, this had created a virtuous circle: unprecedentedly rapid economic growth; an increase in population; and a dramatically changed fiscal environment in which tax rates were falling alongside a spectacular reduction in public sector debt ratio—from 109 per cent of GDP in 1987 to 25 per cent in 2006.'[3]

And then things began to unravel. The first shock was the collapse of the dot.com bubble in 2000, and with it a lot of excited talk about a 'new economy', e-commerce, fibre-optics, and information technology generally. Then the psychic shock of 9/11 hit American confidence, and with it some of the confidence of US hi-tech firms, and this was echoed by a general slow-down in the global economy. Volume growth in Irish exports collapsed from 21 per cent year-on-year in 2000 to a mere 0.3 per cent in 2003.

Though property prices in Ireland shuddered for a while, the property boom, fuelled by massive bank lending, gathered steam and surged happily away. *Accountancy Ireland* tempted its readers with articles about investment in gold and art, and the ways high-net-worth individuals spent their money (mostly on luxury collectibles, it seemed).[4] People spoke comfortingly of a 'soft landing', at least, as it seemed, until 2007.

Table 1: *The rise and rise of accounting*

Census occupational code	*Description*	*1996 Census*	*2002 Census*	*2011 Census*	*1996 to 2011 increase*
250	Qualified accountants	14,822	22,166	27,116	83%
410	Accounts clerks	21,190	25,542	30,538	44%
Total in employment (million)		1.5m	1.8m	2.1m	40%
Accountants and clerks ratio to employees		1:42	1:37	1:36	

Source: Census 2002 Vol. 6 Table 2 gives data for 1996 and 2002; Census 2011 *Employment, Occupations and Industry* Table 2 gives the 2011 data. The codes/job classifications, which are the same for each of the three years, are based on the International Standard Occupational Classification and are described as follows: 250 'Chartered and certified management accountants (inc. taxation experts)'; 410 'Accounts and wages clerks, bookkeepers and other financial clerks'. Data covers persons in the Republic aged 15 or over.

But the worsening position of the US sub-prime market throughout 2007, and the collapse of the British bank Northern Rock in August 2007 began to make financial markets jittery, and caused them increasingly to look askance at property-related investment. The tectonic plates in the international financial environment were shifting, and the weakness of the Irish banking system was about to be revealed. The collapse of Lehman Brothers on 15 September 2008 was the final straw. Some days later the Irish Government took the fateful decision to guarantee the country's banks, and the crisis was acknowledged.

The profession in the 2000s

According to the regular censuses, by 2011 the number of qualified accountants in Ireland had shown healthy, even extraordinary, growth of 83 per cent in the 15 years since 1996 (see *Table 1*). Unsurprisingly, most of this increase occurred in the Celtic Tiger years up to 2002. However there was a long-term trend, similar to one in Britain. It has been written that 'the rise to prominence of accountants has been one of the most decisive trends in British business management over the last 150 years . . . only the United

States has more practising accountants than the UK, while in terms of labour force per accountants the latter (at 198) far undercuts the former (427)'.[5] Much of this growth was in the corporate sector, with 81 per cent of a sample of top UK companies having an accountant on the board.[6] Partly because of the weakness of management education, British and Irish companies have long looked to accountants to contribute professionalism. As a result, 'while in the United States senior managers are associated with the MBA and in Germany with engineering qualifications, the British cadre is dominated by accountants.'[7] If anything this is more striking in Ireland: the 1996 Irish Census showed that in the Republic of Ireland the ratio of accountants to labour force was 1:102, and there had been a four-fold increase in the number of accountants in the 25 years between 1971 and 1996.

The spectacular presence of accountancy-trained managers such as Michael O'Leary and Lochlann Quinn and the high-flying accountants in leading firms such as ESB, Davy, Axa, BNP Paribas, Irish Life, Kenmare, Kingspan, Microsoft, and Paddy Power showed accountants turning into managers at the centre of Irish business. Typical of these high-flyers was Vincent Sheridan of the Voluntary Health Insurance Board, President of Chartered Accountants Ireland 2007–8. After education at Blackrock College he did a commerce degree in UCD (getting a first) and then articles with Reynolds McCarron O'Connor. He qualified in 1972 and went straight into business, resisting the temptation to work abroad. 'I wanted to get into business', he told *Accountancy Ireland*.[8] He joined Norwich Union on the life and pensions side, growing the business until he eventually became Group Chief Executive in 1990. When Norwich Union merged with Hibernia Insurance in 2000 he was in line to become Chief Executive, when the challenge of the VHI was offered. During his eight years with the health insurer perhaps his most significant achievement was the consolidation of the risk equalisation levy on competitors to compensate VHI for its much older client base. He retired in 2008. Like his predecessor Leo O'Donnell, he believed that 'becoming an accountant is a tremendous training for business', but he believed that this is not now enough: 'the Finance Director of a public company must be more than a first class accountant. They're going to have to be experts in corporate finance, in communications, in strategy formulation.'

Ten years before Leo O'Donnell, President of the Institute 1996–7, had described the profession as 'service providers to business'. Now a wider aspiration prevailed. In the words of Brendan Lenihan (ICAI President 2013–4) especially in the larger companies accountants were 'in the engine-room'. The new world, in which business rather than practice was the predominant mode, was thus described by a member of the Institute's Council, Penelope Kenny: 'as a profession, . . . we need to assume a new role, a role in which we become the drivers of corporate change rather than the controllers of corporate destiny. The accountant as innovator, the accountant as visionary, accountants as intrapreneurs within the organisations and society they serve.'[9] This was a long way from the old idea of a learned profession providing disinterested advice to clients.

Of course, most of the 27,000 accountants in the country did not work in multinationals or indeed in the fewer than 500 companies employing 250 or more. Just as the great majority of practitioner firms were not the Big Four, but were one- or two-partner practices who had no thought or expectation of being asked to audit a Stock Exchange-quoted company, so 80 per cent of industrial enterprises and 98 per cent of service businesses employed fewer than 50 people.[10] For them derivatives, exchange-rate swaps and international supply chain management were not hot topics in their corridors. The core activity of these members of the profession has from the earliest post-Famine days been the understanding and translating of the financial (and other numerical) ambiguities of life into formats for decision-making—primarily by fellow board members and fellow managers, and others such as shareholders, clients, tax inspectors, creditors and regulators. This core task remained. Even with computer accounting programs, translating business flows was not automatic; the swirling activity of the shopfloor had to be pinned down; tax returns made; shops, estates and partnerships needed to be sorted out; insolvencies unravelled. Mastery of these flows was of course a high road taken by many to wider responsibilities in small companies as well as large.

The carrying out of the core tasks occurred in a widely varied set of environments and, as we shall see, qualifications. As it had been for decades, the Institute was comfortably the largest Irish body, but not quite so dominant as it had been in the past, when its membership accounted for as much as 60 per cent of the total number of accountants reported in the Census. The Association of Chartered Certified Accountants (ACCA) and the Chartered Institute of Management Accountants (CIMA) had enormously greater world-wide memberships (see *Table 2*).

Table 2: *Accountancy Bodies in the Republic of Ireland 2006* [11]

Name	*Founded*	*Original name*	*Initials*	*In Ireland* *Members*	*Students*
Institute of Chartered Accountants in Ireland	1888	Institute of Chartered Accountants in Ireland	ICAI	10,468	3,732
Association of Chartered Certified Accountants	1904	London Association of Accountants	ACCA	6,368	9,029
Chartered Institute of Management Accountants	1919	Institute of Cost and Works Accountants	CIMA	3,416	2,716
Institute of Certified Public Accountants in Ireland	1943	Society of Public Accountants	ICPAI	2,849	1,883
Institute of Chartered Accountants in England and Wales	1880	Institute of Chartered Accountants in England and Wales	ICAEW	425	21
Association of International Accountants	1928	Association of International Accountants	AIA	195	40
Institute of Incorporated Public Accountants	1981	Institute of Incorporated Public Accountants	IIPA	191	57
Chartered Institute of Public Finance and Accountancy	1885	Corporate Treasurers and Accountants Institute	CIPFA	70	23
Institute of Chartered Accountants of Scotland	1951*	Society of Accountants in Edinburgh	ICAS	51	

* ICAS was formed in 1951 by a merger of the Society of Accountants in Edinburgh (Royal Charter 1854), the Institute of Accountants and Actuaries in Glasgow (Royal Charter 1854) and the Aberdeen Society of Accountants (Royal Charter 1867).

A comfortable majority of accountants now worked in business. The pages of *Accountancy Ireland* reported opportunities for financial controllers, systems accountants, analysts, risk specialists, tax planners, corporate finance and treasury specialists. And not only in Ireland—one advertiser tempted readers with 'the essential wardrobe for Australia: one grey suit and one wet suit'.

The Institute in the new century

The new century started with what the Institute's Chief Executive Brian Walsh described as 'seldom a more challenging time for the accountancy profession'.[12] He instanced the traumatic effects of the Public Accounts Committee's DIRT Enquiry in the Republic, which reported in December 1999. Among other things this report commented on 'serious defects and weaknesses' in the statutory audits of the banks involved. These, declared the Public Accounts Committee, 'contributed to the continuance of the bogus non-resident problem and these require to be addressed urgently'. Three out of the Big Five (this was before the sudden, shocking demise of Arthur Andersen), Ernst & Young, PricewaterhouseCoopers and KPMG, were singled out for adverse comment.[13] In July 2000 a Review Group on Auditing, established by Mary Harney as Minister for Enterprise, strongly recommended the establishment of a dedicated body to oversee the activities of the recognised accountancy bodies.[14] This eventually became the Irish Auditing & Accounting Supervisory Authority (IAASA), which was introduced to the Dáil in 2003 and opened for business in 2006. The role of this body was originally envisaged simply as being to oversee the activities of the nine accountancy bodies (of which six were recognised for audit), but in 2009 it was agreed that it would directly inspect the auditors of big companies. This change, however, was delayed, and in 2013 Institute President Brendan Lenihan called on the Government to act. 'We cannot', he wrote, 'afford to wait for additional negative experiences before we implement this important change.'[15]

In his review of the year 2000 then President David Simpson recorded the 'days of economic prosperity and unprecedented wealth creation', leading to a dynamic and changing environment.[16] Chief Executive Brian Walsh confirmed that there were record numbers of students going through the core training system, as well as over 8,000 participants in the Continuing Professional Development programme. In February 2002, the Institute welcomed its 12,000th member, Emer Joyce from Galway, who trained with Michael Cosgrove in Castlebar before taking up a tax position with KPMG in Dublin. On the downside was the continual heavy drain of the Public Concern cases. These were the Institute's own inquiries into the implications of findings of the McCracken Tribunal (the Blayney Committee), the conduct of members in relation to Powerscreen International, the PAC's DIRT enquiry and an appeal into the findings of the Blayney Committee. Between them these four cases cost the Institute £1.2 million in 1999–2000 and £512,000 in 1998–9, large sums relative to the Institute's reserves of just over £1 million. The accumulated cost was considerably more than the £868,000 raised by special increase in subscriptions to fund such cases. As a result the Institute's income and expenditure account showed a deficit of £238,000. Some of this was funded by adroit profit-taking on investments. At the Special General Meeting in December 2000 the subscription was raised by 17.5 per cent, primarily, as it was put, 'to strengthen its reserves in the context of its self-regulatory role'.

At the beginning of the new century the Institute's day-to-day activities were carried out by a staff of 84 people (15 of whom were based in the Belfast office). The management team consisted of Brian Walsh (Chief Executive), Judy Fay (Secretary), Simone Doran (Director, Business Members), Heather Briers (Director, Quality Assurance), David Butler (Director, Finance), Albert Powers (Director, Education and Training), Paddy O'Boyle (Director, Projects) and Gerry Naughton (Director, Member and Media Relations). Supporting the President was a 29-member Council (including several past-presidents). During the year it was decided that this was an unwieldy group and it would be better to reduce the number of Council members to 17. Under the broad aegis of the Council were 24 specialist committees, involving a total membership of over 200. These committees advised the Council on a range of issues from finance and resources, various education and disciplinary committees, to quality review and committees dealing with the interests of members in business and in practice. The group of committees also included technical committees on tax, insolvency, business law and accounting and auditing standards. Some of these operated on a CCAB–I basis and included representatives from ACCA, CIMA and ICPAI.

The District Societies of Chartered Accountants had their origin in the very successful Belfast Society (renamed the Ulster Society in 1966) which celebrated its centenary in 2006. Seeing the success of the Belfast Society, a Dublin Society was founded soon afterwards, but this did not survive, and was only revived in 1927. Years later societies covering the Munster,

Mid-West, North-West and the Western (mainly Galway) areas were established and there were also overseas Societies in Britain and Australia. Internationally, the Institute was represented on two committees/boards of the International Federation of Accountants (IFAC)—Henry Saville chaired education and Richard George chaired the ethics board—and the General Assembly of the Fédération des Experts-comptables Européen (FEE). Two Irish representatives, Margaret Downes and David Devlin, have served as Presidents of FEE, the latter for two consecutive terms.[17]

Although training of new recruits to the profession remained the core activity, considerable development was made to the Practice Advisory Service, which now had three qualified staff. In 2000, they carried out a Practice Comparison Survey to aid benchmarking, held a residential conference and handled thousands of calls from members on technical and practical issues from buying/selling a practice to accounting, audit or ethical issues. The buoyant economy was good for *Accountancy Ireland*'s advertising sales, up 41 per cent on the year, with a circulation of just under 18,000 copies.

For an organisation that put such a high priority on training, its facilities had for a long time left much to be desired. So it was decided that a new purpose-built 'training centre with an office', as the new Chief Executive Pat Costello (appointed in 2004) described it, would be created in Pearse Street. The new facility had three lecture rooms, one with a capacity for 600 students, training suites and meeting rooms. It was formally opened by President Mary McAleese in December 2009. Just before the Institute moved into its new offices, the opportunity was taken to change its name and logo to something more 'modern and fresh', as Pat Costello put it-Chartered Accountants Ireland.

On being a partner

Before the coming of limited liability companies in the mid-19th century, partnership was the normal way of organisation for businesses larger than sole traders, from banks to department stores, coal merchants and biscuit factories. We have seen how, initially, limited liability was looked on with suspicion, but over time became the acceptable norm. Several Irish businesses took the advantage of the stock market boom of the 1890s to convert to limited liability companies. Professional firms such as solicitors, architects and accountants were however inhibited by law and practice from making the change to this simpler and more straightforward method of corporate organisation. Perhaps in the legislators' minds was some sense of personal professional responsibility and a dim echo of the robust saying 'how can you trust a corporation that has neither a soul to be damned nor a body to be kicked?'[18]

Critically, this meant that every partner was 'jointly and severally' liable for debts, even to the extent of personal assets. As the British judge Lord Lindley put it: 'Every member of an ordinary partnership is liable to the utmost farthing of his property for the debts and engagements of the firm.'[19] In an era of multi-million defaults and associated law suits, this meant that individual partners, working perhaps in the secretarial or insolvency department, faced the possibility of personal bankruptcy (property sold, children taken out of school, savings swallowed) if an audit went sour. The burden of liability was widely felt to be unfair. As Leo O'Donnell put it: 'I find it hard to understand the sense of equity underlying the view that an auditor or anyone else who is responsible for five per cent of the damage can be accountable for 100 per cent of the liability.'[20] Technically, a law of 1907 allowed a form of limited liability partnership, but under the unacceptable conditions that no more than 20 partners could be involved, and that at least one general partner had to accept full liability for all debts and obligations.

In some jurisdictions, notably in the United States, this risk had become very real and in the 1990s a new form of corporate vehicle evolved called the limited liability partnership, which combined the governance of a partnership with the benefits of limited liability. This was introduced to English law in 2000, and was extended to Northern Ireland in 2004. In 2010, firms of auditors in the Republic of Ireland gained the right to incorporate by virtue of the implementation of the Statutory Audit Directive (S.I. No. 220 of 2010), which amended section 187 of the Companies Act 1990.[21] The benefit for incorporated auditors was that the liability of shareholders (who would, at least initially, typically be the partners) in respect of the debts and liabilities of that company was limited to the amount, if any, remaining unpaid on the shares held by them, save in exceptional circumstances. In addition, only the company (as a separate legal person) could be sued for its debts and obligations. So if the audit company was to be sued for negligence, it would be liable to the extent of its assets, including insurance; if these were insufficient, the audit company would have to go into liquidation. Although the lack of limited liability had been identified by Leo O'Donnell during his Presidency as 'a primary concern of the Institute', at the time of writing the large firms had generally not taken advantage of the new regulations. Perhaps this was because, as Aidan Lambe of Chartered Accountants Ireland noted, the solution offered 'only provides a partial answer to the problem of Ireland's liability regime. It does not address the continuing inability of an audit firm (incorporated or non-incorporated) to limit its liability in respect of statutory audit work. Coupled with the legal principle of joint and several liability, audit firms (incorporated or non-incorporated) continue to face the prospect of being liable for losses caused by their own negligence, but also the negligence of others, for example, company directors.' It has also been suggested that firms have been reluctant to undertake the considerable administrative task (including resigning all accounts and reapplying under the new name) given the probability of further changes likely to be initiated by the EU in the near future.

Clearly the governance problems faced by firms whose partners can sit comfortably around a table are quite different from those faced by firms whose multi-specialised partners can hardly fit in a large room. In the former the necessary closeness of relationships, and the fact that the work would be broadly known to each other is one thing. In the latter, the sheer size of the partnership undermined the basic assumption of partnership law, that it was reasonable to expect one partner to be able to judge personally another. In practice, all large accounting firms and most of those with four partners or more have had since the 1980s a managing partner whose job was that of a team leader tasked with overseeing, motivating and orienting the other partners.[22] There would also be a managing partner's committee and partner sub-committees dealing with various aspects of the business. Managing partners typically kept some of their direct client work when appointed (involving perhaps a minimum of a quarter of their time), so as to keep their feet on the ground. As the role evolved, it became similar to but not the same as a corporate CEO. As Terence O'Rourke, previously managing partner of KPMG (and Institute President 2005–6), explained, 'because the partners have to agree, there is a good deal of diplomacy in the job.' He characterised the way in which different firms evolved different styles by the story of the former Arthur Andersen partner who joined KPMG and reported in amazement a few months later: 'I never knew you could say "no" to the boss.'[23]

The most important decision faced by any partnership was that of appointing a new partner. Not least because of the legal implications, this task had long been taken extremely seriously. In the 2000s, typically, potential candidates were initially spotted by the managing partner, perhaps with the help of a special committee. After a general consultation with appropriate senior colleagues, there would be a gruelling interview process, perhaps involving presentations. Intellectual and technical ability was more or less taken for granted—what was important was to convince the interviewers of motivating and interpersonal skills and, crucially, the ability to contribute to the firm's growth in some vigorous way. In some firms, the potential new partner served as a salaried partner for a two-year probation period. It was unusual for new partners to have to 'buy in', i.e. pay for goodwill, though they were normally required to make a contribution to capital. Payment systems also varied with the ethos of the firm; some believed that each partner should get the same (except perhaps the managing partner), others had a more performance-based reward system, usually paying a basic salary plus bonus, depending on achieved targets.

Although it was well-known that the strongest contribution came from partners in the 35–45 age group, partnership was theoretically for life. With the increasing scrutiny and regulation of the profession partnership became riskier and less attractive, and managing partners across the industry were aware that the average age of partners was creeping beyond 50, which John McCarthy, then Practice Advisory Executive of ICAI, described as 'a succession time bomb waiting to go off'.[24] As well as the external risks, partnership, especially in the larger firms, required long hours of intensive, concentrated work together with a substantial after-hours commitment. Despite this, the concomitant high rewards attracted extremely competitive people, for whom peer pressure was sufficient goad to maintain standards.

Ethical, auditing and financial reporting standards

The efforts of companies to produce regular and smoothed earnings year on year has been a persistent theme of this history. The need for this stems from the fact that investors, now as in the past, dislike surprises, and have difficulty discriminating between real trends and mere statistically inevitable fluctuations. In Sweden these accounts-smoothing techniques went under the resounding name of *konjunkturtimingsprincipen* (business cycle smoothing principles) and were regarded as perfectly legitimate by the authorities.[25] In Ireland and Britain secret reserves, off-balance sheet activity and a hundred other techniques have been used, so that the requisite 'smoothing' could be achieved. Because accounts are not just simple statistical artefacts (like counting the cows in a field), but sophisticated constructs with serious financial implications, earnings management could potentially go on at all levels. At the simplest level is the small client who 'forgets' to provide updated stock figures, so the initial draft accounts have to be prepared with last year's stock valuation (to be raised or lowered accordingly); at quite another are sophisticated games of creative accounting.

The remorseless production of standards in an attempt to control the pressure of this earnings management went on throughout the 2000s. Regulation bodies proliferated. The Financial Reporting Council (with an Irish consultative committee) was established in Britain in 1990. Since then it has seen its remit expand over the years from originally comprising an Accounting Standards Board and the Financial Reporting Review Panel, to also including the Auditing Practices Board, previously a separate and independent body. The Professional Oversight Board (with an Audit Inspection Unit) and an Accountancy Investigation and Discipline Board were more recent bodies established within the FRC aegis, as self-regulation in the UK continued to be dismantled. There was also the International Accounting Standards Board (responsible for the increasingly important International Financial Reporting Standards) and the US Financial Accounting Standards Board. By the end of the decade Ireland had its own regulatory body in the Irish Auditing & Accounting Standards Authority (IAASA), which began work in 2006.

The output of standards was continuous, with frequent exposure drafts, standards and revised standards. To those not closely involved, the churning seemed unstoppable: in the issue of *Accountancy Ireland* that featured the Institute's new building at Pearse Street, articles announced 'Clarified ISAs: Auditing Standards are Changing Again' and 'IFRS for SMEs: is this the end for Irish/UK GAAP?'.[26] And as Aidan Lambe noted, the most significant change in a generation had been in 2002 when the EU mandated listed companies to prepare their accounts in accordance with IFRS, effective from 2005. As the process continued, with old standards being replaced with new ones, it was not only Patricia Barker who feared that the old 'rigorous body of theoretical knowledge was being replaced by an enormous body of rules that required memory rather than intellectual reasoning'.[27]

Occasionally, the standards themselves were contradictory—notable differences divided US and European standards.[28] Nonetheless, standards for financial reporting, for auditing and for ethics generally have become the essential backdrop for all practice activity. But for most accountants they were not daily concerns. As we have seen, the overwhelming majority of practitioners were small (five or fewer partners) and were only concerned with equivalently small companies and business. Training and continuous professional development ('CPD') provided quite sufficient familiarity for the problems involved in such clients. Intense daily involvement with standards was the preserve of Technical Partners in large firms with listed clients.

The substantial international effort by the profession put into the policing of auditing and financial reporting (by 2013 Ernst & Young's publication *International GAAP* reached 4,300 pages; the auditing standards were only slightly less voluminous) underlines a widespread acceptance by insiders of a considerable problem, for which the only available solution was increased regulation. The Auditing Practices Board identified six 'threats' to auditor objectivity: familiarity; self-interest; self-review; management threat; advocacy; and intimidation.[29] Opinions differed as to the relative importance of these threats. For both internal and external accountants, the 'dominant senior manager', the driving entrepreneur and his team with very decided views of where the company should go and a disinclination to be deflected, continued to represent a danger indicator behind many of the APB's threats.[30]

The profession in 2006

The first years of the decade were uncomfortable for the international profession. Major corporation financial reporting scandals erupted in Enron, WorldCom, Rite Aid, AOL Time Warner, Quest, Global Crossing and others. But in Ireland the profession continued to go from strength to strength, and this was especially marked in the firms below the level of the Big Four. As Simpson Xavier partner Anthuan Xavier told *Accountancy Ireland* in 2002: 'it is a peculiar thing. Things are very good here . . . we are getting more than our fair share of [Big 4-related] business and have taken on an incredible amount of business this year.' Jim Keane of Russell Brennan Keane agreed: 'despite a public perception that it has been a bad year for accountants we have never been so much in demand.' Joe Carr of Mazars identified an effect of the well-publicised problems from Enron onwards about audit quality: 'there has been no negative reaction to us on a day-to-day basis. However, the issues that have arisen have made people look at their accounting services . . . they are examining the size and quality issues and see that size does not necessarily ensure a quality client service.' Pearse Farrell of Farrell Grant Sparks had also noticed this: 'The move away from the Big 4 is because the middle tier firms have "niched" themselves in certain areas and can provide very competitive service to the Big Four in a local environment and the market is buying that service.'[31]

Despite the media sniping, accountancy firms were doing well. They continued to recruit the brightest and the best from the universities, and the training rooms of the Institute and the other accounting institutions had never been busier. Fee incomes rose and rose, and accountants in practice and business were seen as the go-to solution for all sorts of quantifiable problems. All in all, the profession had never had it so good.

Although the Big Four took almost all of the large audits, and their successes and failures were the stuff of media coverage, the profession as a whole was much more diverse. Of the 1,464 firms from the various bodies licensed to perform audits, the bulk (70 per cent) were sole practitioners. A mere 1.5 per cent had more than five partners, a fact rarely commented on (see *Table 3*).

Table 3: *Registered Republic of Ireland Auditors in 2006*

Body	*No. of principals*			*Total*
	1	*2 to 5*	*5+*	
ICAI	522	252	18	792
ICPAI	254	96		350
ACCA	233	73	5	311
IIPA*	n/a	n/a	n/a	120
ICAEW	10			10
ICAS	1			1

* At the time, the IIPA registered firms, not members, so had no breakdown of principals.

Source: IAASA *Annual Report 2006* (IAASA's first annual report).

As we have seen in previous generations, there was a rich variety of accountants in Ireland. According to the newly created Irish Auditing & Accounting Supervisory Authority, in 2006 there were nine formally recognised groups in the profession in the Republic, with 24,000 members, 60 per cent of whom worked in business and a small number in the public service. The largest body (in Ireland) was the Institute and the smallest the Institute of Chartered Accountants in Scotland, with just 51 members. There were 1,554 new students admitted to the various bodies in 2006, 44 per cent of which came to the Institute. The others went to ACCA, ICPAI and CIMA, in that order. IAASA's listing did not include the members of the Institute of Accounting Technicians of Ireland (IATI) which had been established with the help of the ICAI in 1983 with the aim of providing a basic qualification in book-keeping. In 2002, IATI began to employ its own staff, having previously been administered by staff on secondment from the ICAI, starting with Ben Lynch. When it celebrated its 25th anniversary in 2008, it had over 5,000 members. In 2009 it was rebranded as Accounting Technicians Ireland.

There were also, bizarrely, 29 individuals who did not belong to any of the bodies but had the personal right to sign audits as a result of ministerial licence issued by Ministers before February 1983. (Backhand evidence this of how little the public then understood what the profession was about: it is difficult to imagine a Minister licensing unqualified doctors or lawyers.) It was an ongoing grievance that the term 'accountant' had no statutory protection, so that it was perfectly possible for anyone to put up a plate, and indeed to advertise, announcing themselves to be an 'accountant'. This of course completely undermined the disciplinary effect of expelling a member for misconduct. An international attempt to skirt round this problem and to more fully represent the range of tasks now done by accountants, by establishing a new protected name, 'cognitor', initiated by the American Institute for CPAs, never got off the ground. Cognitor was at least better than the AICPA's first thought—'knologist'.[32]

Each of these bodies had a different make-up of members, but in general about one-third were female and one-third aged under 35. Both of these figures were affected by recent recruiting patterns: the surge of recruits since the 1990s kept the ages low, and only the gradually increasing proportion of women members disguised the fact that 54 per cent of students across the board were female. Women had in fact been entering the profession in equal numbers to men since the late 1980s. However, they were still sparsely represented at the very top of the profession, and odd 'firsts' kept appearing. It was not, for instance, until June 2007 that the Ulster Society elected its first woman chair—we have seen that the Leinster Society had elected Niamh Brennan in 1989. In Ireland, 16 per cent of the Big Four partners were women. In the US, only 13.2 per cent of partners in the Big

Four were women, and in the UK only 9 per cent of the partners in the top 60 firms were women.[33]

But this is not solely a problem for accountancy: the situation is echoed in other professions, such as law and architecture, in the board members of quoted companies in Ireland, in Britain and the US, and, famously, in aspects of public life, such as broadcasting and politics. Even in France and Sweden, whose family-friendly policies have been much touted, very, very, few women make it to the top. Those who do, such as Christine Lagarde of the IMF, are famous for their work ethic. For historical and perhaps biological reasons, women face harder choices between professional success and personal fulfilment. Gender-related impediments to women's equality in all these areas also include: the difficulty of invading a space clearly 'male' (the same difficulty women used to experience going into certain Dublin pubs); the different male and female attitudes to self-confidence, networking and leadership style; and problems as mothers with the work–life balance and excessive hours.[34] The ICAI had by far the largest number of women in practice but women members as a whole represented only a third of all its members in Ireland (see *Table 4*).

Table 4: *Irish Accountancy 2006 (Republic of Ireland data)*

Institute	*Employment*		*Of Members*	
	Practice	Industry	% Female	% age under 35
ACCA	1,681	3,916	39	37
AIA	26	134	3	12
CIFPA	n/a	n/a	34	3
CIMA	171	2,596	30	26
ICAEW	183	157	21	16
ICAI	3,470	6,187	31	38
ICAS	8	30	18	14
ICPAI	1,054	1,371	49	34
IIPA	120	n/a	4	n/a
Totals	6,713	14,391	34	34

Source: IAASA *Annual Report 2006.*

Six bodies were recognised in the Irish Companies Acts (section 187 of the 1990 Act) for the purposes of audit. Under this section a potential auditor had to maintain membership of one of the six 'recognised' bodies and hold a practice certificate issued by them. (For ICAI this is now done by the Chartered Accountants Regulatory Board (CARB).) Consequently, membership of a recognised accountancy body did not automatically entitle an individual or firm to provide audit services. To obtain *audit* registration, a member or firm must satisfy the relevant body's additional criteria (i.e. over and above those required for membership and practising authorisation) which normally included: an audit qualification for any individual who proposed to sign an audit report; and sufficient and appropriate audit-related post-membership experience.[35]

Each body organised quality control procedures, typically involving desk-top reviews of annual returns from members, desk-top reviews of members' individual client engagement files and periodic quality assurance visits to registered auditors' offices by quality assurance reviewers, who were typically employees of the body involved. The process of audit quality control was demanding in terms of time and money. In 2006, for instance, the Institute engaged 21 staff in their 'professional standards' section at a cost of €2.65 million.[36]

Each of the bodies had a slightly different protocol for its quality monitoring. The ACCA, for instance, visited members firms on a six-year cycle with a follow-up in two years if serious problems had been found. The ICAI had had a mandatory practice review in place since the 1980s; it carried out an annual desk-top review and risk analysis of every firm based on an extensive annual return submitted by the firms. Firms were visited on a risk basis; thus firms with listed clients were visited every two to three years, while for firms with other low risk audit clients the cycle was 10 years. The ICPAI, on the other hand, had a general six-year cycle for monitoring, with priority given to firms exposed to risk. Finally, the IIPA had two cycles in operation, comprising three years and five years. Some visits were based on random selection and others will be targeted based on risk assessment. Members in the risk category were visited every three years, while all other members were on a five-year cycle unless their circumstances changed. Elements that triggered risk alerts included previous assessment problems, a problematic number or type of audit clients, with special attention given to the so-called public interest entities (listed companies, credit institutions, insurance brokers, investment firms and pension firms) and weaknesses in the firm's documentation process.[37]

In the year before CARB was established, the Institute's complaints procedure dealt with 160 cases, of which nearly three-quarters related to poor, inadequate or unsatisfactory work either in accounting or liquidation. Although names were generally not made public, we can assume that the vast bulk of these were not the highly publicised complaints against Big 4 firms, but cases that were never likely to reach public consciousness. Only 10 per cent related to breaches of the Institute's *Codes of Ethics* or such matters. In most cases a reprimand was issued, in 15 a fine. Total fines were €36,740 and €44,598 of costs were imposed.

A strategic review

The brunt of the public criticism of the profession in these years fell on the tiny number of firms that audited big and influential corporations. And in Ireland these were (and are) all member firms of the ICAI. So not surprisingly the Institute was self-conscious about the quality of its regulation of members. As CEO Brian Walsh noted, in his last 'Comment' column in *Accountancy Ireland* of August 2004: 'regulation, in one form or another, has dominated the Council agenda for the past ten years.' As the dust from the public concern cases finally settled, and the implications sunk in of the Companies (Auditing and Accounting) Act, which established the IAASA, it was decided to have a 'root and branch review of the Institute'. This decision followed closely on the heels of another decision, to discontinue one more merger proposal, this time with the Institute of Certified Public Accountants in Ireland.

The Strategic Review Group, headed by ex-President David Simpson of Simpson Xavier, reported to Council in November 2004 and the report was published in March 2005. On the members' behalf, the key problem, as the Group put it, was 'maintaining and enhancing the status and standing of the Chartered Accountant; the Chartered Accountant brand is the key strategic issue and the key strategic priority for the Institute. This should be the primary driver in determining future Institute strategy.'[38] (Stripped of modern jargon, this may not in practice be very far from the Institute's original aim of 'respectability'.)

To this end, the Group proposed fundamental changes of direction in two aspects of the Institute's activity. In the first place it proposed that the traditional self-regulatory activity of the Institute, which some had seen as going to the very essence of what it meant to be a professional, be hived off into a 'separate regulatory entity' with full operating autonomy and complete independence. The dramatic extent of the change envisaged can be seen from the fact that from then on the Chartered Accountants Regulatory Board (as the body is called) was independently responsible for setting and monitoring all standards of professional conduct by chartered accountants.

The elaborate and detailed annual practice returns and desk monitoring of practices that had previously been ICAI activity now went to CARB. It was also to be responsible for carrying out quality review visits. It issued practice certificates, insolvency licences, audit licences and authorisation of conduct investment business.[39] It also took on all the disciplinary and complaints activity that the ICAI had previously conducted, including activity enforcing various IFAC standards, such as those relating to continuing professional development and professional indemnity insurance. The responsibility for applying and ensuring compliance with IFAC education standards remains with ICAI.

It was optimistically proposed that 'the Institute should work to bring other accountancy bodies under the umbrella' of this body, which it was hoped would be a significant step 'towards establishing a level playing field in the regulation of the profession generally'. In the short term, however, the new body concentrated on its brief in respect of ICAI, being called the *Chartered Accountants* Regulatory Board and housed in the same building as the Institute. In its first annual report, covering the activities in 2007 Chairman Liam O'Reilly reported that 'from inception our overriding aim has been to deliver a high quality regulatory system which would enhance the trust and respect of our stakeholders. To achieve this, the Board must be seen to act with integrity and in the public interest.'[40] Establishing working relationships with key bodies such as the Chartered Accountants Ireland Council was the first priority.

By 2012 and the sixth annual report, in pursuit of its aim 'to regulate the members of Chartered Accountants Ireland independently, openly and in the public interest', CARB noted that it had registered 986 firms for audit.[41] It issued practising certificates to 2,399 individuals (there were, by comparison, some 2,200 medical consultants practising in the country). As part of the ongoing monitoring process CARB received 1,597 annual returns from practising firms, of which only 12 were marginally incomplete. In total, 126 firms received an audit monitoring visits, of which the great majority resulted either in no action or a request for minor improvements. The Complaints Committee considered 71 cases of complaints against ICAI members, of which most were dismissed as having no prima facie case to answer; of the 28 others, six resulted in no further action and

17 a reprimand with or without a fine and costs.[42] CARB was funded by the Institute and cost €5.9 million in all and emplyed 31 staff.

The second radical proposal of the Strategic Review Group was to 'establish and support new training routes to membership through business, the public sector and other sectors'. This has since led to trainees now becoming chartered accountants without the traditional 'apprenticeship' contract with a principal. Called the 'Elevation' route this was introduced in 2009 and has proved very successful, with 15 per cent of students following that path. Chief Executive Pat Costello, who took up the position in time to contribute to the discussions, perceived this as an important step. 'It is important for the sustaining of the brand that we attract the best students, and it was clear that some of the brightest and best were not attracted by the traditional route. I thought at the time that this would prove more controversial than it did, but the logic was clear.'[43] It would not have escaped the policy-makers' attention that by 2006 ACCA (which did not require articles) had more than twice the number of students as ICAI. Equally, since two-thirds of members were now ending up in business, training them in the traditional disciplines of audit and tax, which had once seemed a good solution to the problem of management education, now looked less obviously useful. As the Group put it 'the Institute should develop a new examination syllabus based on the broader competencies [required] of a leading business professional'.

In 2012, IAASA summarised the data from the nine accountancy bodies it dealt with.[44] They mustered some 32,000 members in the Republic, up by 32 per cent on 2006. Chartered Accountants Ireland and ACCA members made up 72 per cent of the Irish profession with ICAI representing 45 per cent. Two thirds of the active profession were in business, just over a quarter in practice and the balance in the public service. A total of 3,340 practising certificates had been issued. There were in all 1,597 firms registered for audit. Only 25 of these firms had six or more partners (1.5 per cent); among these of course were the Big Four, who had virtually all the audits of Irish Stock Exchange-listed companies. Only 12 firms had more than 10 partners, and 13 had six to 10 partners. Eighty per cent of these larger firms were ICAI members.

Financial reporting in 2012

In 2012 it was, more than 40 years since Bruce Lyster (of Craig Gardner) and Frank Barrett (of Arthur Andersen) began attending the meetings of the Accounting Standards Steering Committee in London. Since those early days, numerous exposure drafts and standards have been produced, discussed, attacked, revised and promulgated. It was difficult, however, to argue that all this work had cracked the world-wide problem of financial reporting. Perhaps the financial stakes were just too high. In his first report as Chairman of IAASA, the distinguished UCD Professor of Economics, Brendan Walsh, noted in 2012 how 'the financial crisis has called into question the quality of audited financial statement and the audit report . . . rebuilding public confidence in financial reporting represents a significant challenge.'[45] This was not of course an Irish problem exclusively and major audit reform proposals published by the EU in 2011, 'including major changes in the European regulatory framework and supervisory structures', were bound in due course to have an effect on the UK and Ireland. Walsh highlighted two other pending developments: the revised accounting framework for Irish and UK entities issued by the Financial Reporting Council and due for implementation by 2015; and the assumption by IAASA of a direct quality assurance role in respect of auditors of public interest entities (following an EU recommendation).

Tax in 2012 – a shift in public attitudes?

The second major plank of the Irish accountancy profession's activity—tax and tax management—came under new scrutiny in the 2000s. As David Devlin of PricewaterhouseCoopers wrote, 'governments have become very concerned recently with the apparent difficulty of taxing corporate profits in a way which corresponds to societal notions of fairness'.[46] As we have seen in previous chapters, the Irish public attitude to tax avoidance had been broadly tolerant. When an opportunity was presented to take part in the game, many Irish people did so with relish, as the DIRT Inquiry made clear.[47] But several high-profile cases of successful tax planning, especially by household-name companies such as Apple, Facebook and Google, aroused public interest. The racy name of one technique, the 'Double Irish with a Dutch, or perhaps Swiss, sandwich', aided public memorability.

A shift in public and political mood in the West generally led to an OECD report called *Addressing Base Erosion and Profit Shifting*.[48] In this report the result of tax planning is described as 'constituting a serious risk to tax revenues, tax sovereignty and tax fairness'. Although the exact amount of the loss to sovereign states was found impossible to quantify, the anomalous position that Bermuda and the British Virgin Islands were among the top Foreign Direct Investment sources into China, Russia and India, and that the top FDI sources for India also included Cyprus and the Bahamas, was suggestive. A follow-up G20 declaration pronounced a determination to crack down on avoidance. It seems likely that, at the very least, corporations will (as David Devlin, former President of FEE and crucially a former member of IFAC's International Ethics Standards Board for Accountants put it) 'have to manage their tax affairs not only from an efficiency and compliance point of view but from a reputational point of view'. He perceived this extra dimension 'as part of the public interest and social responsibility of members of [the] profession'.[49]

The versatile profession

In an article celebrating the 125th Anniversary of the Charter, I described how the profession in Ireland had gone through three incarnations.[50] When the Charter was signed in 1888, the senior members were generally sole principals, employing a number of unqualified seniors, mainly but not exclusively engaged in insolvency, estate and other court work. After the introduction of compulsory audit from 1900 on, firms turned their attention increasingly to that aspect and evolved into multi-partner firms. Each partner was a generalist, handling the audit, tax and other matters, except in highly specialised areas such as secretarial services. Although unqualified seniors still played a prominent part, a new element in the firm were the articled clerks, from whom eventually the next generation of partners would be chosen. The third professional model was that of the professional services firm, with the partners as far as possible specialising in various aspects of the service, whether it was audit, tax or management advice.

Irish accountants are and will remain numerous, active and influential, particularly those in dominant positions in Irish business, practice and public life. But it seems quite unlikely that when the history of the 150 years since the issuing of the Charter come to be written, their professional world will look the same as it does now. Pressures, opportunities and challenges stimulating change abound on all sides. In 2013 it seems that these might be the most significant[51]:

- the increasing globalisation of world business and financial reporting;
- the EU's tendency to insist on continental models for the audit of public interest entities (however these might be defined), these to include mandatory rotation of audit firms and tight rules regarding non-audit services;

- the worldwide trend of re-positioning professional bodies as purely representative bodies for their members rather than bodies that act in the public interest setting and regulating standards;
- the national and international impacts of the US Sarbanes–Oxley Act of 2002, notably the Public Company Accounting Oversight Board;
- the attempts to pre-empt corporate scandals by external regulatory bodies (such as IAASA or the Financial Reporting Council or similar bodies in the US and the EU);
- the ever more detailed international accounting standards, requiring a highly technical approach and producing increasingly indigestible annual reporting;
- a combination of regulation and increasing audit exemption thresholds may see auditing become the preserve of larger firms, perhaps as specialists, thus taking an important tranche of business from smaller firms, but leaving them free to offer other types of consultancy and accounting services;
- it has long been recognised that the profession's general reputation is weakened by the existence of multiple professional bodies (in contrast, for instance, to solicitors, doctors or architects), as the campaigns for registration demonstrated in the past—now as many as nine separate bodies are licensed by IAASA;
- the growing impact of public reputational considerations in financial reporting, tax planning and audit;
- the ever-widening technical sophistication requiring constant professional development and certification;
- new possibilities for IT-driven, real-time models of auditing perhaps combined with 'off-shoring' of some work, leading front-line audit staff to require quite different skills;
- by the end of the 20th century members of the ICAI in business were a majority, and of the profession as a whole a very considerable majority, causing profound but subtle changes in the Irish profession, to the extent perhaps of leading some business accountants to challenge the relevance of professional bodies; decreasing numbers are likely to have gone through the traditional audit and tax training route with all it meant in terms of ethos;
- the challenge of business school graduates, despite the unprecedented recent recruiting success of all the professional accounting bodies;

- the focus on corporate governance, risk and compliance.[52]

Which of these, a combination of these, or indeed some quite different factors, will turn out to have been crucial will be for the historian of the 150th celebrations of the 1888 Charter to describe. All we can say is that the profession has actively evolved several times already, and there is little doubt that further exciting changes are likely.

Notes

Chapter One

1 Quoted in R. J. Chambers, *An Accounting Thesaurus* (London 1995) p 22.

2 There had been a Collegio dei Rasconati (College of Accountants) in Venice in the 16th century, but a new start had to be made in post-Industrial Revolution Britain.

3 H. Howitt, *The History of the Institute of Chartered Accountants in England and Wales 1880–1965* (London 1966) p xi.

4 N. Stacey, *English Accountancy 1880–1954* (London 1954) pp 50–1.

5 See, for instance, J. Aho, 'Rhetoric and the Invention of Double-entry Book-keeping' *Rhetorica* Vol 3.1 (1985) pp 21–43. Like all rhetorics (for instance, sermon writing or sports reporting), it imposed its own conventions, which users simply took for granted. Only when they were codified as Generally Accepted Accountancy Principles was it realised how contentious they could be.

6 I. Origo, *The Merchant of Prato* (London 1957). This book gives a fascinating description of these deals and in other pages aspects of his financial and personal life.

7 See G. Nigro, *Francesco di Marco Datini: The Man, the Merchant* (Florence 2010) pp 76, 92. The book-keepers of the day must have quailed at having to abandon the numerals with which they had been familiar for years, adding instantly and unconsciously *xxvii* to *lxxiii*, just as their professional descendants were able to add 5s 11d to 17s 5d at a glance.

8 P. Clarke, 'The Teaching of Book-keeping in Nineteenth-Century Ireland', *Accounting, Business & Financial History*, Vol. 18, No. 1 (March 2008), pp 21–33.

9 I. Origo, *The Merchant of Prato* (London 1957) p 113.

10 P. Clarke, 'The Teaching of Book-keeping in Nineteenth-Century Ireland' *Accounting, Business & Financial History*, Vol. 18, No. 1 (March 2008) p 29.

11 B. S. Yamey, 'Accounting in England 1500–1900' in W Baxter *et al.* (Eds.) *Studies in Accounting Theory* (3rd ed., London 1962) p 37.

12 D. Anderson, *Recounting: The First Hundred Years of the Ulster Society of Chartered Accountants* (Dublin and Belfast 2006) p 105.

13 J. Crowley *et al.*, *Atlas of the Great Irish Famine* (Cork 2012) pp 30–31.

14 E. Smith, *The Highland Lady in Ireland* (Edinburgh 1991) p 341.

15 E. Smith, *The Highland Lady in Ireland* (Edinburgh 1991) p 349.

16 T. Grimshaw, 'A Statistical Survey of Ireland from 1840 to 1888', *Journal of the Statistical and Social Inquiry Society of Ireland,* Part l XVIII, 1888, pp 331–61.

17 *Report from the Select Committee on Industries (Ireland) 1884–5* BPP 288.

18 W. C. Sullivan to the *Royal Commission on Technical Instruction* C-3981-111, Appendix X, p 492.

19 *Report from the Select Committee on Industries (Ireland) 1884–5* BPP 288, p 359.

20 *Report from the Select Committee on Industries (Ireland) 1884–5*, question 616.

21 *Report from the Select Committee on Industries (Ireland) 1884–5*, questions 4128, 4129.

22 D. Morier Evans, *The Commercial Crisis* (London 1849) p 19.

23 K. B. Nowlan, 'The Transport Revolution: the Coming of the Railways' in K. B. Nowlan (ed.), *Travel and Transport in Ireland* (Dublin 1973) pp 96–100.

24 T. Grimshaw, 'A Statistical Survey of Ireland from 1840 to 1888', *Journal of the Statistical and Social Inquiry Society of Ireland,* Part l XVIII, 1888 pp 331–61.

25 M. Turner, 'Towards an Agricultural Price Index for Ireland 1850–1914', *Economic and Social Review,* Vol. 18, No. 2 (January 1987) p 193.

26 T. Grimshaw, 'A Statistical Survey of Ireland from 1840 to 1888', *Journal of the Statistical and Social Inquiry Society of Ireland,* Part l XVIII, 1888 pp 331–61.

27 R. V. Comerford, 'Ireland 1850–70: Post-Famine and Mid-Victorian' in W. E. Vaughan (ed.) *A New History of Ireland, Vol V: Ireland under the Union 1800–70* (Oxford 1989) pp 376–7.

28 J. R. Edwards, 'The Origins and Evolution of the Double Account System', *Abacus* Vol. 21, No. 1 (1985). See also J. Challone Smith, 'On the form of railway accounts', *Irish Builder* Vol. xviii No. 392 pp 112–3.

29 D. Matthews *et al.*, *The Priesthood of Industry: The Rise of the Professional Accountant in British Management* (Oxford 1998) p 35.

30 D. Matthews *et al.*, *The Priesthood of Industry: The Rise of the Professional Accountant in British Management* (Oxford 1998) p 17.

31 C. Dickens, *Little Dorrit* (London 1857) Chapter XXV.

32 Brown's obituary in *The Irish Times* (2 November 1902) was relied on by Howard Robinson in his *History of Accountants in Ireland.* It states that Brown entered the Bank of Ireland in 1844, having been obliged to curtail his education in Trinity, finally leaving in 1853 to establish his accountancy practice. This was the story Brown promoted in later life in, for example, a report of a meeting of the Institute in December 1893 (*The Irish Times* 1 December 1893). But in fact he continued to advertise his accountancy services regularly in directories after supposedly joining the Bank in 1844. It is not clear how these facts can be reconciled. Perhaps he worked only part-time for the Bank, or possibly he had a spell in private practice from 1844 to perhaps 1850 and then joined the bank where he met his future partner, William Craig.

33 A. M. Sullivan, *New Ireland—Political Sketches and Personal Reminiscences of Thirty Years of Irish Public Life* (Dublin 1877) Chapter XII.

34 A. Longfield (ed.), *The Shapland Carew Papers* (Dublin 1946) p 170.

35 *The Irish Times* 6 June 1863.

36 *The Irish Times* 13 May 1876.

37 P. McClelland and P. Stanton, '"An Ignorant Set of Men": An Episode in the Clash of Legal and Accounting Professions Over Jurisdiction', *Accounting History* (2004) 9:207.

38 T. Farmar, *A History of Craig Gardner & Co.: The first 100 years* (Dublin 1988)

pp 22–5. It is not clear where this ledger is now.

39 *The Irish Times* 7 May 1861 and 14 October 1863.

40 J. Wyse Jackson and P. Costello, *John Stanislaus Joyce: The Voluminous Life and Genius of James Joyce's Father* (London 1997) pp 62–4.

41 *The Irish Times* 4 November 1875.

42 *The Irish Times* 28 February 1882.

43 E. A. French, *Unlimited Liability: The Case of the City of Glasgow Bank* (London 1985) pp 8, 9, 27. The reference to the London *Times* is 31 December 1878.

44 *The Irish Times* 15 March 1881.

45 *The Irish Times* 2 and 7 August 1877.

46 For example, K. Kennedy *et al.*, *The Economic Development of Ireland in the Twentieth Century* (London 1988) p 110.

Chapter Two

1 Based on ICAEW Library *Index of UK and Irish Accountancy and Professional Bodies.*

2 H. Howitt, *The History of the Institute of Chartered Accountants in England and Wales* (London 1966) pp 24–5.

3 His partner William Craig had left the firm in 1875. T. Farmar, *A History of Craig, Gardner & Co.* (Dublin 1988) pp 28–32.

4 *The Irish Times* 5 July 1886; the positions of about 80 per cent of the names listed can be identified from Thom's *Directory*. Many of the guests are listed only by name and initial, such as J. Lyster, W. Fitzgerald, etc., but we can assume that no woman would be so curtly referred to in *The Irish Times.*

5 *The Irish Times* 5 July 1886.

6 W. Dawson, 'My Dublin Year' in *Studies* (Dublin 1912) p 705.

7 K. Kennedy *et al.*, *The Economic Development of Ireland in the Twentieth Century* (London 1988) p 15.

8 A. Trollope, *The Vicar of Bullhampton* (1870) Chapter IX.

9 H. Howitt, *The History of the Institute of Chartered Accountants in England and Wales* (London 1966) p 34.

10 D. Anderson, *Recounting* (Dublin and Belfast 2006) p 104.

11 A. Abbott, *The System of Professions* (Chicago 1988) p 10.

12 Summarised in W. Birkett and E. Evans, 'Theorising Professionalisation' in *Accounting History* (2005) No. 10, pp 118–9.

13 See P. O'Regan, 'Elevating the Profession: the Institute of Chartered Accountants in Ireland and the Implementation of Social Closure Strategies 1888–1909' in *Accounting, Business & Financial History*, Vol. 18, No. 1 (March 2008) pp 35–59. This is a special edition of the journal devoted to Ireland, edited by Professor Ciarán Ó hÓgartaigh of UCD.

14 J. Wyse Jackson and P. Costello, *John Stanislaus Joyce* (London 1997) pp 62–3, 65.

15 *Weekly Irish Times* 17 February 1894.

16 *Weekly Irish Times* issues from 26 December 1891 to 27 February 1892.

17 H. W. Robinson, *A History of Accountants in Ireland* (2nd ed., Dublin 1983) p 53.

18 *Bankruptcy Law Committee Report 1972* (the Budd Report) Prl 2714 (Dublin 1972) Chapter 1.

19 H. W. Robinson, *A History of Accountants in Ireland* (1st ed., Dublin 1964) pp 116–9.

20 M. Annisette and P. O'Regan, 'Joined for a Common Purpose', *Qualitative Research in Accounting and Management,* Vol. 4, No. 1 (2007) p 13.

21 *Studies* (Dublin 1915) reprinted in A. Clery, *Dublin Essays* (Dublin 1919) p 46.

22 Census of Population 1891, Table 19.

23 M. Annisette and P. O'Regan, 'Joined for a Common Purpose', *Qualitative Research in Accounting and Management,* Vol. 4, No. 1 (2007) p 13. The same was said of Robert Gardner, who certainly earned his knighthood by rescuing the finances of the unionist Pembroke Township, but he was not elected to that body until 1902.

24 E. Cahill, *The Framework of a Christian State* (Dublin 1932) p 230; G. Clune, *Freemasonry—its Origins, Aims and Methods* (Dublin 1931) p 14; J. Cooney, *John Charles McQuaid* (Dublin 1999) pp 69–70 describes the future Archbishop of Dublin's view that Freemasons were allies of the Jews in their battle against Christ's church.

25 Quoted in D. Keogh, *Jews in Twentieth Century Ireland* (Cork 1998) p 22.

26 Government of Ireland Act 1920, clause 65.

27 Grand Lodge of Ireland Index of Members from 1875, inspected by courtesy of the Archivist Rebecca Hayes.

28 *The Irish Times* 18 January 1899.

29 *The Irish Times* 11 June 1888.

30 *The Irish Times* 24 September 1868.

31 Quoted in *The Irish Times* 11 June 1888.

32 T. Farmar, *A History of Craig Gardner & Co.* (Dublin 1988) p 44. Unfortunately, the Craig Gardner fee book, a valuable source for the early years of the Irish profession, and possibly the earliest artefact relating to the profession in Ireland, was not available for examination for this history.

33 *The Irish Times* 11 June 1888.

34 It used to be thought that the motto meant 'Serving faithfully in all matters', but recent research has identified that '*servo*' means 'I preserve, guard, look after', not 'I serve', and '*fidemque*' is a noun, not an adverb. See, e.g. Cassells *Latin Dictionary* under '*servo*'.

35 *The Irish Times* 20 November 1888 and 7 May 1889.

36 P. O'Regan, 'Elevating the Profession: the Institute of Chartered Accountants in Ireland and the Implementation of Social Closure Strategies 1888–1909' in *Accounting, Business and Financial History,* Vol. 18, No. 1 (March 2008) pp 47–8.

37 M. Crowley, *Statistics and Directory of Limited Companies Registered in Ireland* (Dublin 1901) p x.

38 W. A. Thomas, *The Stock Exchanges of Ireland* (Liverpool 1986) p 153.

39 H. W. Robinson, *A History of Accountants in Ireland* (1st ed., Dublin 1964) p 149.

40 *The Irish Times* 10 January 1890.

41 *The Accountant* 7 June 1890.

42 D. Matthews *et al.*, *The Priesthood of Industry* (Oxford 1998) p 50.

43 *The Irish Times* 12 July 1905.

44 W. A. Thomas, *The Stock Exchanges of Ireland* (Liverpool 1986) pp 153–7.

45 *The Irish Times* 26 April 1887.

46 W. A. Thomas, *The Stock Exchanges of Ireland* (Liverpool 1986) Appendix 6, pp 263–3, lists 49 companies of which 37 had fewer than 500 shareholders at the time of registration.

47 The modern historian of English auditing has written that 'management letters became the general rule from the 1970s'. D. Matthews, 'From ticking to clicking', *Accounting Historians Journal*, Vol. 33, No. 2 (December 2006) p 87.

48 T. Farmar, *A History of Craig Gardner & Co.* (Dublin 1988) pp 73–4.

49 *The Irish Times* 21 February 1896.

50 *Accountancy Ireland* October 2000.

51 *The Irish Times* 27 January 1900.

52 See examples quoted in R. J. Chambers, *An Accounting Thesaurus* (Oxford 1995) pp 75–6.

Chapter Three

1 R. J. Chambers, *An Accounting Thesaurus* (London 1995) p 75. Chambers quotes numerous other writers to the same effect.

2 W. B Yeats, 'September 1913'.

3 The 'Salaries Book', for staff, not partners, is in two volumes, the first covering December 1896 to May 1921, and recording the arrival, progress and sometimes abrupt departure of over 170 names. The second volume, covering the period from 1921 to 1942 will be analysed in more detail in the next chapter. I am grateful to Terence O'Rourke and Elaine Reynolds of KPMG for arranging access to this archive.

4 His obituary is in *The Irish Times* 13 December 1958.

5 T. Farmar, *A History of Craig Gardner & Co.* (Dublin 1988) pp 100–102.

6 *Dictionary of Irish Biography* (Cambridge 2009), *sub nom* 'Jeremiah Buckley', which corrects *The Irish Times'* obituary error that Buckley had been imprisoned with Parnell.

7 *Dictionary of Irish Biography* (Cambridge 2009), *sub nom* 'Percy Reynolds'.

8 *The Accountant* 27 May 1916. This report of the AGM was probably prepared by the Honorary Secretary J. Harold Pim, and inserted verbatim.

9 E. McCague, *Arthur Cox 1891–1965* (Dublin 1994) p. 49.

10 If 'the course is only open to rich men and not the poor man,' *The Accountant* wrote, 'the matter is not of any consequence to the public . . . things may be made too easy for the impecunious man of ability.' 11 November 1911.

11 Renamed the Society of Incorporated Accountants and Auditors 1954; Society

of Incorporated Accountants 1954–7, merged with the British and Irish Institutes 1957.

12 H. W. Robinson, *A History of Accountants in Ireland* (1st ed., Dublin 1964) p 110.

13 A. Garrett, *History of the Society of Incorporated Accountants 1885–1957* (London 1961) pp 25–6.

14 This and the next paragraph are based on H. W. Robinson, *A History of Accountants in Ireland* (1st ed., Dublin 1964) Chapter 12 *passim.*

15 M. Crowley, *Statistics and Directory of Limited Liability Companies Registered in Ireland* (Dublin 1901).

16 D. Anderson, *Recounting* (Dublin and Belfast 2006) p 36.

17 Until the Entente Cordiale in 1904 and the publication of Erskine Childers' *The Riddle of the Sands,* both statesmen and novel readers believed that if war were to come not only would it be short but that France or possibly Russia would be the enemy. See I. F. Clarke, *Voices Prophesying War 1763–1984* (Oxford 1966) p 116.

18 As reported in the *Weekly Irish Times* 11 March 1906.

19 E. McCague, *Arthur Cox 1891–1965* (Dublin 1994) p 8.

20 His obituary is in *The Irish Times* 16 July 1940.

21 H. W. Robinson, *A History of Accountants in Ireland*, (1st ed., Dublin 1964) p. 193.

22 T. Farmar, *A History of Craig Gardner & Co.* (Dublin 1988) p 72.

23 E. Jones, *Accountancy and the British Economy* (London 1981) p 59–61.

24 H. W. Robinson, *A History of Accountants in Ireland* (2nd ed., Dublin 1983) p 42.

25 *In re The London and Central Bank* (1895).

26 H. W. Robinson, *A History of Accountants in Ireland* (2nd ed., Dublin 1983) pp 40, 97.

27 Quoted by Howard Robinson in 'Published accounts in the Republic of Ireland' *Members' Bulletin* November 1962.

28 Amos & Walton, *Introduction to French Law* (Oxford 1963) p 352.

29 A. Mikol, 'The Evolution of Auditing and the Independent Auditor in France', *European Accounting Review* (1993) p. 3.

30 See H. W. Robinson, *A History of Accountants in Ireland* (1st ed. Dublin 1964) pp. 162–3.

31 See 'Chart of Accounts', *European Accounting Review* (May 1995).

32 See R. J. Chambers, *An Accounting Thesaurus* (London 1995) pp 75–6.

33 F. R. M. De Paula, *The Principles of Auditing* (London 1914) p 6.

34 V. R. V. Cooper, *Manual of Auditing* (London 1966) p 1. The impact of this book will be discussed in Chapter Six in the context of the establishment of Cooper Brothers, Dublin, in 1968.

35 M. Crowley, *The Commercial Handbook and Office Assistant* (London 1891) pp 16–17.

36 F. R. M. De Paula, *The Principles of Auditing* (London 1914).

37 The Editor, *Fraud in Accounts* (3rd ed., London 1919) p 22.

38 Quoted in J. Amernic and R. Craig, 'Reform of Accounting Education in the Post-Enron Era' in *Abacus* (2004) Vol. 40, No. 3, p 343.

39 D. Matthews, 'From Ticking to Clicking', *Accounting Historians Journal*, Vol. 3, No. 2 (December 2006) pp 67–8.

40 Paul Creedon, interview with author, October 2012.

41 Niamh Brennan (chartered accountant and Michael MacCormac Professor of Management at University College Dublin) interview in May 2013.

42 E. Jones, *English System of Book-keeping* (Bristol 1796) quoted in B. S. Yamey, 'Accounting in England 1500–1900' in W. Baxter (ed.), *Studies in Accounting Theory* (3rd ed., London 1962) p 32.

43 E. Peragallo, 'On the History of the Trial Balance', *Accounting Review* (1956) (3) p 389; B. S. Yamey, 'Closing the Ledger', *Accounting and Business Research* (1970) 1 (1) pp 71–7.

44 M. Crowley, *Commercial Handbook and Office Assistant* (London 1891) p 68.

45 L. Dicksee, *Advanced Accounts* (London 1903) Chapter 4.

46 Quoted in J. Maltby, 'A Sort of Guide, Philosopher and Friend' in *Accounting Business & Financial History*, Vol. 9, No. 1 (March 1999) p 41.

47 H. Shannon,'The Limited Companies of 1856–83' reprinted from *Economic History Review* IV (1933) in E. Carus-Wilson (ed.), *Essays in Economic History* Vol. 1. (London 1954) p 391. The background to the specialised meaning given to 'prudence' by the profession is discussed in J. Maltby, 'Prudence', *Critical Studies in Accountancy* (February 2000).

48 *The Accountant* 15 October 1904, quoted in J. Maltby, 'A Sort of Guide, Philosopher and Friend', *Accounting, Business & Financial History* Vol. 9, No. 1, (March 1999) p 45.

49 *Irish Investors Guardian* December 1906.

50 Bell & Graham, quoted in R. J. Chambers, *An Accounting Thesaurus* (Oxford 1995) p 376.

51 *The Accountant* 22 April 1904, quoted in J. Maltby, 'A Sort of Guide, Philosopher and Friend' *Accounting, Business & Financial History* Vol. 9, No. 1, (March 1999) pp 44–5.

52 *Newton v. Birmingham Small Arms* (1906) quoted in R. J. Chambers, *An Accounting Thesaurus* (Oxford 1995) p 376.

53 Financial Reporting Standard 18 Accounting Policies, para. 43.

54 J. Bardon, *A History of Ulster* (Belfast 1992) pp 456–7.

55 D. Matthews, *Priesthood of Industry* (Oxford 1998) Chapter 5, esp. p 180.

56 A. J. P. Taylor, *English History 1914–1945* (Oxford 1965) p 40.

57 J. Edwards, *A History of Financial Accounting* (London 1989) p 132.

58 M. Crowley, *Commercial Handbook and Office Assistant* (London 1891) p 101.

59 *Select Committee on Income Tax 1906*, Question 106 to Sir Henry Primrose, Chairman of the Board of Inland Revenue.

60 *Select Committee on Income Tax 1906*, Question 375 to Bernard Mallet, Commissioner of the Board of Inland Revenue.

61 B. Sabine, *A History of Income Tax* (London 1966) pp 152–5.

62 A. Frydlender and D. Pham, 'Relationship between accounting and taxation in France', *European Accounting Review* (1996). Joseph Caillaux, a senior political figure and eventually Prime Minister, is now better known as a protagonist in a sensational murder case. His wife shot and killed a newspaper editor who had published a politically embarrassing letter that Caillaux had sent to a former mistress. Madame Caillaux was acquitted on the very French grounds that she was upset by the revelations and as a woman she could not be expected to control her emotions. See E. Berenson, *The Trial of Madame Caillaux* (California 1992).

63 H. W. Robinson, *A History of Accountants in Ireland* (1st ed., Dublin 1964) p 219.

64 *The Accountant* 2 June 1917.

65 The letter-book contains 500 pages of copy-letters dealing with the affairs of just over 80 clients, including The Irish Times, the Hammond Lane Foundry, Mitchell's, Elvery's and Bray Cinema.

66 B. Chubb, *A Source Book of Irish Government* (Dublin 1983) pp. 27–8.

67 P. Barker, *The Minority Interest; Women Who Succeed in the Accountancy Profession* (Dublin 2009) pp 26–7. The AGM and the passing of the resolution was some months before the Act was introduced to Parliament (July) and became law (December). Basing themselves on early drafts, the Council, having taken legal advice, believed that a special act of parliament would be necessary because the Charter apparently forbade women to become members. Once the Government's actual wording of clause 1 became clear, this new Bill (which President Stewart Quinn hoped would also include a new attempt at setting up a statutory register) was no longer necessary.

Chapter Four

1 K. Bowen, *Protestants in a Catholic State* (Dublin 1983) pp 85–8.

2 The 1926 Irish Census did not report on religion; the 1911 Census found that 42 per cent of accountants practising in Leinster were Protestant.

3 D. Anderson, *Recounting* (Dublin and Belfast 2006) p 46.

4 K. Bowen, *Protestants in a Catholic State* (Dublin 1983) p 47.

5 *The Irish Times*, 13 May 1922.

6 G. Seaver, *John Allen Fitzgerald Gregg, Archbishop* (Dublin 1963) p 126.

7 Rev. G. Clune, *Freemasonry—its origins, aims and methods* (Dublin 1931). This was a Catholic Truth Society pamphlet.

8 E. Bolster, *The Knights of St Columbanus* (Dublin 1959) pp 34, 57–8, 68.

9 B. Inglis, *West Briton* (London 1962) p 13.

10 This paragraph is based on B. Inglis, *West Briton* (London 1962) Chapter 1. The term 'R.C.' exemplifies the group's detachment. This was an English term seen as simply precise by Protestants and faintly offensive by Catholics, as they called themselves.

11 T. Farmar, *A History of Craig Gardner & Co.* (Dublin 1988) p 133.

12 B. Inglis, *West Briton* (London 1962) p 36.

13 J. Bardon, *A History of Ulster* (Belfast 1992) p 467.

14 J. Bardon, *A History of Ulster* (Belfast 1992) p 496.

15 For details of the causes of this economic war and the annuities question in particular, see R. Fanning, *The Irish Department of Finance 1922–58* (Dublin 1978) Chapter 7.

16 J. J. Lee, *Ireland 1912–1985* (Cambridge 1989) p 190.

17 J. J. Lee, *Ireland 1912–1985* (Cambridge 1989) p 190.

18 M. E. Daly, 'An Irish-Ireland for business?' *Irish Historical Studies* (November 1984) p 24.

19 *Weekly Irish Times* 16 December 1933.

20 *Dictionary of Irish Biography* (Cambridge 2009), *sub nom* 'Frank Lemass'.

21 Anon., *Twenty-one Years of Industrial Financing* (Dublin 1954).

22 P. Clarke, 'The Evolution of Accounting Practice in Ireland', *The Irish Accounting Review* (2006) Vol. 13, p 9. It was only in 1955 that the numbers of members and firms in Dublin exceeded those in Belfast.

23 See estimates by P. Clarke in 'Financial reporting in Ireland' in *The Irish Accounting Review* (2001) Vol. 8, No. 2, p 33.

24 *Commission on Vocational Organisation Report* (Dublin 1943) pp 122, 518–21. The Commission was established in 1939 under the Chairmanship of Bishop Michael Browne of Galway. Its brief was to explore how the principles of corporatism, such as had been applied in Fascist Italy and as were promoted by Pope Pius XI, might be applied in Ireland. The *Report* (actually published in August 1944, by which time Italy had lost the war) fell stillborn from the press, no doubt partly because it recommended a range of elaborate schemes, including the establishment of a National Vocational Assembly backed by parish councils. It remains a useful description of the business and commercial organisations of the day.

25 Seanad Éireann, Vol. 8, 24 February 1927.

26 J. Joyce, *Ulysses* (Harmondsworth 1969) p 489.

27 J. Joyce, *Ulysses* (Harmondsworth 1969) p 632.

28 K. Warnock, 'Auditing Bloom, Editing Joyce' in *Accounting, Business & Financial History* Vol. 18 No. 1, (March 2008) pp 81–95. The firm was always known as Craig Gardner & Co. Keith Warnock is inclined to suppose these apparent errors are subtle artistic signals—others less generously might think they are simply heedless, like Shakespeare assigning a sea-coast to Bohemia (Czech Republic), Jane Austen enjoying apple blossom in June or the literary errors Professor John Sutherland has described in various books.

29 Sir Patrick Hastings, 'The Case of the Royal Mail' in W. Baxter (ed.), *Studies in Accounting Theory* (London 1962) p 452.

30 C. Brooks (ed.), *The Royal Mail Case* (Edinburgh and London 1933) p 187. The publication of the transcript of this City case in the long-running Notable British Trials series, which was normally devoted to sensational murder cases, is evidence of the intense public interest.

31 F. R. M. De Paula, *Developments in Accounting* (London 1948) p 265.

32 J. Edwards, *A History of Financial Accounting* (London 1989) p 127.

33 *The Commission on Vocational Organisation Report* (1943) para. 190.

34 There had never been any ambiguity on the part of the Republican authorities

that such would be the case. S. Réamonn, *The Revenue Commissioners* (Dublin 1981) pp 52, 67.

35 S. Réamonn, *The Revenue Commissioners* (Dublin 1981) p 108. There is no mention in this notably office-centred book of the work of solicitors or accountants in the tax-gathering process.

36 Trevor Morrow, interview with author, September 2012.

37 Seanad Éireann, Vol. 8, 24 February 1927.

38 Dáil Debates, 3 May 1923. Magennis was a Cumann na nGaedheal TD for Dublin South. In his later years he was distinguished for his advocacy of the strictest Catholic public morality and censorship of publications.

39 S. Réamonn, *The Revenue Commissioners* (Dublin 1981) pp 113–14.

40 S. Browne, *The Press in Ireland* (Dublin 1937) pp 227–34 lists no fewer than 27 of these journals from *Irish Accountant and Secretary* to *Irish Vintner*.

41 *Irish Accountant and Secretary* (January 1936).

42 D. Rowe (ed.), *The Irish Chartered Accountant: Centenary Essays 1888–1988* (Dublin 1988) p 152.

43 William Cunningham, ex senior partner Craig Gardner, interview with author in 1985.

44 M. Crowley *Commercial Handbook and Office Assistant* (London 1891) p 73.

45 D. Anderson, *Recounting* (Belfast and Dublin 2006) p 110.

46 The ancestors of the kind of arithmeticians who could add a column of pounds, shillings and pence at a glance would have been equally unphased by the requirement to add, in Roman numerals, xxviii to xix.

47 F. R. M. De Paula, *The Principles of Auditing* (London 1915) p 22.

48 C. Kohler, *Five Years Hard! Memoirs of an Articled Clerk* (London 1987) p 12.

49 F. R. M. De Paula, *The Principles of Auditing* (London 1915) p 8.

50 D. Rowe (ed.), *The Irish Chartered Accountant: Centenary Essays 1888–1988* (Dublin 1988) p 173.

51 C. Kohler, *Five Years Hard! Memoirs of an Articled Clerk* (London 1987) p 13.

52 C. Andrews, *A Man of No Property* (Cork 1982) p 23; T. Farmar, *A History of Craig Gardner & Co.* (Dublin 1988) p 130.

53 Margaret Downes, interview with author, October 2012.

54 Seanad Éireann, Vol. 8, 24 February 1927.

55 *The Accountant* 12 May 1933.

56 See C. Stray, 'From Oral to Written Examinations, Cambridge, Oxford and Dublin' in M. Feingold (ed.) *History of Universities* XX/2 (Oxford 2005).

57 T. Farmar, *A History of Craig Gardner & Co.* (Dublin 1988) p 132.

58 H. Howitt, *The History of the Institute of Chartered Accountants in England and Wales 1880–1965* (London 1966) p 198.

59 H. W. Robinson, *A History of Accountants in Ireland* (1st ed., Dublin 1964) p 311.

60 H. W. Robinson, *A History of Accountants in Ireland* (2nd ed., Dublin 1983) p 218.

61 W. Baxter, *Studies in Accounting* (London 1958), Introduction. Professor Baxter was Professor of Accounting at the London School of Economics.

62 As for instance in M. Glautier and B. Underdown, *Accounting Theory and Practice* (7th ed., London 2001) Chapters 1–5.

63 E. McCague, *Arthur Cox 1891–1965* (Dublin 1994) p 85.

64 J. Gunther, *Inside Europe* (London 1936) p 271.

65 R. de Zouche *et al.*, *Accountants Costs and Time Records* (London 1923) pp 8–9.

66 Quoted in D. Anderson, *Recounting* (Dublin and Belfast 2006) p 75.

67 D. Anderson, *Recounting* (Dublin and Belfast 2006) pp 60–61.

68 *The Irish Times* 2 February 1934.

Chapter Five

1 This letter was in response to one from 'Jesting Pilate' (a Presbyterian) who had heard on the wireless that falsification of income tax returns was not regarded by the Catholic Church as an offence against the moral law, and wanted to know if this was true.

2 Council Minutes, 21 February 1936. Edward VIII was the Head of State of the Irish Free State under the 1922 Constitution.

3 H. W. Robinson, *A History of Accountants in Ireland* (1st ed., Dublin 1964) p 101.

4 Appreciation, *The Irish Times* 12 January 1968.

5 *Leech v. Stokes and Others* (1937).

6 Gabriel Brock's notes on the case are with the Craig Gardner papers.

7 P. Gatenby, *Dublin's Meath Hospital* (Dublin 1966) Chapter 13.

8 See S. Walker, 'Encounters with Nazism: British Accountants and the Fifth International Conference on Accounting', *Critical Perspectives on Accounting* (2000) Vol. 11, No. 2; and E. Lippman and E. Wilson, 'The Culpability of Accounting in Perpetuating the Holocaust', *Accounting History* (2007) Vol. 12, No. 3.

9 This striking result can best be explained by the idea that since the November 1933 Plebiscite, the Nazis did not need to violate the secrecy of the ballot, since everyone assumed that they would, and acted accordingly. Similar reasoning produced majorities for Hitler in the concentration camps. Victor Klemperer, *I Shall Bear Witness: The Diaries of Victor Klemperer 1933–41* (London 1998) 14 November 1933.

10 Irish Times, *Irish Review and Annual* 1938. This extensive annual summary of the previous year in Ireland provides a thoughtful and more or less contemporary view of economic and political events. It was published in early January of the following year, so the 1938 survey was published on 2 January 1939. The series ran from 1932 (the first covering the 10 years since independence) to 1967.

11 *The Irish Times* 12 November 1938.

12 J. Bardon, *A History of Ulster* (Belfast 1992) Chapter 5 *passim*.

13 J. Bardon, *A History of Ulster* (Belfast 1992) pp 580–1.

14 The Stationery Office, *Statistical Abstract* 1941 P No. 5472 (Dublin 1942) p 183.

15 C. Ó Gráda, *Ireland a New Economic History* (Oxford 1994) p 399. This data is

based on a 1948 survey by the Department of Industry and Commerce.

16 A. Prost *et al.*, *A History of Private Life* Vol. V (Harvard 1991) pp 56–7.

17 Statistical Abstract 1942. H. W. Robinson, *A History of Accountants in Ireland* (1st ed., Dublin 1964) p 257.

18 A. A. Garrett, *History of the Society of Incorporated Accountants* (Oxford 1961) p 325; see also the 1958 ICAI *Membership List* which identified the new members.

19 H. W. Robinson, *A History of Accountants in Ireland* (1st ed., Dublin 1964) p 87.

20 D. Rowe (ed.), *The Irish Chartered Accountant: Centenary Essays 1888–1988* (Dublin 1988); reminiscences of David Rowe himself at p 152.

21 *Irish Accountant and Secretary* January 1938.

22 *Irish Accountant and Secretary* August 1954. See also P. Tormey, 'Equipping the office: accounting machines', *Administration* Vol. 2 No. 4 (Winter 1964–5).

23 T. Farmar, *A History of Craig Gardner & Co.* (Dublin 1988) p 170.

24 Typescript reminiscences of Metcalfe Lilburn & Enright by Stewart Lilburn in T. Farmar archive.

25 R. Lewis *et al.*, *Professional People* (London 1952) pp 58, 63.

26 *Irish Accountant and Secretary* September 1941.

27 G. Ivan Morris, *In Dublin's Fair City* (London 1947) pp 62–3.

28 Stokes Brother & Pim Salaries Book 1921–1943.

29 'Other People's Incomes', *The Bell* August–November 1943. The young professional described is actually a solicitor.

30 D. Rowe (ed.), *The Irish Chartered Accountant: Centenary Essays 1888–1988* (Dublin 1988) p 173.

31 *Accountancy Ireland* October 2000. A 'bob' was a shilling, or one-twentieth of a £1.

32 Hugh O'Hare, interview with author, October 2012.

33 T. Farmar, *A History of Craig Gardner & Co.* (Dublin 1988) p 176. In the US, Price Waterhouse appointed its first Catholic partner in 1941.

34 This Protestant reputation for honesty was in curious contrast to the Nationalist rhetoric about the habitual treachery of the English.

35 *Irish Accountant and Secretary* March 1952.

36 D. Anderson, *Recounting* (Dublin 2006) p 104.

37 *Irish Accountant and Secretary* June 1952

38 *The Irish Accountant and Secretary* assembled quotes from the first five of these chairmen in March 1953, and reported the others later in the year.

39 *The Irish Times* 1 March 1958.

40 *The Irish Times* 19 March 1958.

41 *The Irish Times* 23 February 2008.

42 *The Irish Times* 20 September 1945. In *Political Corruption in Ireland 1922–2010* (Manchester 2012), Elaine Byrne implies that on foot of this advance information the Archbishop 'invested heavily in GSR railway shares' (p 45) but the timing rules out Reynolds's advance information as the initiator of these purchases.

43 *Dictionary of Irish Biography* (Cambridge 2009) *sub nom* 'Percy Reynolds'.

44 G. Golding, 'The Clery Case', *Accountancy Ireland* December 1981; T. Farmar, *A History of Craig Gardner & Co.* (Dublin 1988) pp 164–9.

45 *The Irish Times* 7 September 1967.

46 *Irish Review and Annual* 1946.

47 *Irish Review and Annual* 1946.

48 *Irish Review and Annual* 1947.

49 *Irish Review and Annual* 1951.

50 *Irish Accountant and Secretary* August 1952.

51 Department of Finance, *Economic Development* Pr 4803 (Dublin 1958) pp 56, 151, 152.

52 *Irish Accountant and Secretary* December 1956.

53 J. Bardon, *A History of Ulster* (Belfast 1992) p 618.

54 J. Bardon, *A History of Ulster* (Belfast 1992) p 616.

55 *Irish Review and Annual* 1956.

56 Rates listed in O'Neill's *Commercial Who's Who and Industrial Directory* 1958.

57 *Irish Review and Annual* 1957.

58 *Irish Accountant and Secretary* December 1959. Peard exemplified the profession's involvement in sport as a leading light in Irish badminton both as a player and administrator. In 1995 he published *Sixty Years of Irish Badminton* (Dublin 1995).

59 *Irish Accountant and Secretary* March 1956.

60 Department of Finance, *Economic Development* Pr 4803 (Dublin 1958) p 151.

61 Extract in *Irish Accountant and Secretary* March 1956.

62 *Irish Accountant and Secretary* December 1957.

63 T. Cox, *The Making of Managers: A History of the Irish Management Institute* (Dublin 2002) Chapter 1. Sir Hugh is principally famous for having originated the *Guinness Book of Records* in 1955—'it was a marketing give-away, it wasn't supposed to be a money-maker', he said later.

64 *Irish Review and Annual* 1951.

65 P. Kelleher, 'Familism in Irish Capitalism in the 1950s', *Economic and Social Review*, Vol. 18, No. 2 (January 1987) p 75.

66 O'Neill, *Commercial Who's Who and Industrial Directory* 1958.

67 *Accountancy Ireland* June 1994.

68 Institute of Chartered Accountants in Ireland *List of Members* as at August 1958.

69 This paragraph is largely based on S. Brady, *Doctor of Millions* (Tralee 1965).

70 *Irish Review and Annual* 1958 p 24.

71 Report of the District Court case, *The Irish Times* 22 September 1959.

72 T. Farmar, *A History of Craig Gardner & Co.* (Dublin 1988) pp 199–200.

73 J. McCarthy (ed.), *Planning Ireland's Future* (Dublin 1990) p 46.

74 Quoted in J. McCarthy (ed.), *Planning Ireland's Future* (Dublin 1990) p 76.

75 *Irish Review and Annual* 1958. The 'perhaps' reflects the uncertainty of the present.

76 *Irish Review and Annual* 1958.

Chapter Six

1 P. Clarke, 'Introduction of Export Sales Relief', *Accountancy Ireland* February 2006.

2 *Creation* February 1963.

3 *The Irish Times* 13 February 1963.

4 D. Connery, *The Irish* (London 1968) p 29.

5 B. Biever S.J., *Religion, Culture and Values* (New York 1976) quoted in T. Farmar, *Ordinary Lives: The Private Lives of Three Generations of Ireland's Professional Classes* (Dublin 1991) p 153.

6 T. Garvin, *Judging Lemass: The Measure of the Man* (Dublin 2010) p 45.

7 *Hibernia* March 1963.

8 *The Irish Times* 23 March 1965.

9 Gerard O'Brien, interview with author, 1987. The belief was that Catholics dug with the left foot and Protestants with the right. The expression became a more-or-less polite way of signifying religious difference.

10 J. Bardon, *A History of Ulster,* (Belfast 1992) p 618–9.

11 Republic of Ireland *Census*: Occupations Table 2 1961, 1971, excluding clergy, teachers and nurses.

12 H. W. Robinson *A History of Accountancy in Ireland* (1st ed., Dublin 1964) p 324.

13 *The Irish Times* 24 August 1957.

14 Paper originally delivered to the Eighth International Congress of Accountants, New York, September 1962 and published in the Institute of Chartered Accountants in Ireland's *Members' Bulletin* November 1962.

15 B. Tomlin, *The Management of Irish Industry* (Dublin 1966) pp xxii–xxvii.

16 F. Tobin, *The Best of Decades—Ireland in the 1960s* (Dublin 1984) pp 158–9.

17 F. McDonald, *The Destruction of Dublin* (Dublin 1985) p 23.

18 N. Whelan, *Fianna Fáil: A Biography of the Party* (Dublin 2011) pp 135–6.

19 N. Whelan, *Fianna Fáil: A Biography of the Party* (Dublin 2011) p 147.

20 G. Bull, *Bid for Power* (London 1961) p 281.

21 H. W. Robinson, *A History of Accountants in Ireland,* (1st ed., Dublin 1964) pp 225–7.

22 *The Irish Times* 7 April 1959.

23 *The Irish Times* 29 October 1959.

24 ICAI *Members' Bulletin* June 1962.

25 *The Irish Times* 9 March 1966.

26 H. W. Robinson, *A History of Accountants in Ireland,* (1st ed., Dublin 1964) pp 320–1.

27 H. W. Robinson, *A History of Accountants in Ireland (*2nd ed., Dublin 1983) p 299.

28 T. Farmar, *A History of Craig Gardner & Co.* (unpublished 2nd ed.) p 108. In the event, he won first place in Part V of the exams in 1963, and became a partner in 1965.

29 Margaret Downes, in an interview with the author, October 2012.

30 *The Irish Times* 20 June 1963.

31 H. W. Robinson, *A History of Accountants in Ireland (*2nd ed., Dublin 1983) p 177.

32 *The Accountant* July 1944, quoted in A. Higson, *Corporate Financial Reporting* (London 2003) p 148.

33 ICAI *Members' Bulletin* June 1965.

34 The first students to the new Bachelor of Commerce course entered TCD in 1925, see K. Bailey, *A History of Trinity College Dublin 1892–1945* (Dublin 1947) p 86. In 1962 the department of Business and Social Studies took over the course.

35 *The Irish Times* 28 November 1964.

36 *Dictionary of Irish Biography* (Cambridge 2009) *sub nom* 'Robinson, Howard Waterhouse'.

37 ICAI *Members' Bulletin* June 1965: to one brought up speaking English, the idea that other languages might struggle to comprehend so basic a concept as 'fair' seems extraordinary. But so it is. See A. Wierzbicka, *English Meaning and Culture* (Oxford 2006) Chapter 5.

38 Quoted in T. Cox, *The Making of Managers: A History of the Irish Management Institute 1952–2002* (Cork 2002) p 287.

39 J. Wilson, *The Making of Modern Management* (Oxford 2006) p 248.

40 B. Tomlin, *The Management of Irish Industry* (Dublin 1966) pp 167–252. The conclusions are based on an extensive survey in 1962–6 of a sample of all industries employing between 20 and 499 people, and 100 per cent of the small number employing 500 or more.

41 B. Tomlin, *The Management of Irish Industry* (Dublin 1966) p 217.

42 Published from June 1961 to February 1969 when its functions were taken over by *Accountancy Ireland.* What is probably the only surviving set (it is not in the National Library) is kept by Chartered Accountants Ireland.

43 ICAI *Members' Bulletin* June 1961.

44 A. Abbott, *The System of Professions* (Chicago 1988) p 2.

45 H. W. Robinson, *A History of Accountancy in Ireland* (1st ed., Dublin 1964) p 323.

46 *The Irish Times* 9 May 1963; T. Farmar, *A History of Craig Gardner & Co.* (Dublin 1988) p 215. The offices then occupied by Craig Gardner had been built on the site of the house of former President of the ICAI, Thomas Geoghegan. When Craig Gardner moved in 1984, they became the offices of the Institute.

47 Memo re Forsyth & Co from David Rowe to Geoffrey Perrin of KPMG, 27 January 2000.

48 Trevor Morrow, interview with author, November 2012.

49 *Accountancy Ireland* June 1994.

50 *The Irish Times* 25 March 1966.

51 *Dictionary of National Biography* (Oxford 2004), *sub nom* 'Benson, Henry Alexander 1909–1995' by Professor J. R. Edwards.

52 Margaret Downes, interview with the author, 2012.

53 *Accountancy Ireland* June 1990.

54 ICAI *Members' Bulletin* March 1963.

55 *Dictionary of National Biography* (Oxford 2004) *sub nom* Benson, Henry Alexander.

56 V. R. V. Cooper, *Manual of Auditing* (London 1966) para 215.

57 Review by J. Staunton, *Abacus* (December 1967) Vol. 3, No. 2 pp 188–90.

58 V. R. V. Cooper, *Manual of Auditing* (London 1966) para. 101.

59 V. R. V. Cooper, *Manual of Auditing* (London 1966) para. 103.

60 V. R. V. Cooper, *Manual of Auditing* (London 1966) para. 102.

61 V. R. V. Cooper, *Manual of Auditing* (London 1966) para. 117.

62 V. R. V. Cooper, *Manual of Auditing* (London 1966) e.g. paras. 296–7.

63 V. R. V. Cooper, *Manual of Auditing* (London 1966) paras. 202, 252.

64 V. R. V. Cooper, *Manual of Auditing* (London 1966) para. 319.

65 V. R. V. Cooper, *Manual of Auditing* (London 1966) Appendix C, p 297.

66 V. R. V. Cooper, *Manual of Auditing* (London 1966), paras. 245–6.

67 D. Matthews, *A History of Auditing* (London 2006) pp 44–6.

68 *The Irish Times* 29 October 1962.

69 Irish Independent *Guide to Careers* (Dublin 1968) p 236.

70 His doings are detailed in C. Raw, *Slater Walker: An Investigation of a Financial Phenomenon* (London 1977).

71 Details from B. Tomlin, *The Management of Irish Industry* (Dublin 1966) pp 294–99, and the ICAEW Library *Index of UK and Irish Accountancy and Professional Bodies.*

72 This organisation does not appear to have survived the 1960s, as it does not appear in Thom's *Directory* for 1971. Nor does it appear in the ICAEW Library *Index of UK and Irish Accountancy and Professional Bodies.*

73 Described in detail by Thomas Kenny in ICAI's *Members' Bulletin,* October 1968 and in H. W. Robinson, *A History of Accountants in Ireland* (2nd ed., Dublin 1983) pp 257–8.

74 D. Anderson, *Recounting* (Dublin and Belfast, 2006) pp 103–8.

75 ICAI *Members' Bulletin* February 1969.

76 J. M. Keynes, *The General Theory of Employment, Interest and Money* (London 1936) p 383.

Chapter Seven

1 The author's principal.

2 Hugh O'Hare, interview with author, October 2012.

3 J. Bardon, *A History of Ulster* (Belfast 1992) p 720.

4 D. Anderson, *Recounting* (Dublin and Belfast 2006) pp. 102–113, 123.

5 Michael Smurfit, interview with author, June 1997.

6 Technically she was the second woman cabinet minister, since Countess Markievicz served as Minister for Labour from 1919 to 1922, but spent most of that time either in gaol or on the run.

7 *The Irish Times* 4 February 1972.

8 M. Fogarty, *Report of Banks Inquiry* (Prl 1859) (Dublin 1971) Appendix O.

9 Irish Women's Liberation Movement, *Chains or Change? The Civil Wrongs of Irishwomen* (Dublin 1971). This pamphlet points out 'a comic anomaly in regard to the marriage bar is the fact that an unmarried woman may have two children in the Civil Service (three in wartime) but if she gets married she loses her job.'

10 This association has been through a succession of names: it was the Corporation of Accountants 1891–1939; the Association of Certified and Corporate Accountants 1939–1971; the Association of Certified Accountants 1971–1984; the Chartered Association of Certified Accountants 1984–1996; and has been the Association of Chartered Certified Accountants since 1996. *Source*: ICAEW Library *Index of UK and Irish Accountancy and Professional Bodies.*

11 *The Irish Times* 20 April 1971.

12 *Accountancy Ireland* December 1978. It is unlikely that the Ulster and Munster Societies were any more inclusive, but since their committee members were listed only by name and initials, it is impossible to tell.

13 *The Irish Times* 19 and 21 September 1978.

14 Although bank industrial relations operated on a 32-county basis, even including the British-owned Ulster and Northern Banks, there were always separate agreements. The 1970 dispute arose out of negotiations in the Republic and was accordingly confined to the Republic, though after the dispute the new terms gained in the South were extended to the North. See M. Fogarty, *Report of the Banks Enquiry* Prl 1850 (Dublin 1971) para. 5.

15 M. Fogarty, *Report of Banks Inquiry* (Prl 1859) (Dublin 1971) para. 183.

16 M. Fogarty, *Report of Banks Inquiry* (Prl 1859) (Dublin 1971) paras. 8–11.

17 M. Fogarty, *Report of Banks Inquiry* (Prl 1859) (Dublin 1971) para. 114.

18 A. E. Murphy, 'Money in an economy without banks: the case of Ireland', *The Manchester School* (March 1978) pp 41–50.

19 A. E. Murphy, 'Money in an economy without banks: the case of Ireland', *The Manchester School* (March 1978) pp 41–50.

20 M. Fogarty, *Report of Banks Inquiry,* (Prl 1859) (Dublin 1971) para. 56. The reference was to Horace's line 'The mountain groaned in labour and gave birth to a ridiculous mouse.'

21 ICAI *Members' Bulletin* February 1969.

22 *The Irish Times* 28 April 1971.

23 *The Irish Times* 16 February 1972.

24 *The Irish Times* 20 July 1973.

25 *Accountancy Ireland* December 1983.

26 D. O'Hearn, 'Estimates of New Foreign Manufacturing Employment in

Ireland', *Economic and Social Review* (April 1987) Vol. 18, No. 3, p 173.

27 W. Bruce Lyster, interview with author, February 2013.

28 These arrangements are expounded on in exhaustive detail in H. W. Robinson, *A History of Accountants in Ireland* (2nd ed., Dublin 1983) Chapter 22.

29 As head of perhaps the most prestigious firm in the country, Frank Barrett became one of the most respected accountants in Ireland and was President of the Institute 1982–3. Obituary, *The Irish Times* 30 June 2012.

30 ICAI *List of Members,* 1980.

31 *The Irish Times* 25 October 1972.

32 *The Irish Times* 21 June 1978. The writer, Ronnie Hoffman (later of *Business & Finance*), does not say where his figures come from, and there is an indication from the Craig Gardner archive, which has audit alone at 60 per cent in 1982, that they may be exaggerated, though no doubt in the right direction.

33 For instance in Price Waterhouse, see E. Jones, *True and Fair* (London 1995) pp 266–9.

34 *Accountancy Ireland* December 1978.

35 The Report was discussed by the Committee in the Derryhale Hotel, Dundalk and issued in November 1970.

36 Ben Lynch, interview with author, June 2013.

37 V. R. V. Cooper, *Manual of Auditing* (London 1966) – see also Chapter Six.

38 Council of the Institute of Chartered Accountants in England and Wales, Presentation of Balance Sheet and Profit and Loss Account (October 1958) para. 4. Discussed in E. Stamp, 'Establishing accounting principles', *Abacus* (1970) Vol. 1, p 101.

39 B. Rutherford, *Financial Reporting in the UK: A History of the Accounting Standards Committee* (London 2007) pp 3–25.

40 P. Taylor and S. Turley, *The Regulation of Accounting* (Oxford 1986) p 49.

41 *Report on the Affairs of Maxwell Scientific International and Pergamon Press* (HMSO London 1973) para. 1147.

42 R. Sterling, 'A Statement of Basic Accounting Theory: a review article', *Journal of Accounting Research* (Spring 1967) p 95.

43 B. Rutherford, *Introduction to Modern Financial Reporting Theory* (London 2000) p 109.

44 Although he is often credited with the remark, this quote does not come from the Chinese sage Sun Tzu's *Art of War.*

45 P. Taylor and S. Turley, *The Regulation of Accounting* (Oxford 1986) p 77.

46 *Accountancy Ireland* July 1972.

47 See T. Farmar, *Privileged Lives: A Social History of Middle-class Ireland 1882–1989* (Dublin 2010) p 308.

48 B. Rutherford, *Financial Reporting in the UK: A History of the Accounting Standards Committee* (London 2007) p 17.

49 T. Lee *et al.*, 'The dominant senior manager and the reasonably careful skilful and cautious auditor', *Critical Perspective on Accounting* 19 (2008) pp 677–711 .

50 E. Cahill, *Corporate Financial Crisis in Ireland* (Dublin 1997) p 381.

51 K. Kennedy *et al.*, *The Economic Development of Ireland in the Twentieth Century* (London 1988) p 73.

52 H. W. Robinson, *A History of Accountants in Ireland* (2nd ed., Dublin 1983) pp 270–1.

53 J. J. Lee, *Ireland 1912–1985 Politics and Society* (Cambridge 1989) p 466.

54 D. Yergin, *The Prize* (New York 1991) p 567.

55 See, for instance, S. Alexander, 'Income Measurement in a Dynamic Economy' in W. Baxter (ed.), *Studies in Accounting Theory* (London 1965) p 126. This article was originally written in 1948 for the American Institute of Accountants (which was renamed the AICPA in 1957).

56 *Accountancy Ireland* February 1978.

57 B. Rutherford, *Financial Reporting in the UK: A History of the Accounting Standards Committee* (London 2007) p 231.

58 *The Irish Times* 15 and 16 February 1977.

59 *The Irish Times* 7 March 1977. It is difficult to imagine the modern *Irish Times* devoting so much space to a technical accounting issue.

60 *The Irish Times* 1 and 14 June 1977.

61 B. Rutherford, *Financial Reporting in the UK: A History of the Accounting Standards Committee* (London 2007) pp 234–7.

62 *The Irish Times* 8 November 1979.

63 C. Brooker, *The Seventies* (London 1980) p 167.

64 Derived from P. Taylor and S. Turley, *The Regulation of Accounting* (Oxford 1986) pp 60–1, 82–3, 200–3.

Chapter Eight

1 G. FitzGerald, *All in a Life: An Autobiography* (Dublin 1991) p 353.

2 *Economist* 24 June 2006, Obituary of Charles J. Haughey.

3 Anne Elliott in Jane Austen, *Persuasion*, Book I, Chapter XI.

4 *The Irish Times* 31 December 1980.

5 *The Irish Times* 31 December 1980.

6 G. FitzGerald *All in a Life* (Dublin 1991) p 354.

7 T. Quin, 'A Centenarian Renders his Account' in D. Rowe (ed.), *The Irish Chartered Accountant Centenary Essays* (Dublin 1988) p 63.

8 J. Bardon, *A History of Ulster* (Belfast 1992) Chapter 15.

9 Noel MacMahon was MAS specialist with Craig Gardner. He served as President in 1980–1. MacMahon's views were expressed in an article in the 10th anniversary issue of *Accountancy Ireland* in 1979.

10 *Accountancy Ireland* June 1979.

11 S. Zepp, 'How the US Accounting Profession Got Where It Is Today' Part II, *Accounting Horizons* (2003) Vol. 17, No. 4. p 273–4. The US Financial Accounting Standards Board was established in 1973.

12 *Accountancy Ireland* June 1979.

13 *Accountancy Ireland* November 1981.

14 *The Irish Times* 18 May 1981. This article, by the respected business commentator Bill Murdoch, highlights the opposition to Current Cost Accounting.

15 *The Irish Times* 4 July 1980; the Association of Certified Accountants became the Chartered Association of Certified Accountants in 1984 and finally the Association of Chartered Certified Accountants in 1996 (see ICAEW Library *Index of UK and Irish Accountancy and Professional Bodies*).

16 Speaking at the Annual Conference of the ICAI in Limerick, *The Irish Times* 22 October 1982.

17 *Accountancy Ireland* April 1982.

18 *Accountancy Ireland* November 1981.

19 Advertisement in *Accountancy Ireland* in March 1979.

20 *Accountancy Ireland* March 1979.

21 December 1980.

22 Ben Lynch edited *Accountancy Ireland* from its first issue in 1969 until 1989 when he concentrated on his role as Director of Education. He retired in 1998.

23 M. Cairnduff, *Who's Who in Ireland* (Dublin 1984) p 1.

24 Obituary *The Irish Times* 20 June 2012.

25 'Life begins at 5.30' in *Accountancy Ireland* May and September 1988.

26 *The Irish Times* 9 April 1985.

27 *Southside* 26 August 1981.

28 *The Irish Times* 13 April 1984; *Dictionary of Irish Biography* (Cambridge 2009) *sub nom* 'Charles Russell Murphy'.

29 *The Irish Times* 16 April 1984.

30 *The Irish Times* 14 May 1984.

31 *Accountancy Ireland* June 2001.

32 S. Zeff, 'How the US Accounting Profession Got Where it is Today' in *Accounting Horizons* (2003) Vol. 17, No. 4, p 270.

33 *The Irish Times* 25 April 1985.

34 *Accountancy Ireland* February 1987.

35 *Accountancy Ireland* December 1995.

36 *Accountancy Ireland* February 1987.

37 *Accountancy Ireland* February 1987.

38 G. Hanlon, *The Commercialisation of Accountancy in Ireland* (London 1994) p 73.

39 *Accountancy Ireland* October 1994.

40 *Accountancy Ireland* December 1995.

41 M. Brewster, *Unaccountable* (New Jersey 2003) p 163.

42 Deloitte CEO J. Michael Cook quoted in S. Zeff, 'How the US Accounting Profession Got Where it is Today' in *Accounting Horizons* (2003) Vol. 17, No. 4, p 271.

43 Terence O'Rourke, interview with author, July 2013.

44 R. Lewis *et al.*, *Professional People* (London 1952) p 58.

45 L. Spacek, *The Growth of Arthur Andersen 1928–1973: An Oral History* (New York 1989) p 124. No doubt unconsciously, he had adopted the policy once followed by London society ladies: 'always be kind to the girls—you never know who they might marry.'

46 M. Brewster, *Unaccountable* (New Jersey 2003) pp 136–40.

47 Author's archive. As far as I can discover, examples from other firms do not survive, but it is unlikely that the focus and presentation of this was markedly unusual.

48 Author's archive.

49 *Accountancy Ireland* February 1987.

50 *The Irish Times* 29 January 1987.

51 *Accountancy Ireland* February 1987.

52 *Accountancy Ireland* February 1982.

53 H. W. Robinson, *A History of Accountants in Ireland*, (1st ed., Dublin, 1962).

54 *The Irish Times* 19 August 1989.

55 *The Irish Times* 1 August 1989, based on *Finance* magazine.

56 *The Irish Times* 14 March 1987.

57 *The Irish Times* 23 January 1980.

58 P. Clarke, 'Inflation and taxation', *Accountancy Ireland* June 1984.

59 *The Irish Times* 29 March 1980.

60 What changes in the tax system that did occur over the next 10 years were prompted more by Europe and a response to inflation than the Commission's 'internationally acclaimed tax reform package'. F. O'Toole, 'Tax reform since the Commission on Taxation', *Journal of the Statistical and Social Inquiry Society of Ireland* (1993), Vol. XXVII, Part 1, p 89.

61 *The Irish Times* 13 February 1980.

62 S. Réamonn, *History of the Revenue Commissioners* (Dublin 1981) p 78.

63 J. O'Broin *et al.*, *Tax and Business Decisions* (2nd ed., Dublin 1979). This book was written by O'Broin with two Craig Gardner colleagues and published by Craig Gardner 'for clients of the firm'. It is notable that all three authors had worked as tax inspectors. One of them, Sean Cleary, was described as 'a specialist in tax research'.

64 *The Irish Times* 8 May 1989. The technical and jurisprudential issues were discussed by KPMG Partner Shaun Murphy in *Finance* magazine (September 2000). The result seems to confirm the old saying that the law is open to all—like the Ritz Hotel. If designers, fish farmers and book publishers had been able to afford such high-priced help, perhaps they too would be accounted 'manufacturers'.

65 *McGrath v. McDermott (Inspector of Taxes)* (1988).

66 *The Irish Times* 23 January 1989.

67 *The Irish Times* 9 February 1989.

68 The term used by Peter Cassells of the ICTU in *The Irish Times* 19 May 1995.

69 *The Irish Times* 1 February 1984.

70 *The Irish Times* 2 February 1984

71 *Accountancy Ireland* November 1984.

72 Irish Women's Liberation Movement, 'Five good reasons to live in sin', *Chains or Change* (Dublin 1971) pp 30–2.

73 Marie O'Connor, interview with author, 1990.

74 P. Barker, 'The True and Fair Sex' in D. Rowe (ed.), *The Irish Chartered Accountant Centenary Essays* (Dublin 1988) pp 211–2.

75 P. Barker, 'The True and Fair Sex' in D. Rowe (ed.), *The Irish Chartered Accountant Centenary Essays,* (Dublin 1988), p 218.

76 T. Quin, 'A Centenarian Renders his Account' in D. Rowe (ed.), *The Irish Chartered Accountant Centenary Essays* (Dublin 1988) p 64.

77 T. Quin, 'A Centenarian Renders his Account' in D. Rowe (ed.), *The Irish Chartered Accountant Centenary Essays* (Dublin 1988) p 66.

78 *Accountancy Ireland* July 1988.

79 T. Quin, 'A Centenarian Renders his Account' in D. Rowe (ed.), *The Irish Chartered Accountant Centenary Essays* (Dublin 1988)p 66.

80 *Accountancy Ireland* May 1988.

Chapter Nine

1 E. Hobsbawm, *The Age of Extremes* (London 1995) p 5.

2 For example, see *Hibernia* May 1963. Why the Soviets would want to disrupt the international balance of power so dramatically was not explained. *Hibernia* was then published by the Knights of St Columbanus.

3 For example, *The Irish Times* 23 October 1961.

4 Interview, *The Irish Times* 30 January 2010.

5 P. Honahan, 'Fiscal Adjustment and Disinflation in Ireland' in F. Barry (ed.), *Understanding Ireland's Economic Growth* (London 1999) pp 85–6.

6 *The Economist* 17 May 1988, quoted in D. Donovan and A. E. Murphy, *The Fall of the Celtic Tiger: Ireland and the Euro Debt Crisis* (Oxford 2013) p 15. The analysis in the following paragraphs is largely based on this book.

7 A. E. Murphy, 'The Celtic Tiger: An Analysis of Ireland's Economic Growth Performance' *EUI Working Paper,* RSC No. 2000/16 (San Domenica 2000) p 11.

8 D. Donovan and A. E. Murphy, *The Fall of the Celtic Tiger: Ireland and the Euro Debt Crisis* (Oxford 2013) p 24.

9 A. E. Murphy, 'The Celtic Tiger: An Analysis of Ireland's Economic Growth Performance', *EUI Working Paper,* RSC No. 2000/16 (San Domenica 2000) pp 11–8, 21–2. Data from the Census of Industrial Production.

10 *Finance* August 1999.

11 K. Gardiner, 'The Irish Economy: A Celtic Tiger', *Morgan Stanley Newsletter* 31 August 1994.

12 *The Economist* 16 January 1997, quoted in D. Donovan and A. E. Murphy, *The Fall of the Celtic Tiger: Ireland and the Euro Debt Crisis* (Oxford 2013) p 15.

13 *Census 1991*—unfortunately a redefinition of categories makes these figures not comparable with previous years.

14 *Accountancy Ireland* August 1996.

15 *Accountancy Ireland* December 1991. Haughey resigned as Taoiseach in 1992. The McCracken Tribunal first revealed details of his Ansbacher accounts, gifts from businessmen, etc., in 1997. No doubt the satisfaction of celebrating a Taoiseach as 'one of us' overwhelmed such doubts as may have arisen.

16 *The Irish Times* 29 October 1990.

17 Here, 'IFAC' refers to the specialised agency dealing with farm accounts originally set up by the Irish Farmers' Association in 1974; originally voluntary, its first chief executive was employed in 1978.

18 *Accountancy Ireland* November 1989.

19 *Accountancy Ireland* August 1992.

20 *Accountancy Ireland* April 1993.

21 *Accountancy Ireland* March 1989. At least he did not say 'on the mainland'.

22 P. Barker and K. Monks, 'Irish Women Accountants and Career Progression' in *Accounting Organisation and Society* (1998) Vol. 23, No. 8, p 816.

23 *The Irish Times* 5 May 1992.

24 D. Matthews, *A History of Auditing: the Changing Audit Process from the Nineteenth Century to the Present Day* (London 2006) p 1.

25 *The Irish Times* 19 November 1990.

26 E. Cahill, *Corporate Financial Crisis in Ireland* (Dublin 1997) p 199.

27 Financial Reporting Commission, *Report of the Commission of Enquiry into the Expectations of Users of Published Financial Statements* (Dublin 1992) p 80.

28 See p 40. In the famous case *Re Kingston Cotton Mills* (1896) Lord Justice Lopes had declared: 'It is the duty of an auditor to bring to bear on the work he has to perform that skill, care, and caution which a reasonably competent, careful, and cautious auditor would use. An auditor is not bound to be a detective, or, as was said, to approach his work with suspicion, or with a foregone conclusion that there is something wrong. He is a watchdog, but not a bloodhound. Auditors must not be made liable for not tracking out ingenious and carefully laid schemes of fraud, when there is nothing to arouse their suspicion . . . So to hold would make the position of an auditor intolerable.'

29 This analysis is based on D. Matthews, *A History of Auditing: the Changing Audit Process from the Nineteenth Century to the Present Day* (London 2006). Later models did not replace the older ones—a modern firm, especially a small firm, might regularly be called to carry out each of them.

30 V. R. V. Cooper, *Manual of Auditing* (London 1966). This *Manual* became the standard audit manual with the formation of Cooper Brothers in Ireland in 1968.

31 D. Matthews, *A History of Auditing* (London 2006) p 163.

32 R. Adams, 'Audit risk' in M. Sherer and S. Turley, *Current Issues in Auditing* (London 1991) p 145.

33 *The Irish Times* 3 March 1995.

34 Later published as G. Hanlon, *The Commercialisation of Accountancy* (London 1994) p 83. This book is based on a Trinity College, Dublin PhD thesis; part of the research consisted of interviews with a large number of Big Six staff, from partners to trainees. Hanlon is now Professor of Organisational Sociology at

Queen Mary College, University of London.

35 G. Hanlon, *The Commercialisation of Accountancy* (London 1994) p 86.

36 *Report of the Tribunal of Inquiry into the Beef Processing Industry* Pr 1007 (Dublin 1994) pp 315–16.

37 G. Hanlon, 'The Emigration of Irish Accountants' in *Irish Journal of Sociology* (1991) Vol. 1, p 5.

38 G. Hanlon, *The Commercialisation of Accountancy* (London 1994) pp 110–11.

39 E. Cahill, *Corporate Financial Crisis in Ireland* (Dublin 1997) Chapter 5.

40 N. Brennan, A. Pierce, F. O'Brien, *Survey of Irish Published Accounts* (Dublin 1992) p 92.

41 T. Smith, *Accounting for Growth* (London 1992) p 4. An article in *Business & Finance* magazine (August 1992) noted several of the identified techniques, such as off-balance sheet finance, capitalisation of costs and amortisation of goodwill, being used by leading Irish companies.

42 N. Brennan, A. Pierce, F. O'Brien, *Survey of Irish Published Accounts* (Dublin 1992) pp 63, 81.

43 N. Brennan, A. Pierce, F. O'Brien, *European Financial Reporting Series: Ireland* (London 1992) p 80.

44 *Report of the Financial Reporting Commission* (Dublin 1992) paras. 4.34–4.41.

45 We have seen in previous chapters the resistance by industrial managers such as Howard Kilroy and Noel Griffin to standards. In 1990, Peter Clarke of UCD asked a panel of Irish accountants to rank the future importance of 70 different skill and knowledge areas. Top of the list came written and oral communications and computer systems; and at the bottom was the history of accounting (*Accountancy Ireland* April 1991).

46 *Accountancy Ireland* February 1992.

47 *Accountancy Ireland* December 1992.

48 *The Irish Times* 5 April 1991.

49 *Report of the Tribunal of Inquiry into the Beef Processing Industry* Pr 1007 (Dublin 1994) p 331.

50 The row and the often over-the-top arguments are amusingly covered in P. Bougen *et al.*, 'Accountants and the everyday: or what the papers said about the Irish accountant and tax evasion', *European Accounting Review* (1999) 8: 3, pp 443–61.

51 *Accountancy Ireland* April 1997.

52 *Accountancy Ireland* July 1989.

53 Auditing Practice Board, *Standards and Guidance 2011,* Ireland Edition (Dublin, Chartered Accountants Ireland 2011); International Accounting Standards Board, *International Financial Reporting Standards* (January 2011); S. Bragg, *GAAP 2012* (New Jersey 2009).

54 *Accountancy Ireland* October 1999.

55 *The Irish Times* 21 May 1992 discusses the Lafferty Report.

56 *The Irish Times* 19 September 1997.

57 Interview with managing partner of Coopers & Lybrand, Dick Lane, *The Irish*

Times 16 November 1990.

58 *Finance* July 1990 and September 1999.

59 ICAI *Membership Directories.*

60 *Accountancy Ireland* October 1999.

61 *Accountancy Ireland March* 2000.

62 *Accountancy Ireland* May 1998.

63 N. Hanna, *The Rough Guide to the Millennium* (London 1998) p 18.

64 ICAI, *Annual Report and Financial Statements* 2000.

65 *The Irish Times* 16 and 20 December 1999.

66 E. Cahill, *Corporate Financial Crisis in Ireland* (Dublin 1997) p 394.

67 The case, and KPMG's expression of concern, are described in E. Cahill, *Corporate Financial Crisis in Ireland* (Dublin 1997) Chapter 4.

68 M. Power, 'The audit society—second thoughts', *International Journal of Auditing* (2000) 4: 114, reconsiders his 1999 book *The Audit Society*, which describes the growth in non-financial auditing.

69 *Accountancy Ireland* October 1997.

70 *Accountancy Ireland* February 1999.

71 *Accountancy Ireland* February 1999.

Chapter Ten

1 Data from a promotional video produced by Chartered Accountants Ireland, *Driving Ireland Forward* (2012).

2 This paragraph is based on D. Donovan and A. E. Murphy, *The Fall of the Celtic Tiger* (Oxford 2013) pp 61–5.

3 D. Donovan and A. E. Murphy, *The Fall of the Celtic Tiger* (Oxford 2013) p 59.

4 *Accountancy Ireland* October 2007.

5 J Wilson *et al.*, *The Making of Modern Management* (Oxford 2006; pb 2009) p 248.

6 D. Matthews *et al.*, *The Priesthood of Industry* (Oxford 1998) p 125.

7 J Wilson *et al.*, *The Making of Modern Management* (Oxford 2006) pb 2009 p 252.

8 *Accountancy Ireland* June 2007.

9 *Accountancy Ireland* February 2000. The *American Heritage Dictionary* defines 'intrapreneur' as 'a person within a large corporation who takes direct responsibility for turning an idea into a profitable finished product through assertive risk-taking and innovation'.

10 CSO, *Small Business in Ireland 2008* (Dublin 2008) pp 6, 62.

11 *Source:* Irish Auditing & Accounting Supervisory Authority, *Annual Report 2006*, plus information from respective websites.

12 *Accountancy Ireland* February 2000.

13 *Report of the Review Group on Auditing* Pn 8683 (Dublin 2000) pp 38–9.

14 ICAI, ICAS, ACCA, ACPAI, ICAEW and IIPA. See p 227 for details of these organisations.

15 B. Lenihan, 'Simple changes could significantly improve regulation of accountants', *The Irish Times* 22 July 2013.

16 ICAI, *Annual Report and Financial Statements* 2000.

17 In 2010 David Devlin of PricewaterhouseCoopers received a Lifetime Achievement Award from ICAI (*Accountancy Ireland* June 2010).

18 It is alas likely that Lord Chancellor Thurlow (1732–1806) much less memorably said, 'corporations have neither bodies to be punished nor souls to be condemned, they therefore do as they like'.

19 Quoted in a Law Society submission on the desirability of limited liability partnership submitted to Mary Harney, TD, Tánaiste and Minister for Enterprise, Trade and Employment, 2001.

20 *Accountancy Ireland* August 1996.

21 B. Moloney and A. Fahy, 'Incorporation of an audit practice', *Accountancy Plus* June 2011.

22 This paragraph is based on John McCarthy, then Practice Advisory Executive with ICAI, 'Accountancy Practices' in *Accountancy Ireland* February 2005.

23 Terence O'Rourke, interview with author, July 2013.

24 *Accountancy Ireland* February 2005.

25 *European Accounting Review* (1996) Vol. 5, p 795.

26 *Accountancy Ireland* October 2009.

27 *Accountancy Ireland* August 2004.

28 US standards were long called 'generally accepted accounting principles' or GAAP, a term that has been adopted in the UK and Ireland. In fact, they were often very far from being 'generally accepted': US and European GAAP were sometimes different. By the end of the decade they were increasingly converging with the International Financial Reporting Standards that had been mandatory for certain entities in the EU since 2005.

29 Quoted in A. Pierce, *Ethics and the Professional Accounting Firm: A Literature Review* (Edinburgh 2006) p 96.

30 T. Lee *et al.*, 'The dominant senior manager and the reasonably careful, skilful and cautious auditor', *Critical Perspectives on Accounting,* 19 (2008) pp 677–711.

31 Mary Canniffe, 'Annus Horribilis—but not in the Irish Accountancy Market', *Accountancy Ireland* December 2002.

32 *Accountancy Ireland* October 2001.

33 P. Barker, *The Minority Interest: Women who Succeed in the Accountancy Profession* (Dublin 2009) p 31.

34 P. Barker, *The Minority Interest: Women who Succeed in the Accountancy Profession* (Dublin 2009) Chapter 3.

35 Irish Auditing & Accounting Supervisory Authority, *Annual Report 2006.*

36 Irish Auditing & Accounting Supervisory Authority, *Annual Report 2006.*

37 Irish Auditing & Accounting Supervisory Authority, *Annual Report 2006.*

38 Strategic Review Group, *What are the Aims and Objectives of the Institute?*, (Dublin 2005) para. 3.4, p 9.

39 Chartered Accountants Regulatory Board, *Annual Report 2007* (CARB's first annual report).

40 Chartered Accountants Regulatory Board, *Annual Report 2007*.

41 Chartered Accountants Regulatory Board, *Annual Report 2012*.

42 The Irish Auditing & Accounting Supervisory Board *Annual Report 2011* (at p.25) noted that it had imposed a substantial fine on CARB for failing to follow its own procedures.

43 Pat Costello, interview with author, October 2013.

44 IAASA, *Profile of the Profession 2012* (Dublin 2013).

45 IAASA, *Annual Report* 2012, Chairman's Report.

46 T. Farmar, 'A Versatile Profession', in *Accountancy Ireland* August 2013.

47 'Investigation by the C&AG established that evasion of DIRT was pervasive throughout the Irish deposit-taking system', Public Accounts Committee *Report on DIRT 1999–2000*. This may be balanced by a comment from the *Final Report of the Commission on Taxation* 1980–85: 'the administration of taxation in Ireland has virtually broken down. Non-compliance is a major problem.'

48 *Addressing Base Erosion and Profit Shifting* (OECD 2013).

49 *Accountancy Ireland* August 2013.

50 *Accountancy Ireland* August 2013.

51 I am grateful to Brendan Lenihan, Aidan Lambe and Ronan O'Loughlin of Chartered Accountants Ireland for their contributions to this list.

52 A recent UK paper by Grant Thornton notes that 40 per cent of FTSE 350 companies now have separate audit and risk committees.

Index